ReFocus: The Films of Alejandro Jodorowsky

ReFocus: The International Directors Series

Series Editors: Robert Singer, Gary D. Rhodes and
Stefanie Van de Peer

Board of advisors:
Lizelle Bisschoff (Glasgow University)
Stephanie Hemelryck Donald (University of Lincoln)
Anna Misiak (Falmouth University)
Des O'Rawe (Queen's University Belfast)

ReFocus is a series of contemporary methodological and theoretical approaches to the interdisciplinary analyses and interpretations of international film directors, from the celebrated to the ignored, in direct relationship to their respective culture – its myths, values, and historical precepts – and the broader parameters of international film history and theory.

Titles in the series include:

edinburghuniversitypress.com/series/refocint

ReFocus:
The Films of Alejandro Jodorowsky

Edited by Michael Newell Witte

EDINBURGH
University Press

Edinburgh University Press is one of the leading university presses in the UK. We publish academic books and journals in our selected subject areas across the humanities and social sciences, combining cutting-edge scholarship with high editorial and production values to produce academic works of lasting importance. For more information visit our website: edinburghuniversitypress.com

Grateful acknowledgement is made to the sources listed in the List of Illustrations for permission to reproduce material previously published elsewhere. Every effort has been made to trace the copyright holders, but if any have been inadvertently overlooked, the publisher will be pleased to make the necessary arrangements at the first opportunity.

Edinburgh University Press Ltd
The Tun – Holyrood Road
12(2f) Jackson's Entry
Edinburgh EH8 8PJ

Typeset in 11/13 Ehrhardt MT by
IDSUK (DataConnection) Ltd, and
printed and bound in Great Britain

A CIP record for this book is available from the British Library

ISBN 978 1 3995 0594 9 (hardback)
ISBN 978 1 3995 0596 3 (webready PDF)
ISBN 978 1 3995 0597 0 (epub)

Contents

Figures

Contributors

Jorge Ayala Blanco is a renowned film historian and critic, author and professor at the Universidad Nacional Autónoma de México (UNAM). His major contribution to the study of cinema is his "Abecedario" series on Mexican film. This series comprises *La Aventura del Cine Mexicano* (1968), *La Búsqueda del Cine Mexicano* (1974), *La Condición del Cine Mexicano* (1986), *La Disolvencia del Cine Mexicano* (1991), *La Eficacia del Cine Mexicano* (1994), *La Fugacidad del Cine Mexicano* (2001), *La Grandeza del Cine Mexicano* (2004), *La Herética del Cine Mexicano* (2006), *La Ilusión del Cine Mexicano* (2012), *La Justeza del Cine Mexicano* (2011), *La Khátarsis del Cine Mexicano* (2016), *La Lucidez del Cine Mexicano* (2016), *La Madurez del Cine Mexicano* (2017), *La Novedad del Cine Mexicano* (2018) and *La Ñerez del Cine Mexicano* (2019). Professor Ayala Blanco has granted the editor permission to translate and print his commentary on Jodorowsky's *Fando y Lis* and *El Topo*, from his *La Búsqueda del Cine Mexicano* (1974).

Henri-Simon Blanc-Hoang (PhD, University of Florida) is an expert on *bande dessinée*, cinema, as well as science fiction. His publications include articles on film and graphic novels produced in Latin America, Spain and the French-speaking world. His work has addressed topics such as: old and new nationalisms in Europe, cultural identities in Spanish, Galician, Brazilian, Belgian, and French films and graphic novels, as well as the questioning of pigmentocratic societies in Chilean, Brazilian and Argentine science fiction. His most recent projects include not only a book chapter on Alejandro Jodorowsky's graphic novels that focus on this author's interpretation of messianism, but also an article on Jewish identity in the films of this Chilean-French director. Blanc-Hoang's articles on Jodorowsky's œuvre have appeared in the following academic journals and book series: *Revista*

Iberoamericana, Studies in Comics, Post Script: Essays in Film and the Humanities and *Jewish Fantasy Worldwide*. Before joining the Modern Languages and Cultures department at the City College of San Francisco, Blanc-Hoang taught Spanish, French, Afro-Francophone studies, Latin American studies, and Postcolonial and Globalization studies at the US Army Defense Language Institute.

Amy Sara Carroll is Associate Professor of Literature and Writing at the University of California, San Diego, and a winter 2021 artist in residence at the University of California, Los Angeles's Luskin Institute on Inequality and Democracy. Her books include *SECESSION*; *FANNIE + FREDDIE/The Sentimentality of Post-9/11 Pornography*, chosen by Claudia Rankine for the 2012 Poets Out Loud Prize; and *REMEX: Toward an Art History of the NAFTA Era* which received honorable mentions for the 2017 MLA Katherine Singer Kovacs Prize, the 2018 Latin American Studies Association Mexico Section Best Book in the Humanities, and the 2019 Association for Latin American Art-Arvey Foundation Book Award. Since 2008, she has been a member of Electronic Disturbance Theater 2.0, coproducing the *Transborder Immigrant Tool*. She also co-authored *[({ })] The Desert Survival Series/La serie de sobrevivencia del desierto*. Previously she taught at The New School in New York City, was a 2018–2019 Fellow in the University of Texas at Austin's Latino Research Initiative, and was a 2017–2018 Fellow in Cornell University's Society for the Humanities.

William Egginton is the Decker Professor in the Humanities and Director of the Alexander Grass Humanities Institute at the John Hopkins University in Baltimore. His research and teaching focus on Spanish and Latin American literature, literary theory, and the relation between literature and philosophy. Egginton is the author, editor or translator of more than a dozen books on such topics as the relationship between psychoanalysis, literature, and philosophy; religion and politics; and science and literature. Widely recognized for his work on early modern culture, philosophy, psychoanalysis, and the baroque, he is the author of *How the World Became a Stage* (2003), *Perversity and Ethics* (2006), *A Wrinkle in History* (2007), *The Philosopher's Desire* (2007), *The Theater of Truth* (2010), *In Defense of Religious Moderation* (2011), *The Man Who Invented Fiction: How Cervantes Ushered in the Modern World* (2016), *The Splintering of the American Mind* (2018), *The Rigor of Angels: Borges, Heisenberg, Kant, and the Ultimate Nature of Reality* (2023) and *Jodorowsky: Philosopher and Filmmaker (2023)*. He has also co-authored with David Castillo *Medialogies: Reading Reality in the Age of Inflationary Media* (2017) and *What Would Cervantes Do? Navigating Post-Truth With Spanish Baroque Literature* (2022).

Daniel Escoto holds a Master's degree in Art History from the Universidad Nacional Autónoma de México (UNAM) and a Ph.D. in Communication from the Universidad Iberoamericana in Mexico City. His research has focused on Mexican avant-garde literature, theater, cinema, radio, and music of the 1960s and 1970s and their intersections with global pop culture of the period. He has authored the article "El reino combatiente. Jaime García Terrés y la difusión cultural universitaria [The Combatant Kingdom. Jaime García Terrés and University Cultural Diffusion]," included in the exhibition catalogue *Desafío a la estabilidad. Procesos artísticos en México 1952–1967 [Defying Stability. Artistic Processes in Mexico 1952–1967]* (ed. R. Eder).

Francisco Javier Fresneda-Casado is an artist and researcher whose work explores models of material culture, space, and heritage, through the combination of sculpture, archival investigation, editorial projects, digital platforms, and public events. He is a PhD student in the Art History, Theory, Criticism, and Art Practice program at the University of California San Diego (U.S.), and obtained his Master's degree in the Contemporary Art program of UEM – European University of Madrid (Spain). Some of his most relevant artistic projects have been presented at the Queens Museum New York (U.S.), Scharaun Berlin (Germany), Harvard University (U.S.), CA2M – Centro de Arte Dos de Mayo, (Spain), MCASD – Museum of Contemporary Art of San Diego (U.S.), AKV St. Joost (The Netherlands), Kunsthaus Bethanien (Germany), and The Getty Research Institute (U.S.). He has given workshops and presentations at ELa – École Libre d'architecture Paris (France), UC Irvine, UC San Diego (U.S.), UCM-Universidad Complutense Madrid (Spain), UADY – Universidad Autónoma de Yucatán (Mexico), receiving awards and scholarships from FONCA-PROTRAD, SRE-Ministry of Foreign Affairs-Government of Mexico, Ministry of Culture of Spain, City Council of Madrid-Spain, Rijksdienst voor het Cultureel Erfgoed – The Netherlands. His editorial projects have been part of events such as The New York Book Art Fair in MOMA PS1, ARCO (e)ditorial, PaperWorks Mexico, and Offprint London, among others.

Peter Scott Lederer holds a Ph.D. in American Film and Culture from Queen's University Belfast, where he researched Jewish-American filmmakers, dark comedy, and performance. His recent work includes "'Differentness' and the American Jew-Gentile Heterosexual Romantic-Comedy" (*Question*, vol. 5 [2020]), "Comic Chameleon: Lenny Bruce's Stage Personas" (*Comedy Studies*, vol. 11, no. 2 [2020]), "Presence: An Existential-Humanistic Analysis of Body-mind Unity in The Graduate" (*The Dovetail Journal*, vol. 2 [2016]) – and a chapter in *Jewish Radicalisms*, "Mel Brooks' Subversive Cabaret" (2020). He is currently researching the occult's influence on modern psychotherapeutic practices. He is interested in creative arts therapies: how an individual's relationship to a film or literary work is valuable in the process of healing and wisdom-seeking.

Jesse Lerner is a filmmaker, curator and writer. His documentaries *Frontierland/Fronterilandia* (1995), *Ruins* (1999), *The American Egypt* (2001), *Atomic Sublime* (2010), and *The Absent Stone* (2013) have screened at New York's Museum of Modern Art, the National Anthropology Museum in Mexico City, the Guggenheim Museums in New York and Bilbao, and the Sundance, Rotterdam, and Los Angeles Film Festivals, among many other venues. Washington's National Gallery, the Anthology Film Archives, and Mexico's Cineteca Nacional have presented mid-career surveys of his films. His books include *The Maya of Modernism*, *F is for Phony*, *The Shock of Modernity*, *Ism Ism Ism* and *The Catherwood Project*.

Naomi Lindstrom is the Gale Family Foundation Professor in Jewish Arts and Culture and Professor of Spanish and Portuguese at the University of Texas at Austin, where she is the director of the Gale Collaborative on Jewish Life in the Americas at the Schusterman Center for Jewish Studies. Her teaching and research lie at the crossroads of Latin American studies, gender studies, and Jewish studies. She specializes in the analysis of writing and film from Jewish Latin America. She is the author of, among other books, *Jewish Issues in Argentine Literature: From Gerchunoff to Szichman*, *The Social Conscience of Latin American Writing* and *Early Spanish American Narrative*. Also a literary translator, she has been involved in the effort to offer English-language readers access to the writing of the Argentine writer Roberto Arlt, translating his 1929 novel *The Seven Madmen* and encouraging students and colleagues to create English versions of his other works.

Matthew Melia is a Senior Lecturer in Film, Literature and Media at Kingston University, U.K., where he is also currently Course Leader for the Humanities Foundation degree. His doctorate was on the Theatre of the Absurd, Architecture, and Cruelty, and his current research interests include the work of both Ken Russell and Stanley Kubrick. He is co-editor of *The Jaws Book* (2020) and the forthcoming *Anthony Burgess, Stanley Kubrick and A Clockwork Orange* (2022). He is editor of *The Films of Ken Russell* (Edinburgh University Press, 2021) and is working on a monograph on Russell's *Gothic* (2023). Matt has previously published on Jodorowsky with the chapter "Landscape, Imagery and Symbolism in *El Topo*" in *Reframing Cult Westerns* (ed. Lee Broughton, 2020).

Alessandra Santos is Associate Professor of Latin American Literature and Culture at the University of British Columbia. Her research focuses on modern and contemporary literature, cinema, and arts in comparative contexts. She is interested in gender, race, and indigeneity, technology and media, performance and embodiment, aesthetics and politics, and social justice. Her publications include the books: *Arnaldo Canibal Antunes* (2013); *The Holy Mountain* (2017); and *The Utopian Impulse in Latin America* (2011) and *Performing Utopias in the Contemporary Americas* (2017) (both co-edited with Kim Beauchesne). Her research has been funded by multiple awards, including Social Sciences and Humanities Research Council of Canada grants.

Peter Sloane is a Lecturer in English at the University of Lincoln, U.K., specializing in avant-garde and experimental arts of the twentieth and twenty-first centuries. He has published widely on contemporary literature, film, and theater, including the monographs *David Foster Wallace and the Body* (2019) and *Kazuo Ishiguro's Gestural Poetics* (May 2021). He is currently writing his third monograph, *Altruism and Culture 1900–Present*, editing a collection of new essays on Kazuo Ishiguro (2022) and contributing a chapter on "Screenplays and Film Scripts" to the *Cambridge Companion to Kazuo Ishiguro* (ed. Andrew Bennett, 2022).

Andrew Ventimiglia is an Assistant Professor of Mass Media with a specialization in Media Law and Ethics in the School of Communication at Illinois State University. His research focuses on the history and cultural effects of intellectual property law. He was formerly a Postdoctoral Research Fellow in the TC Beirne School of Law at the University of Queensland. He was awarded his Ph.D. in Cultural Studies from the University of California, Davis in 2015, during which he conducted research into the intersection of religion and intellectual property law in the American spiritual marketplace. Dr. Ventimiglia additionally holds a Master of Arts in Cinema Studies and a Certificate from the Culture and Media Program from New York University. His first book *Copyrighting God: Ownership of the Sacred in American Religion* was published in 2019.

Michael Newell Witte is a Lecturer of Art and Art History with the Department of Art at California State University, Northridge, in Los Angeles. He holds his Ph.D. in Art History, Theory, and Criticism from the University of California, San Diego. His research explores neo-avant-garde art and theory, dissident and ethnographic surrealism, late surrealism in Latin America, and global contemporary art and film. He is currently working on a monograph investigating the experimental films of the celebrated Mexican artist and theater director Juan José Gurrola. He has published texts on film and video history, theory and aesthetics, covering such figures as Alejandro Jodorowsky, Narcisa Hirsch, Juan Downey, Raúl Ruiz and J.-F. Lyotard.

Florian Zappe is a cultural critic and interdisciplinary scholar based in Berlin. He is the author of books on Kathy Acker (*Das Zwischen schreiben – Transgression* *und avantgardistisches Erbe bei Kathy Acker,* transcript, 2013) and William S. Burroughs (*'Control Machines' und 'Dispositive' – Eine foucaultsche Analyse der Machtstrukturen im Romanwerk von William S. Burroughs zwischen 1959 und 1968,* 2008), the editor of the forthcoming volume *ReFocus: The Films of Abel Ferrara* (Edinburgh University Press) as well as the co-editor of the essay collections *The American Weird: Concept & Medium* (2020), *Surveillance | Society | Culture* (2020) and *Spaces and Fictions of the Weird and the Fantastic: Ecologies, Geographies, Oddities* (2019). In addition to that, he has published widely on literary and visual culture.

CHAPTER I

Introduction: The Films of Alejandro Jodorowsky

Michael Newell Witte

"My name is Alejandro Jodorowsky and I have come from Chile to save Surrealism!" These were the words delivered by the 24-year-old Alejandro Jodorowsky to the "pope of Surrealism" himself, André Breton.

According to the story, Jodorowsky's first act in Paris, upon stepping down from his train at two o'clock in the morning, was to telephone Breton, whose number Jodorowsky knew by heart (as it was given to him by the Chilean Surrealist group La Mandrágora, who had maintained relations with Breton since the group's founding in 1938). A half-awake Breton answers the phone and listens to Jodorowsky's proclamation, along with the demand to meet at once in order to plan out, with Breton, the future developments of the movement. Breton, reasonably enough, tells Jodorowsky to try again in the morning, to which Jodorowsky replies "Not tomorrow! Now! A true surrealist," he says, "is not guided by the clock!" When Breton insists again on "tomorrow," Jodorowsky replies, "then never!" and hangs up the phone.[1]

These are the events according to one (apocryphal) story circulated by Jodorowsky years after the alleged phone encounter. The quotation, meanwhile, regarding Jodorowsky's quest to "save Surrealism" has since become preserved in Jodorowsky's 2016 film *Endless Poetry*, a fictionalized "pseudo-memoir" where he, the young artist (played by Jodorowsky's son Adán), proclaims his intention to radically intervene and reconfigure the Western art world. However, what lies ahead, in reality, for the young Jodorowsky, is a journey that will lead him to train intensively, not with the French Surrealists, but with the performance group of the legendary mime Marcel Marceau in Paris, before eventually falling into the company of his early collaborators in theater, Roland Topor and Fernando Arrabal, with whom he launches his first concept of a performance practice.

Now whether we believe the story of Jodorowsky's encounter with Breton (or, better put, *failed encounter*) is, as the film historian Michael Richardson says, in direct correlation to our willingness to be swept up in the mythologies that Jodorowsky has constructed around himself. According to Richardson, the event, as told by Jodorowsky, is itself dubious: "When he arrived in Paris he could, by his own admission, hardly speak a word of French, and Breton, we know, was unable to speak Spanish."[2] Fair enough. On his own account, Jodorowsky himself relays conflicting versions of the story, as evidenced in the various interviews where he's spoken on the subject. In one version, he comes to know Breton albeit briefly; on other occasions, he claims to have trained closely with Breton, playing surrealist games with him and other members of the earlier generation of Surrealist poets. What every telling of the story has in common, however, is Jodorowsky's ultimate decision to move on from "Surrealism" (or from "surrealism of the likes of Breton"), and into the direction of what he would eventually call, with Arrabal and Topor, the "Panic Movement." Whatever the case, no matter what version of events are being described, the critical moment is always the *dismissal*, which will be necessary for the more advanced neo-avant-garde project to emerge out of the ashes of the former movement. According to Jodorowsky, "Panic" – that is, the movement that he fashions in the period following this failed mythical encounter with Surrealism – far surpasses the activities of the old Surrealist masters, so much so that it is no longer necessary, nor even desired, to carry the old moniker.[3]

Whether or not we take Jodorowsky at his word, he paints nonetheless an interesting picture, inscribing a relationship between himself and Surrealism in this (imaginary, yet still instructive) encounter with André Breton. If, say, Breton had agreed to meet Jodorowsky after the 2 a.m. phone call, how might Breton have received him? Would he have been delighted to hear his plans? Would he have been impatient? Would he have agreed with Jodorowsky that the now senescent movement called "Surrealism" indeed required saving?

Of course, we know what happens to Surrealism in the decades following its climax in the 1930s. Writing in Mexico City decades later, the renowned critic Jorge Ayala Blanco summarizes it best when he says that Surrealism, far from being associated with the impulse of artistic revolution as it once had, becomes better known in his country "by way of erudite essays and fastidious volumes of poetry."[4] In other words, what Surrealism represents in the second half of the twentieth century is not the "shock" to the system as it was conceived originally by Breton and his colleagues in the pages of *La révolution surréaliste*, but was now instead a historical relic rather comfortably assimilated into the mid-century bourgeois literary culture. This is the rather downgraded situation of "Surrealism" as it appears to the vantage point of Ayala Blanco, and undoubtedly also Jodorowsky at the time of his arrival.

Many critics have indicated with some accuracy that Jodorowsky, in fact, better resembles the kind of surrealist that would have been *thrown out* of the movement in its heyday. Chief among Jodorowsky's influences is the most notorious of Surrealism's historical dissidents, Antonin Artaud, who had a falling out with Breton, was excluded from Surrealist activities, and was officially excommunicated from the group in 1926. (To be fair, Breton continued to advocate for Artaud in some limited capacity, but strictly always outside the Surrealist context, and always marking a careful separation between Artaud's methods and those of the official group). Indeed, Artaud's surrealism was antithetical to Breton's movement for the very reasons it would appeal to Jodorowsky later. His theorization of an avant-garde theater of cruelty was, first of all, central to his surrealist practice. Breton thought of theater in general as "bourgeois," therefore counter-revolutionary, and so dismissed Artaud's theater works out of hand. Secondly, Artaud's rejection of militant politics – insofar as "concepts" and "representations" are the very things Artaud's theater wished to destroy – went directly against the currents of Surrealism in the late 1920s, which sought to align itself with the aims of international communism (including, naturally, an adherence to communism's necessary concepts and representations).

It is curious, then, that Jodorowsky, with a reading list comprised of figures on Surrealism's periphery (not only Artaud, but also the dissident Bataille, Klossowski, and Caillois), would go pounding on Breton's door as his first act in Paris . . . if indeed Breton's version of Surrealism was well *en route* to becoming the respectable antique of Ayala Blanco's description. It would make sense for Breton – star of the few post-war Surrealist exhibitions that were staged during that decade and the following – to receive Jodorowsky's proclamation as a threat. "To save Surrealism" means conceivably that the orthodox surrealism of Breton is dead (or, at least, dying). And, to add a greater insult, its savior, this young brash Chilean, has arrived with a copy of Artaud's *Le Théâtre et son double* in his back pocket. In other words, what Jodorowsky was in actuality proposing to Breton that night, in this perhaps fictionalized but nonetheless, in many respects, *true* event, was not so much an offer to *resuscitate* the old Surrealism. More accurately, what he (and thus also his Panic Movement) represents is the threat to re-animate Surrealism with a demon spirit, to possess it with the same terror, sensationalism, and dissident sexuality that was once exorcized in the official renunciation of the figure of Antonin Artaud and his exiled Theater of Cruelty.

***

Of course, knowing what we know, the case is made rather easily that Jodorowsky did in fact "save Surrealism," one way or another. Whether Breton was taking 2 a.m. visitors or not, the moment for a late Surrealism had already begun with an active center shifted away from Paris to various coordinates in the Caribbean, Latin America, and the global south. For Jodorowsky's generation in Mexico City, it starts with a small group of cohorts coming together to invent a new set of aesthetic principles, working in performance and media, in theater, comics, graphic arts, situational actions, and film. The story, therefore, takes us away from Jodorowsky's early exploits in Paris back to the situation in Latin America, where Panic comes together in the theatrical works and "stage ephemerals" put on by Jodorowsky and his colleagues in Mexico, as the generation that establishes, in a truly radical and heterogeneous fashion, the neo-avant-garde of Mexico City of the 1960s and 1970s.

Leaving Paris, Jodorowsky arrives in Mexico in 1960 as a member of the touring performance group led by Marcel Marceau. There, in Mexico, he decides to stay, a decision to leave behind the life he had developed in Paris since his arrival there in 1953, years marked by formative experiences in the practice of mime (under the tutelage of Étienne Decroux and Marcel Marceau) and avant-garde theater, having staged numerous works by Beckett, Adamov, and Ionesco. Back in Paris, Jodorowsky also co-produced his first film, *Les têtes interverties* (1957), also known as *La cravate*, a loose adaptation of Thomas Mann's novella, *The Transposed Heads*, from 1940. An examination of metaphysics through the art of mime, this short film stands separate from Jodorowsky's later works in the medium. An excellent comparative analysis of the film, written by the film and media theorist, historian, and filmmaker Jesse Lerner, is included as Chapter 2 of this volume. The film, which for many decades was thought to be lost before it was eventually recovered in 2006, is the only surviving record of Jodorowsky's work prior to the Panic Movement. In his contribution to this volume, Lerner establishes Jodorowsky's minimalist first film effort in contrast to the massive undertaking of Fernando Birri's three hour long film *Org*, an adaptation of the same source material produced between 1967 and 1978. Lerner's chapter is, in many ways, an excellent entry into Jodorowsky's work, not solely for reasons of chronology, but for clarifying Jodorowsky's early and evolving approach to performance, production design, and, of course, mysticism, as three elements that will come to orient his work and his methodologies for the rest of his career. *La cravate* indeed presents a striking contrast, as it is detailed in Lerner's examination, with the works produced afterwards in Mexico City, both in theater production and in the eventual, more substantial return to filmmaking in 1968's *Fando y Lis*, Jodorowsky's experiment to produce a "Panic cinema."

Upon Jodorowsky's arrival to the art scene of Mexico City in the 1960s, he enters on a social milieu characterized by an ever-intensifying atmosphere of revolt, sexual dissent, and political and philosophical experimentation that typifies the critical spirit of the youth counterculture of Mexico and the social and political agitation that would come to a head by the end of the decade. This atmosphere of counterculture and political, sexual, and aesthetic experimentation marks the background for Jodorowsky's own experiments in performance, building from the influences he garnered in Paris, but especially around the figure, as mentioned above, of Antonin Artaud, whose theories Jodorowsky carries with him into the elaboration of Panic. Panic is, for all intents and purposes, Jodorowsky's interpretation (and, you could say, *realization*) of Artaud's Theater of Cruelty, as outlined by Artaud in *The Theater and its Double*, but existing predominantly in theory: a theater "freed" from text, from representation, and from the rational limit, from language itself. For Jodorowsky, the task, as indicated by Artaud, was to produce a theater of the turbulent body, which is precisely what the Panic Movement sought to present. Panic generates, under the watchful eye of the ancient Greek deity Pan (for whom it is named), a series of (first loosely scripted and then, from there) improvised performance works dedicated to the interrelated principles of laughter, violence, chaos, and destruction.

Whereas the Panic theater was conceived originally by Jodorowsky and the Spanish playwright Arrabal from within the more traditional vocabulary of scripted theatrical exercises, the form of the *panic ephemeral*, meaning theatrical events that were one-off productions (organized around improvisation), developed for reasons both theoretical and practical: *practical* insofar as Jodorowsky's longer-run presentations would inevitably be met with censorship in the places they ran (in Mexico City); *theoretical* insofar as the ephemeral format brought Jodorowsky closer to the precepts of Artaud, as indicated in *The Theater and its Double*, against representation, and against the bourgeois theater. For Jodorowsky, following Artaud, the ephemerals allowed for the production of *mises-en-scène* that defy traditional forms of theatrical representation, and that allow for the bodies of the actors *to speak* in a language all their own. From 1962 onwards, Jodorowsky's endeavor comprised the singular production of collaborative, non-scripted scenarios that would push the limits of representation – improvisations premised around staged ritual acts and their violent interruption in order to produce the achieved effect of "crisis" in the bodies of the actors and in the minds of the spectators in attendance.

Jodorowsky's first feature-length film, *Fando y Lis*, represents Jodorowsky's translation of the Panic spectacle to the cinema screen. At the Acapulco Film Festival of 1968, "Panic," in the form of Jodorowsky's film entry to the festival, reached suddenly a wider audience. The first screening, due to the graphic representations of violence, sex, and human malformity contained within the film, incited nothing less than a full-scale riot amongst the festival-goers, with Jodorowsky himself narrowly fleeing the event. After the riot in Acapulco, the film was immediately banned across Mexico. Writing within the wake of Jodorowsky's first endeavor to translate "Panic" into the realm of cinema is the legendary Mexican film critic Jorge Ayala Blanco, whose text on Jodorowsky,

"The Panic and/or Freak Aesthetic," is provided as Chapter 3 of this volume, excerpted from the second edition of his "abecedario" series on Mexican film, *La búsqueda del cine mexicano*.[5] The first section of this review was written by Ayala Blanco in the wake of the 1968 Acapulco Film Festival and recounts the riot that the film provoked amongst its spectators. In his analysis of the film, Ayala Blanco recounts why the film invited such a vitriolic reaction, understanding the scandal as the culminating point within Jodorowsky's iconoclastic art practice of the late-1960s, which defined Panic against the backdrop of the performance practices. These performances ranged from the smashing of pianos live on television to the infamous stomping to death of baby chickens on stage. But what Ayala Blanco locates as the key to understanding the "shock" of *Fando y Lis* requires, above all, the acknowledgment of Jodorowsky's philosophy regarding stage direction. Jodorowsky's well-documented practice of torturing and humiliating his actors, subjecting them to the worst indignities and physical risks in order to observe a cultish set of sado-masochistic rituals, is investigated by Ayala Blanco in his review of the film, in negotiation of what might be best described as the torture of *Fando y Lis*'s two main actors, Diana Mariscal and Sergio Kleiner. This chapter, translated for the first time into English by the art and literary scholar Amy Sara Carroll, negotiates Jodorowsky's "outsider" reception by the Mexican art world as a luminary Surrealist provocateur within the late-1960s Mexican counterculture. The reception of Jodorowsky as a troublesome institutional "outsider" exploding the conventions of aesthetic good taste is what situates Ayala Blanco's response to the film, and his categorization of Jodorowsky as a maverick (albeit dilettantish) filmmaker who produces an intriguing art cinema adjacent to the political and aesthetic debates occurring within the context of Mexican contemporary art in the late 1960s.

The elaboration of Panic, across the various media that the movement occupies, has several influences that bear mention here for their continued relevance as they carry over into the more well-known products of Jodorowsky's film practice. Jodorowsky's preoccupation, for instance, with disabled bodies in his earliest films and performances is something that he developed in collaboration with the artist José Luis Cuevas. Cuevas collaborates with Jodorowsky on a series of illustrations for the book *Teatro Pánico* (1965), as well as for Jodorowsky's 1964 science fiction editorial *Crononauta*. As literary theorist and historian Marisol Luna Chávez writes, observing the drawings of Cuevas, "disfigurement is an instrument for both formal and conceptual aesthetic speculation . . . At the same time, deformity is a resource through which he enquires into the human condition and its limitations."[6] It's a sentiment that resonates especially well with the analysis of *Fando y Lis*, a "road movie" concerning two lovers who search for the mythical city of Tar on the promise that the city will heal the disabled body of the young paraplegic Lis. The two instead embark on a journey that explodes into an orgy of grotesqueries. Included as Chapter 4 of this volume, Peter Sloane analyzes the film as the starting point for Jodorowsky's career-long obsession with the "brute facticity of the human body in its myriad forms and malformations," his interests in corporeality and the equality of human and animal form, and a fascination with the anomalous body as material object, presented in his films in ways that distort and challenge concepts of the filmic, the spectacular, and the beautiful. Sloane argues for the inscription of the anomalous body in Jodorowsky's films as operating beyond the gratuitous, towards rather a consistent exploration of the realities of disability and a heroic centering of the marginalized body, something realized in even greater detail in Jodorowsky's next two films, *El Topo* (1970) and *The Holy Mountain* (1973).

El Topo's promotional materials in 1969 billed the film as a "Panic Fable" in the tradition of the *Fábulas pánicas* comic strips produced by Jodorowsky between 1967 and 1972, which appeared each week in the culture section of the daily newspaper *El Heraldo de México*. These comic strips, conceived and drawn by Jodorowsky himself, attacked bourgeois social mores while at the same time exploring issues of mysticism and Zen philosophy, as influenced by his study of esotericism under the tutelage of Japanese Zen Buddhist monk Ejo Takata in Mexico City. Out of the many ideas sketched out in Jodorowsky's *Fábulas pánicas* emerged the idea for a feature film, a "Panic-Western." *El Topo* depicts the enlightenment quest of a black-clad gunslinger/prophet, played by Jodorowsky, who must defeat the four masters, each one representing, in their own idiosyncratic way, some allegorical relationship to mystical experience. This volume offers, as Chapters 5 and 6 respectively, a pair of chapters that deal with Jodorowsky's mystical learnings and their relevance on the scenario and production of *El Topo* as well as his 1973 follow-up *The Holy Mountain*, another (perhaps even more elaborate) enlightenment tale of Gurdjieffian mystical proportions. The first of these chapters, written by literary critic Naomi Lindstrom, situates *El Topo* and *The Holy Mountain* as the first and most significant examples from among several of Jodorowsky's films that focus on characters who perform the function of a prophet or communicate in prophetic discourse, whether verbally or through mime, channeling influences and exposures as varied as the philosophy of George Gurdjieff, Buddhism, divination by Tarot, alchemy, and other New Age mysticisms, towards, definitively, the prophetic current in Jewish thought, which Lindstrom analyzes as an essential aspect of Jodorowsky's work, embedded in the prophet character of *El Topo* and extended well beyond, with a significance relevant to Jodorowsky's entire filmography. Chapter 6, meanwhile, continues the discussion of Jodorowsky's mysticism with Peter Scott Lederer's excellent comparative analysis of Jodorowsky's work alongside Russian theosophy. Lederer provides the background for understanding the ideas of the performance-therapy that will come to characterize Jodorowsky's own interpretation of *El Topo* and *The Holy Mountain* as forms of *Psychomagic*, a therapy that is formally introduced and then practiced by Jodorowsky later, as the subject of his 2019 documentary *Psychomagic, a Healing Art*, which documents the treatment's applications in the field (among several public performances by Jodorowsky). As such, Lederer traces the psychomagic method, first elaborated in *El Topo*, from its historical theosophical forebearers, as it channels the powers of symbolism to a psychotherapeutic use.

Jodorowsky's fascination with art as a "healing therapy" has its roots in the earlier Panic ephemerals, wherein Jodorowsky developed, along proper Artaudian lines, the notion of the performance work as an exploration of an actor's trauma. From the mid-1960s onward, Jodorowsky's interests in trauma and psychotherapy were formulated at the intersection of several cultural currents to which he was directly exposed: psychoanalysis (and, in particular, the concepts of the counter-Freudian, religion-infused social psychology developed by Erich Fromm, who founded the psychoanalytic department at UNAM), Eastern mysticism (from Jodorowsky's work with the Zen master Ejo Takata, who had arrived in Mexico via California, and who introduced Jodorowsky to Fromm, as well as to a host of mystical writings and practices),[7] and, lastly, most elusively, indigenous mysticism, along the axis of the ritual use of indigenous psychoactive substances, a phenomenon that occupied a continuing interest for a number of countercultural forces across Latin America as well as internationally.

Jodorowsky's *The Holy Mountain* of 1973 can be seen as a diagrammation of these interests, and therefore also as the fitting culmination of Jodorowsky's Panic Fables. *The Holy Mountain* proceeds as a (loose) adaptation of the unfinished masterpiece by French mystic novelist René Daumal entitled *Mount Analogue* (1952), a story of "symbolically authentic non-Euclidean adventures in mountain climbing" (per the description that serves as the novel's subtitle). Daumal's story was inspired by the lessons of the esotericist George Gurdjieff, to whom he was introduced in 1938. Gurdjieff's teachings on consciousness and his methods towards "awakening oneself" merged with Daumal's own satirical, late Surrealist-inspired sense of humor in this tale of a mystical expedition of a group of adventurers to the top of the world's holiest mountain where heaven and earth are said to meet. Jodorowsky's *The Holy Mountain* involves a set of characters similar to Daumal's, insofar as there is a master, a protagonist, and a set of "specialists" who embark on an expedition of spiritual self-awakening. Jodorowsky himself, during the production of *The Holy Mountain*, received instruction from Óscar Ichazo, a Gurdjieff disciple and the founder of the Arica Institute in Chile, a center dedicated to "cosmic consciousness-raising." On the set of *The Holy Mountain*, Ichazo administered LSD to Jodorowsky, which inspired in him a vision: "He [Ichazo] sat me in a meditation position in front of a luminous circle on a terrace. It was a spinning Coca-Cola logo. As it spun, it became a line, then a circle, and then the Coca-Cola logo, which I stared at for six hours. It was the Coca-Cola circle, a ring of light in the city, on top of a roof. And that's when I had a flash of inspiration, a tremendous mental change."[8] As such, the production of Jodorowsky's film, whose plot entails the unfolding of a mystical initiation of a group of holy mountain climbers, takes the form of an initiation itself around the spiritual exercises that Jodorowsky required daily of his actors, with a symbolic imaginary mirroring the film's own complex *mise-en-scène*, a combination of recurring symbols situated around mandalas and other striking geometric constructions borrowed from a mix of different iconographies, from Eastern esotericism to indigenous Amerindian designs.

In Chapter 7, Florian Zappe categorizes *The Holy Mountain*, alongside *El Topo* and Jodorowsky's later "comeback" film *Santa Sangre* (1989), as having to do with the creation of an "aesthetics of intoxication" that characterizes these three (Jodorowsky's most popular) films. These films, in particular, due to their popularity as "midnight movies" in the U.S. and the U.K. (in fact, *El Topo* is said to have inaugurated the midnight movie phenomenon internationally), have been labeled by critics as "pill films," or what David H. Fleming has called "head cinema," an attempt to classify a genre of films whose appeal is specifically to an audience where the preference is to spectate with some form of pharmacological assistance.[9] These audiences, far from being undiscerning consumers of culture, sought films with the capacity to involve their participation (very much unlike the majority of films produced in the West, which maintain the classic Hollywood protocols of inducing a passive spectatorship). Fortuitously, Jodorowsky was well suited to meet the demands of this audience, having conceptualized his films as "accelerants" for transforming the consciousness of these very populations. Much of the cult cinema studies orientation to Jodorowsky's work thus far has been dedicated to analyzing the ways in which Jodorowsky's films were suited for this moment, to meet the needs of this Anglo-American LSD youth counterculture. In his contribution to this volume, Zappe moves beyond this trend in the cult studies formation to analyze Jodorowsky's "pill films" in the longer tradition of artwork, cinematic or otherwise, that identifies "inebriation" as its aesthetic paradigm. Jodorowsky's transgressive cinema can therefore be understood, says Zappe, as a modern resuscitation of a "Dionysian aesthetics of intoxication," which recognizes the representational schema of cinema as an affective dispositive, something achieved in Jodorowsky's films by means of shocking and overwhelming (and even repulsing) the audience, "mobilizing the weaponry of aesthetics against the stifling conventionality, predictability and unimaginativeness of the film industry's conservative standards."

Another important aspect of Jodorowsky's film production, when considered in its collision with other popular forms of aesthetic invention in the long 1960s and 1970s period, is the centrality of the film's score, often composed by Jodorowsky himself (as is the case with the exceptional soundtrack of *El Topo*). Included as Chapter 8 of this volume, Daniel Escoto provides a history and analysis of the soundtrack of Jodorowsky's *The Holy Mountain*, an endeavor that brought together Jodorowsky with legendary jazz trumpeter Don Cherry and studio musician Roger Frangipane, in order to produce an eclectic and experimental surrealist soundtrack of the highest order. In this chapter, Escoto gives a bird's-eye view of Jodorowsky's career in sonic experimentation, leading eventually to the collaboration with Cherry and Frangipane. This history includes, notably, the inclusion of rock music in the stage spectacle *La ópera del orden* (1962), free jazz in the filmed ephemeral *Melodrama sacramental* (1965), and then, of course, discussion of Jodorowsky's band *Las Damas Chinas*, whose music accompanied the theater production *Zaratustra* (1970). In his analysis of *The Holy Mountain*'s soundtrack, Escoto investigates the way that *pastiche* functions not only in Jodorowsky's scoring of the film, but in the larger concept of Jodorowsky's entire aesthetic project, the way in which, for instance, a pastiche of styles is activated in his work, whether it be in the realm of film, music, or comic writing, where concepts of genre are readily subverted in order to invent various new means of expression. In *The Holy Mountain*, this project yields a soundtrack with extremes at the antipodes of generic musical expression in a way that mirrors in a sometimes one-to-one, sometimes disjunctive relationship with the eclectic imagery of the film and its surprisingly deep well of intertextual references. Escoto refers to the soundtrack as part of the "Jodorowskian Machine" that typically "[devours] everything and anything needed for the project." The soundtrack itself, under these conditions of synthetic and disjunctive intertextuality, is best understood as proceeding from a "collage logic" that devours rock, free jazz, chamber music, and Hollywood orchestration in equal measure. As Escoto aptly summarizes, "*The Holy Mountain* remains a remarkable example of this intertextuality, an exercise of the cerebral that coexists with an appeal to emotions and the cathartic . . . Apart from its endless spilling of images," he continues, "the Jodorowskian machine is designed to entice the ears."

Among Jodorowsky's admirers after the success of *El Topo* were Yoko Ono and her husband John Lennon. Yoko and John, who saw the film at a midnight showing at New York's Elgin Theater, then convinced the businessman Allen Klein of the Beatles' ABKCO Records to front a million U.S. dollars for the production of Jodorowsky's next film project, which would turn out to be *The Holy Mountain*. Lennon also convinced Klein to secure the rights to *El Topo* in order to further distribute the film in the U.S. What began as a productive relationship between Jodorowsky and Klein, however, turned sour.

During production of *The Holy Mountain*, Klein went around collecting investors for "Jodorowsky's *next* project," which Klein had handpicked himself, unbeknownst to Jodorowsky, an adaptation of *The Story of O*. When *The Holy Mountain* was complete, Klein then demanded Jodorowsky begin preparing for the next project. Jodorowsky refused, leading then to Klein, in his rage, locking away the two films that were now owned by ABKCO (*El Topo* and *The Holy Mountain*), barring any (legal) exhibition of the films for the next thirty-plus years. Included as Chapter 9 of this volume, "Outlaw Artists and Esoteric Media: International Copyright and Alejandro Jodorowsky's Illicit Media Practice," Andrew Ventimiglia, a specialist in the history of media and intellectual property law, recounts the history of the copyright dispute with ABKCO and Jodorowsky's response: to become a bootlegger of his own films. Ventimiglia argues that Jodorowsky's public airing of the copyright dispute and the ensuant link to an "outlaw" distribution strategy were designed to further promote his films as countercultural products, both illicit in their content and clandestine in their guerrilla exhibition. The strategy, says Ventimiglia, demonstrates Jodorowsky's savvy at the level of strategic circulation in the face of institutional opposition, both at the hands of government censorship and capital. Moreover, Ventimiglia links Jodorowsky's strategies with similar problems faced by Óscar Ichazo at the Arica Institute, which was itself embroiled in a copyright dispute around the ownership of the esoteric symbol of the enneagram. The similarities between Jodorowsky and Ichazo's situations and their responses exhibit a larger tendency with religious media producers of the era to use copyright law to strategically shape the distribution and control of their media. In Jodorowsky's case, the piracy of his own media was not a singular case with ABKCO, but has continued in defiance of the copyright holders of even his most recent releases. In 2015, for example, Pathé Distribution, which holds the distribution rights for Jodorowsky's *The Dance of Reality* (2013) filed a DMCA (Copyright) Complaint to Vimeo, LLC, when Jodorowsky uploaded the film to the free streaming website's servers. When Pathé had the video removed, Jodorowsky responded via Twitter.com, in all caps: "PERDER UNA BATALLA NO ES PERDER LA GUERRA, @PatheFilms HA DETENIDO EL DON DE 'LA DANZA DE LA REALIDAD' VOLVEREMOS A LA CARGA PRONTO" ["LOSING THE BATTLE IS NOT LOSING THE WAR, @PatheFilms HAS BLOCKED THE GIFT OF 'THE DANCE OF REALITY' WE WILL STRIKE BACK SOON"] (1:03 PM 24 Mar 2015).

Following the debacle with ABKCO, Jodorowsky was, more or less, a free agent in 1974. It was then that he was approached by French producers Michel Seydoux and Jean-Paul Gibon, who, after an effort of fundraising, offered the director a budget of 9.5 million dollars for the next film project. When asked what film he would most like to make following his epic *The Holy Mountain*, Jodorowsky's response was "*Dune*." The rights for Frank

Herbert's 1965 sci-fi novel *Dune* had been previously owned by the producer Arthur P. Jacobs, of *Planet of the Apes* fame. When Jacobs died in 1973, Gibon purchased the rights. By 1976, Jodorowsky had enlisted an illustrious set of collaborators for the project, while also having already, in pre-production expenses, blown through a little more than 20 percent of the film's total budget. The assembled cast and crew comprised Jodorowsky's twelve-year-old son Brontis in the role of Paul Atreides, Orson Welles as the Baron Harkonnen, Salvador Dalí as the emperor, Mick Jagger as Feyd-Hautha, and David Carradine as Duke Leto, with a score by Pink Floyd, visuals by H. R. Giger, Chris Foss, and Jean Giraud (aka Mœbius), and special effects by Dan O'Bannon (who was brought on only after Jodorowsky met with and rejected the special effects legend Douglas Trumbull of *2001: A Space Odyssey*). For all the pre-production wrangling involved in the run up to *Dune*, what Jodorowsky had to show for his efforts by 1976 was a thick book of storyboards and a collection of concept art conceived by Jodorowsky with the collaboration of Mœbius and Giger. The storyboards, illustrated magnificently by Mœbius, are themselves a veritable masterpiece, existing as a 3,000-panel visualization of the entire film (of which, sadly, few copies exist, one of which resides in the personal collection of Jodorowsky).[10]

After roughly two and a half years of development, the project stalled for financial reasons when the film's early backers reportedly caught wind of Jodorowsky's baroque and, in their minds, *excessive* plans for the film, a visually stunning, special effects-laden *fourteen-hour-long* space opera that veers significantly from its source material. Although much of the legend of Jodorowsky's *Dune* likely stems from its existence as one of the great *unrealized films of cinema history* – a film that "*could not be*" for reasons of Jodorowsky's own heroic uncompromising vision for it – the failure of the project, as experienced by Jodorowsky, had nonetheless some lasting negative effects on Jodorowsky's career, as well as his attitude towards the film industry.[11] Jodorowsky's critical attitude towards the more orthodox forms of commercial film production (and financing) was cemented in 1980 with the realized project of *Tusk*, based on Reginald Campbell's novel *Poo Lorn of the Elephants*. *Tusk* was a film of compromise, according to Jodorowsky, a film that was indeed "*made for money*," insofar as its producer Éric Rochat wrestled a significant amount of control from Jodorowsky during production for precisely the reason of protecting his investment. The product – a somewhat paint-by-numbers adaptation of Campbell's novel – bore none of the characteristics of a "Jodorowsky film," despite the promise of being the newest "fable panique" in its promotional materials. After the project was completed in 1980, the film failed to garner a U.S. distributor, after which point it was disavowed by its maker. Today the film remains seldom seen, circulating predominantly in the form of a few out-of-print and heavily degraded VHS tapes.

After several years of inactivity in filmmaking (strictly speaking), Jodorowsky's late-1980s "comeback" to cinema takes place in the form of the exceptional *Santa Sangre* (1989). The film, a Mexican/Italian co-production conceived by Jodorowsky alongside the Italian producer Claudio Argento and screenwriter Roberto Leoni, takes place in Mexico City in a setting that spans the asylum, the circus, and the late-night cabaret. Starring Jodorowsky's son Axel, the film is organized around a concept that is loosely inspired by the infamous 1940s serial killer Gregorio "Goyo" Cárdenas, aka "Goyo the strangler," who Jodorowsky met once at a bar in Mexico City sometime after the killer's rehabilitation and release from prison in 1976. Much like Goyo, who strangled women to death in – so he claims – *hallucinatory fits*, Fenix too, the protagonist of *Santa Sangre*, is compelled to kill by an obscure force, materialized in the super-egoic commands of his dead apparition mother, ordering Fenix to murder the various women he comes into contact with over the course of the narrative. In Chapter 10 of this volume, Alessandra Santos delves into Jodorowsky's film in order to recover the potent allegory of political violence contained within its scenario, an allegory that crosshatches and telescopes an array of social problems that are the usual fodder of exploitation films, from violence against women to problematic queer representation and portrayals of disability. Chapter 10, "Resistance in Alejandro Jodorowsky's *Santa Sangre*," therefore, launches a close reading of the film in order to negotiate its place as a work of "resistance," functioning within Jodorowsky's oeuvre as a critical study of the types of violence typified in exploitation cinemas that culminates in the spectacularized depiction of femicide occurring in the film. Santos argues, in a brilliant counterintuitive gesture, that within the gendered violence portrayed in the film there is an advocacy against such violence, a maneuver that separates *Santa Sangre* from the types of exploitation films that it usually evokes. In a tradition of cult cinema where "shock value" and "spectacle" work as vehicles for promoting the idea of an unrestrained violence as itself the sign of a radical social and aesthetic progress, Santos instead provides a reading of *Santa Sangre* relevant for understanding the less evident layer of meaning comprised in the film's dealings with trauma, whose spectacularization in Jodorowsky's film is posed against the hegemonizing regimes of patriarchal authoritarianism that deny trauma's existence as an organizing principle. This reading of the film demonstrates how, in the words of Santos, "collective and personal traumas persist in internalized structures of domination, power relations and hierarchical structures," a key argument for understanding, as well, Jodorowsky's later works in cinema: *The Dance of Reality* (2013) and *Endless Poetry* (2016), works of memoir that deal both directly and indirectly with the psychological operations of colonial domination, inspiring in turn the psychological and aesthetic forms of resistance that Jodorowsky develops in his art practice.

Although the film was met with mixed reviews at the time of its release, *Santa Sangre* was a triumph on a number of levels, not least of which was the much anticipated "return to form" that the film represented for Jodorowsky. Following the collapse of the *Dune* project and the unmitigated artistic and commercial failure of *Tusk*, the concern that Jodorowsky had, in fact, abandoned cinema once and for all was palpable. It was only with some luck and determination that the director was able to gain full artistic control of a feature film. If the failure to realize *Dune* had signalled to financiers that Jodorowsky, in 1980, was incapable of producing a feature film within reasonable economic constraints, the success of *Santa Sangre*, a film made on a relative shoestring budget, proved otherwise. In 1989, following the successful production of *Santa Sangre*, Jodorowsky was signed on to direct *The Rainbow Thief*, with a significantly larger budget at his disposal. The film was a British production starring the actors Peter O'Toole and Omar Sharif (in a much-anticipated *Lawrence of Arabia* reunion), and offered audiences the chance to see these two screen legends perform in a wild surrealist film captained by a proven master of the genre. Far from realizing that promise, however, the actual production of the film mirrored the experience of *Tusk* in practically every way, and the product itself, in its final form, came to resemble the chaos of the conditions under which it was produced. Creative control of the film was wrestled from Jodorowsky early on, with the production allowing the director no leniency with the script, constraining his every move and reducing him, so Jodorowsky says, to the level of an abused technician. Making matters worse, the director, for his part, turned out to be no match for the domineering presence of O'Toole (nor the kind of production culture that an ego of that size fosters). *The Rainbow Thief*, released in 1990, yielded both a commercial and critical failure in Europe and was ultimately denied a wider international distribution. Opportunities to return to the director's chair, unfortunately, did not come pouring in after *The Rainbow Thief*, and it was at this point that *Santa Sangre* was understood as an exception, produced within a set of circumstances that simply weren't replicable in the years following its release. In the 1990s, Jodorowsky shopped around a sequel to *El Topo* that failed to gain any financial backing, and much the same in the 2000s, with an idea for a gangster film (*King Shot*), which remains unproduced. There would be a total of twenty-three years separating *The Rainbow Thief* and Jodorowsky's next feature, *The Dance of Reality*, the first part of a surrealist, semi-autobiographical duo of films based on Jodorowsky's 2001 memoirs of the same title.

However, it would be an error to say that Jodorowsky produced nothing "filmic" outside of *Santa Sangre* and *The Rainbow Thief*, within the two "dry spells" that characterize the decades-long separation between these films and the triumphant works on either side (*El Topo* and *The Holy Mountain*, and *The Dance of Reality* and *Endless Poetry*, respectively). After the collapse of the *Dune* project, Jodorowsky returned to comic book writing, much as he had occupied himself with earlier in his career in the production of the *Fábulas pánicas*. The difference, in the 1980s, was that Jodorowsky now had Mœbius, a veritable genius of the Franco-Belgian *bandes dessinées* tradition, in his orbit. With the pen of Mœbius at his disposal, Jodorowsky no longer relied on his own naïve illustrations to realize an increasingly complex set of visual ideas, as were fostered in the concept art in the failed run up to *Dune*. Whereas the constraints, financial and otherwise, proved a tragedy for the realization of the project in film, Jodorowsky's *Dune* was "completed," in some sense, in the collaborative effort of its storyboards. Although those storyboards remain unreleased, many of the ideas generated in that original collaboration take on a more polished form under yet another name. A series of science fiction graphic novels, written by Jodorowsky and illustrated by Mœbius, and based loosely on the original art of *Dune*, was born under the title of *The Incal*, beginning in 1980, with *L'Incal Noir*, published originally as installments in the French magazine *Métal Hurlant*. The series took shape in a number of editions between 1981 and 1989, and was followed then by a prequel (*Before the Incal*, 1988 to 1995), a set of sequels (*After the Incal*, 2000, and *The Final Incal*, 2008 to 2014), and several spinoff series (*The Metabarons*, 1992 to 2003; *The Technopriests*, 1998 to 2006; *Megalex*, 1999 to 2008; *Metabarons Genesis: Castaka*, 2007 to 2013; *Weapons of the Metabaron*, 2008; and *The Metabaron*, 2015 to 2018). The overall collection of works is referred to by its readership as "the Jodoverse," or, alternatively, "The Metabaron Universe," signifying the interconnected system of narratives that unifies the series of graphic novels produced in the wake of Jodorowsky and Mœbius's original collaboration.

Chapter 11, "Inherit and Repair: Self-erasure and Allegoric Montage in Jodorowsky's *The Caste of the Metabarons*" by Francisco Javier Fresneda-Casado, examines the relationships between body and imperial structure as featured in the graphic novel *The Metabarons* (*La Caste des Méta-Baron*, 1992–2004) through the study of its narrative and visual organization. Conceived by Jodorowsky as a "space-opera saga" mixed in with elements of Greek tragedy and employing Central European and Japanese imperial iconographies in the story's visual regime, the series focuses on a dynasty of invincible warriors known as "the metabarons." (The last of the metabarons was featured in the original *L'Incal*, for which the *Metabarons* series functions as "prequel.") In this chapter, Fresneda engages a close reading of *The Metabarons* in order to analyze the critique of imperial iconography inherent in the work. Jodorowsky, argues Fresneda, takes advantage of the multidimensional properties of the graphic novel in order to make a *cinematic montage* that problematizes linear notions of genealogy. A complicated notion of dynastic "genealogy" is what structures the series. The term that Fresneda uses to describe Jodorowsky's narrative inventions in the graphic format is "allegorical montage," in order to characterize the narrative distribution evident in the complex unfolding of the Metabarons saga, profuse as it is in retroactive storytelling and differential visual authorships where the images conflict with their own representational field. What Jodorowsky presents is a narrative style realized in the graphic novel that would be *otherwise resistant* to the suture of linear (cinematic) continuity. Fresneda's intricate analysis of temporality in the Metabaron universe situates Jodorowsky's adoption of the graphic novel as a form sought not merely for its convenience (as a way to communicate "cinematic ideas"), but as an important and complex site of intervention into the medium of the graphic novel itself, *beyond* the cinematic, in a modality of the graphic novel conducive for a more radical (but nonetheless *legible*) set of narrative possibilities: the thematizations of the suspension of time, the disintegration of bodily integrity/identity, and the introduction of alternative timelines and subjectivities that characterize the narrative organization of the work.

The idea of the "unmade," alongside Jodorowsky's departure into other media to pursue new forms of authorship, is taken up again in Chapter 12, "Alejandro Jodorowsky, the Unmade and *The Sons of El Topo*," by Matthew Melia. In this chapter, Melia constructs a historical timeline linking the failure of *Dune* to Jodorowsky's works in the graphic novel medium, including the graphic novels produced by Jodorowsky that depart from the visual iconographies explored originally with Mœbius in the *Dune* pre-production. As such, Melia's chapter centers on Jodorowsky's unmade sequel to 1970's *El Topo*, in *The Sons of El Topo* (or *Abel Cain*), and its afterlife as a graphic novel (*The Sons of El Topo, vol. 1: Cain* and *The Sons of El Topo, vol. 2: Abel*). Unlike *The Incal* and *Metabarons* series (which originated as graphic novels), *The Sons of El Topo*, published in 2016, is a cross-media hybrid, containing in its pages a latent, "unmade" film, necessarily conceived "cinematically," as the follow-up to *El Topo*. In this entry, Melia considers how Jodorowsky's "unmade text" extends and develops the themes and ideas present in his original 1970 film, connecting his analysis to his own previous explorations of Jodorowsky's use of cinematic landscape and his inheritance of the legacy of the theater of the absurd (which Melia investigates in his previous text "Landscape, Imagery and Symbolism in *El Topo*" in *Reframing Cult Westerns*).[12] This chapter, building from Melia's earlier study, provides an in-depth examination of the advantages that the graphic novel/comic format provides for Jodorowsky's development of the *El Topo* narrative. Therein Melia explores the industrial and cultural reasons which led to the project's initial failure as a feature film. In the course of his argument, Melia nonetheless instills an optimism that the realization of "the unmade" in graphic form represents the project's realization in an adjacent, but certainly not *inferior*, format, very much in line with Jodorowsky's own thinking on the subject, of the graphic novel as a ready alternative for an otherwise fully conceived (and uncensored) "film authorship."

Regarding the contemporary reception of *El Topo*, alongside talk of sequels and Jodorowsky's endurance as a lingering controversial character in international film, one must address the moment in 2019 when a retrospective of Jodorowsky's work at El Museo del Barrio in New York City was canceled after comments made by Jodorowsky in an interview promoting the film in 1972 were once again unearthed in the run-up to the retrospective. In Jodorowsky's 1972 book, *El Topo: A Book of the Film*, Jodorowsky made claims that he committed a nonconsensual act of unsimulated sexual violence on his co-star Mara Lorenzio: "After she had hit me long enough and hard enough to tire her, I said, 'Now it's my turn. Roll the cameras.' And I really raped her."[13] After protests erupted during the resurfacing and publicity of these comments in 2019, and in the midst of the #MeToo movement's drive for holding institutions accountable, the retrospective was canceled. El Museo director Patrick Charpenel said in a statement to *The New York Times* that "[w]hile the issues raised by Jodorowsky's practice should be examined, we have come to the conclusion that an exhibition is not the right platform for doing so at this time."[14] The publication *Artforum*, in the wake of the museum's decision, allowed Jodorowsky an opportunity to respond to the controversy:

These words: 'I've raped my actress,' was said fifty years ago by El Topo, a bandit dressed in black leather that nobody knew. They were words, not facts, Surrealist publicity in order to enter the world of cinema from a position of obscurity. I do not condone the act of rape, but exploited the shock value of the statement at the time, following years in the Panic Movement and other iterations of harnessing shock to motivate energetic release.[15]

He continued by saying, "I acknowledge that this statement is problematic in that it presents fictional violence against a woman as a tool for exposure, and now, fifty years later, I regret that this is being read as truth. My practice is centered on healing and love. I invite further dialogue in the spirit of progress."[16]

Of course, 1972, when the original comments were made, also marks the year that *Last Tango in Paris* was released, a film that has since been re-evaluated according to its own controversial production history involving the stated abusive treatment of the actor Maria Schneider by the film's director Bernardo Bertolucci, regarding what Schneider has called an unscripted rape scene that led to her sexual humiliation on set. Recent decades have likewise seen a critical reappraisal of the gender politics of many famous male auteurs, in the ways in which certain of these filmmakers have treated their female actors, from Alfred Hitchcock's well-documented abuse of Tippi Hedren, to Stanley Kubrick's methods for instantiating a near perpetual state of psychological duress for the actor Shelley Duvall during the filming of 1980's *The Shining*, and also

Quentin Tarantino's alleged abuse of Uma Thurman on the set of 2003's *Kill Bill* (to name just three famous examples from a devastatingly long catalogue of gendered abuse in film history).

The protests around and subsequent cancellation of Jodorowsky's retrospective at El Museo del Barrio place the comments of Jodorowsky within the continuum of these other stories of abuse. The trials of Harvey Weinstein are evoked in the grotesque image of the abusive, exploitative, and overall masculinist framework of commercial and independent film production. Considering, however, both the 1972 claim by Jodorowsky, and likewise his various apologies and defensive statements *for* the claim, made on separate occasions between 2007, 2017, and 2019, we might be able to produce a commentary that links the story that Ayala Blanco was telling his readers in the early 1970s about the kinds of abuse that Jodorowsky inflicted on his *Fando y Lis* actors, Diana Mariscal and Sergio Kleiner, and about how important these tales of abuse were to the mythologizing of Jodorowsky's character as a late Surrealist. Bertolucci, after all, produced *real* tears from Maria Schneider ("I feel guilty, but I don't regret it," he says).[17] And Kubrick's *The Shining* likewise produced an image of a woman living in *actual* terror. "Art" justifying "abuse," or so the argument goes. Perhaps the difference, however, between these other isolated examples of on-set abuse and Jodorowsky's 1972 claim is that unlike these other abusive auteurs, Jodorowsky actually *campaigned* on the abuse in 1972. He attempted to *mythologize himself* with the concept of abuse, which he now alleges as nothing more than a trait of Surrealist provocation.

Indeed, again, whether or not we accept Jodorowsky at his word (and I have already alluded to the dangers of accepting *any* of Jodorowsky's words, if you recall the opening paragraphs of this introduction), there is still nonetheless something to be said about our ambivalent relationship with whatever it is historically that we want to call "Surrealism" in the twenty-first century. Jodorowsky's comments resurfaced first in 2017 and again in 2019, around the same time that protestors, in a separate and unrelated incident, were gathered outside the Metropolitan Museum of Art in New York City to condemn a work by the French Surrealist painter Balthus, along with a petition of nearly 9,000 signatures to remove a painting from the Met's collection that, in their words, "romanticizes the sexualization of a child." That work (Balthus's *Thérèse Dreaming*, 1938) was carefully defended as a work of Surrealist provocation. The Met's spokesperson, in response to the petition, released a statement saying:

Moments such as this provide an opportunity for conversation, and visual art is one of the most significant means we have for reflecting on both the past and the present, and encouraging the continuing evolution of existing culture through informed discussion and respect for creative expression.[18]

What the Met spokesperson and the director of El Museo del Barrio have in common is their admission for the need to examine the issues raised in these works in connection with contemporary cultural issues. For Jodorowsky, however, his "creative expression," insofar as he claims the comment as part of a performance of the "El Topo character" in the 1972 promotion of the film, is something that, due to the circumstances of the 2019 protests, he at last faced consequences for, and apologized for, while feeling the need also to contextualize the comment: to explain that this particular idea of "Surrealism," as a form of violent provocation, whose relationship to the effects of reality is based solely on the logic of publicity and exposure, but not truth, is a method of garnering attention that *is* in fact contradictory to the evolution of his overall artistic practice toward, instead, in his words, methods of "healing and love."

This volume concludes, appropriately, with two chapters on Jodorowsky's practice of "Psychomagic," conceived in cinematic terms and also in terms of Jodorowsky's evolving performance practice, which Jodorowsky has taken internationally. Both chapters, in different ways, negotiate what Jodorowsky, in the last instance, makes of "surrealism." Hence, to the place we started. In Chapter 13, "Jodorowsky, Psychomagic, and Subjective Destitution," the literary critic and philosopher William Egginton engages the intellectual history of the therapeutic practice of psychomagic as essentially "cinematic" in nature. Psychomagic, says Egginton, represents "a coherent picture of human existence that finds its highest expression in cinema," and therefore requires cinema, as a conceptual form, in order to understand and to extrapolate on both its practical and philosophical dimensions. "Surrealist poetry," he writes, "and the specifically visual forms of it that [Jodorowsky's] filmmaking takes, is a prime example of this existential therapy." Egginton, therefore, returns to the site of Jodorowsky's filmmaking in order to say something of psychomagic as a form of therapy, as a therapy that relies on a series of impressions mapped out in his cinema and theater practice, and situated especially around the "role of the guru" as conceived in such films as *El Topo* and *The Holy Mountain*. Where Ayala Blanco, in Chapter 3, noted the centrality of the "guru figure" as the phenomenon organizing Jodorowsky's relationship with his production team (by both consulting gurus on set and by taking the form of one himself), Egginton extends this analysis to the narrative organizations of the films that mirror this process whereby the provocative teacher (or "the alchemist") functions as a catalyst for provoking forms of "enlightenment" in the student. In this volume's penultimate chapter, Egginton compares the relationship between the psychomagical guru (a.k.a. Jodorowsky) and his student/patient to the relationship of the analyst and analysand in the Lacanian conception of the *sujet supposé savoir* (the "*subject supposed to know*"), whose interventions, writes Egginton, "find their efficacy in the power they have to shatter the ego's complacent attachment to the normative structure of power and submission"). Egginton's comparative study, moreover, is necessary for a deeper understanding of the complexity, as well as the perversion and controversy, of Jodorowsky's psychomagical therapy practice, materialized in the interactive performance art demonstrations that Jodorowsky has toured with around the globe under the name of psychomagic, performances marked by shamanistic initiations, Tarot readings, and other forms of auto-suggestion, mobilized in order to precisely – as Egginton argues – disturb the relationship between the guru and his follower, by which Jodorowsky's guru, the *subject supposed to know*, is, in the end, *emptied* of his vast knowledge when the cards are revealed and the camera "zooms back" to reveal the artifice at its core.

Chapter 14, "Talmudist and Kabbalist Practices in Alejandro Jodorowsky's *Psychomagic, a Healing Art*," by Henri-Simon Blanc-Hoang, concludes the volume with a brilliant alternative historicization of Jodorowsky's conception of therapy through the rabbinic and Kabbalist tradition. Instantiating a close reading of Jodorowsky's latest film *Psychomagic, a Healing Art* (2019), a document of Jodorowsky's psychomagical performance roadshow, Blanc-Hoang draws a connection between the narrative organization of the documentary film to the lesson plan of a Talmudic class, which he demonstrates as the film's precedent in terms of its formal structure. Where the film appropriates a host of shamanistic practices, notably indigenous Latin American, Blanc-Hoang highlights the particular strain of the Talmudist tradition that acts as a binding agent for all the practices that enter into this New Age blender of psychomagical performance art. Although Jodorowsky's performance practice, at a certain level, defies categorization, Blanc-Hoang shows how the pedagogical traditions of Judaism make sense for a reading of *Psychomagic, a Healing Art*, placing the film in a continuum with Jodorowsky's two meta-fictional "memoir" films, *The Dance of Reality* and *Endless Poetry*, as two works among the canon of otherwise fiction films that are cited in the documentary. Jodorowsky's free mixing of documentary footage and excerpts from his earlier filmography proceeds in a way that harmonizes the entire body of work in the form of a recognizable Judaic strategy of biblical exegesis, with the film itself functioning as the culminating circle of Jodorowsky's entire body of work, where the fictional narratives intersect with the pseudo-sacred performances of psychomagic. Taken together with Egginton's study of psychomagic in the chapter that precedes it, Blanc-Hoang's study of the Judeo-mystical practices at the heart of Jodorowsky's final film provides an excellent case study for how a form of Surrealist poetry *qua* therapeutic practice morphs over the course of Jodorowsky's entire body of work, from the original radical form of theater, whose intention it was to cultivate an understanding of its participants' trauma, to the theorization of the guru figure as the *subject supposed to know* in Jodorowsky's films, at last to the documentary "conclusion" of Jodorowsky's therapeutic practices in his final work, an endeavor to "complete the circle" for our understanding of Panic theater and, more generally speaking, of Jodorowsky's trajectory as a late (dissident) Surrealist.

NOTES

1. Alejandro Jodorowsky and Ariel Godwin, *The Dance of Reality: A Psychomagical Autobiography* (Rochester, VT: Inner Traditions International, Limited, 2014), 172–173.
2. Michael Richardson, *Surrealism and Cinema* (Oxford: Berg, 2006), 137.
3. There is no record of an apprenticeship with Breton.
4. See the review by Ayala Blanco contained in this volume.
5. Jorge Ayala Blanco, *La búsqueda del cine mexicano (1968–1972)* (Mexico City: Universidad Nacional Autónoma de México, 1974).
6. Marisol Luna Chávez, "Disfigurement and Monstrosity in the Work of José Luis Cuevas" in *Desafio a la Estabilidad/Defying Stability: Procesos Artisticos en Mexico/Artistic Processes in Mexico 1952–1967*, ed. Rita Eder (Madrid and Mexico: Turner and Universidad Nacional Autónoma de México, 2014), 267.
7. For an account of Jodorowsky and Takata's relationship in English, see Ken Martin's "Mexico City, Koans, and the Zen Buddhist Master: Alejandro Jodorowsky, Ejo Takata and the Fundamental Lesson of the Death of the Intellect," *Transmodernity: Journal of Peripheral Cultural Production of the Luso-Hispanic World*, vol. 8, no. 3.
8. Jodorowsky, from an interview with Olivier Zahm for *PURPLE magazine*, F/W 2009, issue 12.
9. David H. Fleming, "Head Cinema as Body without Organs: On Jodorowsky's Bitter Pill Films and Their Spinozian Parallels" in *Unbecoming Cinema: Unsettling Encounters with Ethical Event Films* (Bristol: Intellect, 2017).
10. In November 2021, a "crypto" group called Spice DAO purchased one of the exceedingly rare copies of the Mœbius-Jodorowsky *Dune* concept art for roughly $3 million (USD). The group, financed by crypto currency, was reportedly under the (legally misguided) impression that ownership of a physical copy of the book meant ownership of the book's intellectual property and claimed that they would make an animated series based on the acquisition. See David Barnett, "Jodorowsky Animated Dune in Development, Says Crypto Group," *The Guardian*, January 24, 2022, https://www.theguardian.com/film/2022/jan/24/dune-animation-based-on-jodorowsky-concept-art-in-development-says-cryptocurrency-group-spice-dao-frank-herbert
11. Much of the concept, artwork, and assembled crew of Jodorowsky's unrealized *Dune* was cannibalized by other productions, including, notably, *Alien* (1979), whose screenplay was written by O'Bannon and whose concept art was designed by Giger, a collaboration initiated by Jodorowsky. For more, see Frank Pavich's 2013 documentary, *Jodorowsky's Dune*, recounting the rise and fall of the *Dune* project, including its legacy in science fiction cinema.
12. Matthew Melia, "Landscape, Imagery and Symbolism in Alejandro Jodorowsky's *El Topo*" in *Reframing Cult Westerns: From The Magnificent Seven to The Hateful Eight*, ed. Lee Broughton (New York: Bloomsbury Academic, 2020).
13. Alejandro Jodorowsky, *El Topo; A Book of the Film* (New York: Douglas Book Corp., distributed by the World Pub. Co., 1972).
14. Qtd. in Colin Moynihan, "El Museo del Barrio Cancels Jodorowsky Show." *The New York Times*, January 28, 2019, https://www.nytimes.com/2019/01/28/arts/design/el-museo-del-barrio-cancels-jodorowsky-show.html

15. "Alejandro Jodorowsky Speaks Out After El Museo del Barrio Calls Off Retrospective." *Artforum*, January 31, 2019, https://www.artforum.com/news/alejandro-jodorowsky-speaks-out-after-el-museo-del-barrio-calls-off-retrospective-78538

16. Ibid.

17. "Bertolucci over Maria Schneider." *College Tour*, February 5, 2013. Archived from the original on December 11, 2021, https://ghostarchive.org/varchive/RMl4xCGcdfA

18. Qtd. in Peter Libbey, "Met Defends Suggestive Painting of Girl After Petition Calls for Its Removal." *The New York Times*, December 4, 2017, https://www.nytimes.com/2017/12/04/arts/met-museum-balthus-painting-girl.html

Two Tales of Transposed Heads: "La Cravate" and "Org"

Jesse Lerner

By almost any measure, *La Cravate* (also known as *Les têtes interverties*, 1957) is an exceptional entry within Alejandro Jodorowsky's filmography; his first film, it is the only film he co-directed (sharing the directorial credits with fellow actors Saul Gilbert and Ruth Michelly), and the only surviving cinematic record of his work prior to the Panic Movement, which he co-founded with Francisco Arrabal and Roland Topor in 1962.[1] *La Cravate* was assumed to be lost for close to half a century, only to reappear in 2006 in a German attic. In part for this reason, it is relatively little seen, especially when compared with Jodorowsky's subsequent feature films, the midnight movie staples and renown cult films *El Topo* (1970) and *La montaña sagrada/ The Holy Mountain* (1972), both of which enjoy a devoted fan base, transgress numerous norms, and undermine "basic poles of good and bad"[2] in ways that *La Cravate* does not. Like fellow avant-garde filmmakers Kenneth Anger (*Rabbit's Moon*, 1950–1971) and Arthur and Corinne Cantrill's collaboration with the mime Will Spoor (*Moving Statics*, 1968), *La Cravate* draws on a European performance tradition going back to Jean-Louis Barrault and commedia dell'arte, if not further back into traditions of the classical Mediterranean.[3] Of Jodorowsky's years in the world of Parisian pantomime, his work with Étienne Decroux and Marcel Marceau, it is the only film documentation to have appeared to date. At an intersection of French mime, pre-dictatorship Chilean experimental theater, German literature, performance art, and encounters with Breton and the writings of Artaud, the film is as atypical of Jodorowsky's cinema as it is revealing. This chapter will explore *La Cravate*, Jodorowsky's adaptations of Thomas Mann's novella *The Transposed Heads*, as a window into the beginnings of the artist's long career in what, for want of a better word, I will call "experimental film."[4]

Jodorowsky states that his interest in mime dates to a 1948 viewing (in Santiago de Chile) of the epic historical drama *Les enfants du paradis* (Marcel Carné, 1945), when he was nineteen years old. The film performances of Jean-Louis Barrault (in a role based on the life of the famed Bohemian-born French performer Jean-Gaspard Deburau) and Étienne Decroux inspired the young artist to form a five-person mime troupe, the *Teatro Mímico*, which first performed at the Santiago campus of the University of Chile in 1951. Two years later Jodorowsky relocated to Paris to study with Decroux, leaving his former collaborator, the mime Enrique Noisvander, in charge of the Chilean ensemble. His instruction under Decroux proved to be a profoundly disappointing, nothing less than an insufferable, experience: "I never imagined that this mythical creator of modern mime language . . . had such cruelty, such bitterness, such envy of another's success."[5] The relationship with Marcel Marceau grew to be much more productive and positive. *La Cravate* is, among other things, very much a reflection of this milieu. The film score by the Romanian composer Edgar Bischoff, who later composed music for film and stage performances by Marceau (*Der Mantel*, 1951, an adaptation of Nikolai Gogol's 1842 short story *The Overcoat*, and *Les Trois Perruques* [*The Three Wigs*], 1953) represents one of many points of connection.

La Cravate is ostensibly an adaptation, albeit an extremely loose one, of Thomas Mann's 1940 novella *The Transposed Heads: An Indian Legend* (*Die vertauschten Köpfe: Eine indische Legende*), though the setting is shifted from India to an unspecified, presumably Western city and all dialogues are omitted, among many other transformations. Coincidentally, an important contemporary of Jodorowsky, Fernando Birri, the so-called "father of the New Latin American cinema," also adapted this short novel of Mann's, though the results could not be more different. Nearly three hours long and incorporating over 26,000 cuts, the resultant film, Birri's *Org* (1967–1978), is as sprawling, excessive, and maximalist as Jodorowsky's is jocular and modest. Beyond the curious novella by Mann, the central image of transplanted heads recurs in mythology and popular culture, including the Soviet science fiction classic by Alexander Belyaev, *Professor Dowell's Head* (1925, reworked as a novel in 1937), and the animated Fleischer Brothers short with Betty Boop, *Crazy Town* (1932). This conceit raises numerous questions of the mind/body relationship, of the nature and source of human identity, and of the cruelty of corporeal dismemberment.

Mann's novella is set in an ahistorical India, and is written in a light-hearted, playful tone that contrasts with the tragedies it narrates. It is based on Mann's reading of the German folklorist Heinrich Zimmer's compendium *Maya: Der Indische Mythos*, an anthology of South Asian myths and legends.[6] Mann dedicated the book to Zimmer, "the great Indian scholar."[7] Significantly, neither Mann nor Zimmer ever visited Asia, though the latter developed an encyclopedic knowledge of Indian mythology, exclusively from secondary sources.

And despite the novel's reworking of Indian folklore, the central premise echoes Western myths as well. Giovanni Boccaccio's *Decameron* includes the tale of Cimon and Iphigenia, told by the fictional Panfilo. Cimon is described as having been born into wealth, and being very handsome and physically fit, though intellectually challenged. Like Mann's novel and Jodorowsky's adaptation, it is the sight of a beautiful woman, the sleeping Iphigenia (not the daughter of Agamemnon and Clytemnestra sacrificed to Artemis, but a Cypriot commoner of the same name), that provokes the simpleton to transform himself into an intellect, though as told in the *Decameron*, without decapitations or a tragic ending. The story of Cimon and Iphigenia has been a favorite among painters, including Peter Paul Rubens, Sir Joshua Reynolds, and Benjamin West. The Indian origins of the tale which inspired Mann and Jodorowsky are even older than Boccaccio's fourteenth-century collection of tales; Zimmer's telling is derived from one in the eleventh-century collection of myths and legends, *The Kathāsaritsāgara*, compiled by Somadeva Bhatta.[8] That Boccaccio drew on diverse sources for his stories, both European and Asian, suggests the possibility of cross-fertilization, though scholars believe the tale of Cimon is Italian in origin.[9]

Even more so than Mann's, Jodorowsky's adaptation takes many liberties with the original. It transposes the setting from the distant Indian past to a contemporary, unspecified Western city. The relationship between the two male leads is not one of friendship, as described in the novella; rather, the muscular, weak-minded Nanda character (played by Raymond Devos) is presented as a macho bully, who pushes around the sensitive (and presumably more learned and brainier – though there's little indication of this in the film) Shridaman character, played by Jodorowsky. In fact, Shridaman is not portrayed as possessing "a noble headpiece" or mind, as Mann describes him, "and correct diction – which, of course, was inseparable from wisdom and philosophy, and one with these,"[10] but rather comes off as a bit slow and very immature. The fact that the film is without dialogue means we have no opportunities to hear or judge his diction, but throughout his actions are guided by a naïve desire to win favor with the opposite sex, and there are no indications of wisdom or nobility. When challenged to a game of checkers by the shopkeeper/head transplanter, he quickly loses. The child and the goddess of the novella are eliminated, as are both the tragic ending and, again, the dialogues. While the novel gives the three members of the love triangle equal weight, the film is decidedly Shridaman's story, a male ingénue's journey from romantic rejection to satisfaction. Sita, the love interest, is divided into two female roles, one the shopkeeper/head transplanter, who falls in love with Shridaman's head, and the other a manipulative femme fatale (played by Rolande Polya), only seen haughtily resting in a chaise longue. It is the latter's rejection, rather than the goddess' rage, that leads to Shridaman's multiple decapitations. He proceeds to try on multiple heads, hoping to find one that pleases the scornful female, and his comportment changes with each one. When he ends up with the Nanda's head, equipped with a deficient brain, he becomes desperate in his search to recover his original. The storefront head shop has gone out of business, and the storefront now sells hats. But the alluring young shopkeeper at the head shop (played by Jodorowsky's future wife Denise Brosseau), who also performs the swapping of heads for her clients, found Shridaman's head attractive, and has brought it home with her, without a body. She keeps on the fireplace mantle and uses it for entertainment. They play chess together, and the head blows on a recorder while she performs the fingering – an echo of Fenix's devoted, Oedipal tending to his armless mother's needs in *Santa Sangre* (1989). Spotting his own head through the window, stored under a glass bell jar, Shridaman's body (with Nanda's head attached) attempts to steal it, but when the shopkeeper awakens, she agrees to reunite the original head and body. Their love for each other – or at least their desire – can now find physical expression, and Nanda's head is thrown in the trash, where it becomes a plaything for a simple-minded homeless man.

Beyond this brief synopsis, a few words about the production design are necessary. For all of their surreal imagery, Jodorowsky's other films take place in what we recognize as the real world. Many of the locations used in the later films – Mexico City's Zócalo, Mathias Goeritz and Luis Barragán's *Torres de Satélite*, the ruins of Chichén Itzá and Uxmal – are instantly recognizable. *La Cravate*, however, true to its roots on the stage, all transpires in what is essentially a theatrical space, drained of most real-world references. On the studio set, these locations are suggested by a bare minimum of props. The shop is nothing more than a set of shelves, a chair for the transposing of heads, and a storefront display window. The city is little more than a theatrical flat with painted, caricatures of building façades. Rather than realism, the locations, costumes, and props all have a simplified, color-coded quality that transports the narrative far from the real world. Though the strategy used is very different, the apparent artifice (as well as the impossibility of the premise of head transplants) consistently reminds the viewer that what we are watching is not real, just as the well-known dolly-back at the end of *The Holy Mountain* (1973) reveals the film crew and equipment. "Is this life reality?" the Master asks in that film. "No. It is a film," he replies, answering his own question. "Zoom back, camera. We are images, dreams, photographs." Both achieve a Brechtian alienation affect in the viewer, precluding audience identification with the characters or the misrecognition of the staging for the real. Elsewhere Jodorowsky has reflected on the differences between stage and screen. The latter, he claims lends itself to representations of the universal: "Theater is a cry in the city. Cinema is a cry in the world. Theater's address is a place. Cinema's address is the entire planet. In theater, the actor is man. In cinema, the actor is humanity."[11] Despite the evident theatrical quality of *La Cravate*, there is no question that the characters represent archetypes, not individuals, and the story aims to be an allegory on the human condition, not a particular set of circumstances. Though based in theater we are asked to take the dilemma of the actor (Shridaman, as played by Jodorowsky) as that of mankind.

The titular *cravate*, or lavender necktie, marks the dividing line on the body between the head and rest. The neck, being the site of the removal and replacement of heads, is a locus of anxiety and concern at numerous moments in the film. One customer, head newly reattached to a body, makes a point of donning a detached shirt collar. The necktie, initially presented as an adornment designed to make the wearer more attractive, is likewise the source of anxiety for those who have had their heads removed and replaced. Freudians would be quick to identify this as castration anxiety. At the film's end, with his head and body reunited, the protagonist looks in horror at his earlier neckwear, stumbles, wobbles, and reels before reconfirming his head's firm attachment and throwing away the cravate. Jodorowsky has stated repeatedly that filmmaking for him is a form of therapy, a means of resolving deep-seated issues. While one would be hard-pressed to connect this or any other sequence from the film to the director's accounts of his inner conflicts, difficult childhood, or to wider philosophical debates about the mind-body relationship, some of those questions are lurking playfully in the background. As to the mind-body dialectic, the director's statements emphatically endorse one possible interpretation: "I am saying 'you are not a body who has a spirit, you are a spirit who has a body.'"[12] One's body, the director would like us to think, is nothing more than a vessel for one's mind. Despite the Indian origins of the narrative, this position is closer to a Western, Cartesian understanding of the mind as equivalent to the conscious self than to the dualism of some Hindu or Buddhist philosophies.

The echo of Fenix's armless mother in *Santa Sangre* is only one of many ways in which *La Cravate* anticipates themes of Jodorowsky's more mature films. Though the genders are reversed, the relationship between the able-bodied shopgirl and the detached head of Shridaman is a less abusive, less perverse variation on that of Fando and the physically disabled Lis, as portrayed in Jodorowsky's feature film debut, his 1968 adaptation of Arrabal's play. More generally the co-dependent relationship between the body-less head of Shridaman and the lonely shopkeeper/head-transplanter echoes multiple dysfunctional relationships depicted in his later films. The image of a warehouse of severed body parts returns in *The Holy Mountain*. However anomalous and adolescent it may appear to be, *La Cravate* hints at many of the themes of Jodorowsky's mature work.

The humor of *La Cravate* is derived from its sense of absurdity and incongruity. In Kant's reflections on humor, he proposes: "in everything that

is to excite a lively convulsive laughter there must be something absurd . . .
Laughter is an affection arising from the sudden transformation of a strained
expectation into nothing."[13] Similarly Schopenhauer postulates: "In every
case, *laughter* arises from nothing other than the sudden perception of an
incongruity between a concept and the real objects that are, in some respect,
thought through the concept."[14] Here, the real objects, the heads, operate
differently than in the real world. We all know that decapitation is inevitably
fatal and that brain transplants or head transplants have never succeeded. The
head transplant scenes, more than a sense of shock or fear, call for a suspension
of disbelief, and later, and more sustained, reflection on where we (or our souls,
our beings) reside. Do we divide ourselves or see ourselves as an integrated
whole? And if we were to divide ourselves, how?

There are some striking contrasts between *La Cravate* and the works
Jodorowsky created immediately afterwards in Mexico City (having arrived
as part of Marcel Marceau's touring troupe): *La lección* (a staging of Ionescu's
1951 play at *La casa del lago* in 1960), *Había una muchedumbre en la mansión*
(a 1960 staging of the 1955 play *Il y avait Foule au Manoir* by Jean Tardieu at the
Teatro de la Esfera), *Fin de partida* (a staging of Beckett's 1957 *Endgame*), and
La ópera de la orden (at the *Teatro de los compositores*, 1962). While the program
for the latter promises actors and mimes, there is also a monologue (performed
by Beatriz Sheridan), something inconceivable in the theater of Barrault,
Decraux, and Marceau. Language, albeit absurdist language deprived of
meaning or selected by a chance operation, becomes an increasingly important
part of Jodorowsky's work with his "*efímeros pánicos*," made in 1962 and 1963
in collaboration with the sculptor Manuel Felguérez (who later would make
the "sex machine" seen in *The Holy Mountain/La montaña sagrada*, 1972).
The "*efímeros pánicos*" include *Poema dinámico para un inmóvil de hierro*,
Efímero en la sala Villaurrutia, and *Efímero en la Escuela de San Carlos*. The
impulse to scandalize and shock, so prevalent in his feature films, is perhaps
best evident in what was his most ambitious performance of this era, *Canto al
océano*, at the inauguration of Felguérez's monumental mural for the *Deportivo
Bahía* (owned and sponsored by artist and filmmaker Gelsen Gas). Inspired
by the Comte de Lautréamont's *Les Chants de Maldoror* (Isidore Ducasse,
1868–1869), the action involved dancers, *tableaux vivants*, and film projections.
Jodorowsky, in the role of the transgressive Maldoror, was to make his entrance
lowered from a helicopter, but during rehearsal the aircraft crashed into the
swimming pool, where it remained during the performance. That said, the
use of disquieting imagery and grotesque themes is a constant in his work; as
part of Marceau's mime troupe, Jodorowsky had developed a sketch called *The
Heart Eater*, in which the protagonist murders a man, a woman, and a child,
and removes and consumes their hearts before committing suicide.[15] Marceau
stated: "it goes beyond Artaud in the concept of cruelty."[16] Artaud's *Theater*

and its Double (1938) has elsewhere been referred to as "Jodorowsky's bible."[17] Jodorowsky's first book, *Teatro Pánico* (1965, dedicated to Artaud, among others) is suggestive of both a radical departure from the world of *La Cravate* as well as points of continuity between the works. On the one hand, he states his intention is to make a break from all previous theater, which up until that point had been, in his eccentric taxonomy, either figurative or abstract. Panic theater, in contrast, is aligned with the absurd juxtapositions one finds on a page of the daily newspaper. Yet the book includes the scenarios of two of the skits Jodorowsky created for Marceau, *El fabricante de mascaras* (*The Mask Maker*) and *La jaula* (*The Cage*). In 1967, Jodorowsky began publishing cartoons called *Fábulas pánicas* in *El Heraldo*, and one of the first of these involved the gradual dismemberment of man, ending with two panels of the head, placed on a bizarre, psychedelic end table. "I really want to roll around naked in the grass" ["Tengo muchas ganas de revolcarme desnuda en la hierba"], the head laments, a sentiment his character in *La Cravate* might have felt.[18] And while the documentation of these early Mexican works is extremely scant, from what can be garnered in the available sources, the move from Parisian mime to Panic was paradoxically both a radical rupture and a point of continuity.

   Co-founder of the film school at San Antonio de los Baños and "father" of the New Latin American Cinema Fernando Birri also adapted the same Thomas Mann novella for the screen, more than two decades after *La Cravate*. The expansive, anarchic, epic adaptation called *Org* is screened even less frequently than Jodorowsky's short adaptation, though it was recently restored by Berlin's Arsenal. The results could not be more different from Jodorowsky's short. The film's epigraph is from William Blake – "La strada della eccesso conduce al palazzo della saggezza" ["The road of excess leads to a palace of wisdom"] – and the film is nothing if not excessive. Inspired by renegade Freudian Wilhelm Reich, Birri imagined this film viewed not in a movie theater, but in an environment, a variation on the orgone accumulator, a "scientific receptacle projected by W. Reich with the object of verifying, experimenting, and regulating orgone energy" ["receptáculo proyectado científicamente por W. Reich con el objeto de verificar, experimentar y regular el uso de la energía orgónica con fines terapéuticos liberadores"[19]]. In preparation for the film's premiere in Venice, he described his vision in a telegraph: "Beyond cinema beyond no-cinema but still cinema Stop Metacinema Stop To get to the screen where *Org* is projected: diaphragms sesame labyrinths . . . in front of a membrane-hymen-screen made of sheets" ["Más allá del cine más allá del no-cine todavía cine Stop Metacine Stop Para llegar a la pantalla donde se proyecta *Org*: diafragmas sésamo laberintos . . . delante de una membrana-himen-pantalla hecha con sábanas"[20]]. Despite their shared inspiration, only a handful of elements connect the excesses of *Org* with *La Cravate* and Mann's fiction: a love triangle, the head transplants, and the absence of any references to India. Birri's main interest, based in Reich but of little apparent interest to either Jodorowsky or Mann, is the possible connection between political and sexual liberation. In his words, "we want neither revolution without orgasm nor orgasm without revolution" ["no queremos revolución sin orgasmo ni orgasmo sin revolución"[21]].

That filmmakers and writers as diverse as Birri, Jodorowsky, and Mann can all find artistic inspiration in the myth recorded by Somadeva Bhatta and Heinrich Zimmer is a testament to the resonance of its basic premise. The myth has similarly inspired an opera, a stage play, and a musical.[22] Each of these takes the fundamental proposition in very different directions and strikes a very different tone, but the fact that elective cosmetic surgery is a multi-billion-dollar industry suggests that the desire for a different face, a larger (or smaller) nose (or breasts, etc.), is not an uncommon one. While head transplants remain the terrain of fiction, the notion that for romantic fulfillment (or enhanced self-esteem) our heads ought to be shaped differently, or attached to a body shaped differently, is omnipresent in contemporary life. *La Cravate* suggests that the ultimate satisfaction is found in reconciling ourselves to the mind and body with which we were born.

NOTES

1. Thomas John Donahue, *The Theater of Fernando Arrabal: A Garden of Earthly Delights* (New York: NYU Press, 1980), 28; Alejandro Jodorowsky, *Teatro pánico* (CDMX: Ediciones Era/Alacena, 1965); Frédéric Aranzueque-Arrieta, *Panique: Arrabal, Jodorowsky, Topor* (Paris: Harmattan, 2008).

2. Ernest Mathijis and Xavier Mendik, eds., *The Cult Film Reader* (New York: Open University, 2008), 2.

3. Karl Toepfer, *Pantomime: The History and Metamorphosis of a Theatrical Ideology* (San Francisco: Vosuri Media, 2019).

4. Jesse Lerner and Luciano Piazza, "Introduction" in *Ism Ism Ism: Experimental Film in Latin America* (Oakland: University of California Press, 2017), 2.

5. Alejandro Jodorowsky, *La danza de la realidad: (psicomagia y psicochamanismo)* (Madrid: Siruela, 2009), 195.

6. Heinrich Zimmer, *Maya: Der Indische Mythos* (Stuttgart: Deutsche Verlags-Anstalt, 1936).

7. Thomas Mann, *The Transposed Heads: A Legend of India*, trans. by H. T. Lowe Porter (New York: Alfred A. Knopf, 1941), n.p.

8. Somadeva Bhatta, *Stories from the Kathāsaritsāgara*, trans. by P. V. Ramanusaswamy, ed. by Aryendra Sharma (Hyderabad: Sanskrit Academy, Osmania University, 1959–1965).

9. Giovanni Boccaccio, *The Decameron*, 2nd ed., trans. by G. H. William (London: Penguin, 1993), 831–832.

10. Mann, *The Transposed Heads*, 9.

11. Sergio Guzig, trans. by Joanne Pottlitzer and Sandy MacDonald, "A Mass Changes Me More: An Interview with Alejandro Jodorowsky," *TDR/The Drama Review*, vol. 14, no. 2 (1970), 76.

12. Quoted in Ben Cobb, *Anarchy and Alchemy: The Films of Alejandro Jodorowsky* (London: Creation Books, 2006), 25.

13. Immanuel Kant, *Critique of Judgement*, trans. by J. H. Bernard (London: Macmillan, 1892), part I, div. I, 54.

14. Arthur Schopenhauer, *The World as Will and Idea*, trans. and ed. by Judith Norman and Alistair Welchman, ed. by Christopher Janaway (Cambridge: Cambridge University Press, 2010), 84.

15. The sketch is described in Ben Cobb, *Anarchy and Alchemy: The Films of Alejandro Jodorowsky* (London: Creation Books, 2006), 24–25.

16. Quoted in Cobb, ibid., 25.

17. Alessandra Santos, *The Holy Mountain* (London: Wallflower, 2017), 99.

18. This comic, originally published June 25, 1967, is reprinted in Alejandro Jodorowsky, *Fábulas pánicas* (Grijalbo, 2003), 10. See also Olivier Debroise and Cuauhtémoc Medina, eds., *La Era de la Discrepancia, Arte y cultura visual en México, 1968–97* (CDMX: UNAM, 2007), 104–105.

19. Fernando Birri, "Carta al pintor escenógrafo portugués Henrique Rulvo," in *El Alquimista Democrático: Por un nuevo nuevo nuevo cine latinoamericano* (Santa Fe, Argentina: Sudamérica, 1999), 107.

20. Birri, "Org," in ibid., 102.

21. Birri, "Revolución y Orgasmo" in ibid.,78.

22. I refer to the opera *The Transposed Heads* by the Australian composer Peggy Glanville Hicks (1954), the play *Hayavadana* by the Indian actor and director Girish Karnad (1971), and the musical *The Transposed Heads* by Julie Taymor and Sidney Goldfarb, with music by Elliot Goldenthal (1986).

CHAPTER 3

The Panic and/or Freak Aesthetic

Jorge Ayala Blanco
Translated by Amy Sara Carroll

*I*n *the late 1960s and early 1970s, the legendary Mexican film critic Jorge Ayala Blanco reviewed Jodorowsky's films* Fando y Lis *(1968) and* El Topo *(1970). His commentaries were later collected in the second volume of his "abecedario" series on Mexican film,* La búsqueda del cine mexicano *(1974). His remarks are presented here for the first time in English.*

Putting forth a formula for "Panic theater," [Fernando] Arrabal specified the import he intended to bestow on the notion of Ceremony: Theater can no longer settle for a text or its animation, it must encompass and express everything through the raw and brutal means of the primal scream and exhibitionism, sadism and poetry, up to and even including necrophilia and sacrilege. "Eroticism in all its pathological distortions is the first god of this Dionysian cult," Michel Corvin asserts in his compendium, *Le théâtre nouveau en France* (Presses Universitaires, Paris).[1] This formulation of Panic theater was introduced to Mexico by a Chilean mime who'd worked under Marcel Marceau: Alejandro Jodorowsky (b. 1928). For several seamless years – in the early 1960s – the stage novelty of the director garnered him the well-earned reputation of being a destroyer of theatrical habits in an environment still dominated by *costumbrista* realism, laborious academicism, and the decried vices of fin-de-siècle Spanish theater.[2]

The old stage structures were shaken, demolished, and relegated to base commercial theater. Invention and imagination replaced rote recitation. The set production of [Samuel] Beckett's *Endgame* situated pantomime as an intermediary between two existential garbage cans while *The Dream* of [August] Strindberg was reduced to two lonely characters. Jodorowsky exuberantly flexed his God-complex. His egotism and narcissistic excesses inaugurated a brand of sublime show business as snobbish religion, as a cult of provocation, as the surest method to *épater* (shock) the recently acculturated Mexican bourgeoise.

On Jodorowsky's watch, the force of scandal emerged as still possible in a country where Surrealism had hitherto only been known by way of erudite essays and fastidious volumes of poetry. It was a scandal to break pianos with hammers on television screens, edit books of *Panic Games* or comics steeped in cheap philosophy called *Panic Fables*, mount as a cultural challenge a pedestrian but profitable piece like Luis G. Basurto's *Cada quien su vida* ("To Each His Life"), write like an illuminated "Orientalist," train masochist actors to withstand being slapped or exposed to the worst indignity and physical risk in the name of obedience to the master.[3]

The inflated ego of Jodorowsky in turn pivoted, in an almost natural manner and with independent financing, to cinema. His first film *Fando y Lis* (1967), a loose adaptation of a homonymic piece by Arrabal, starred Sergio Klainer and Diana Mariscal, the very actors who had performed the piece on the boards in OPIC theater in the second staging of the play by Jodorowsky (its first unforgettable run having taken place in 1962 with Beatriz Sheridan and Héctor Ortega).[4] It mattered little that the new director didn't have the slightest inkling of what could be achieved with a camera or that a basic, easy-to-learn cinematographic language was already widely in circulation. Jodorowsky's filmic adventure was fundamentally mystic: Enticed by the light of the demiurge, cameraman [Rafael] Corkidi would point and shoot; the producers would be burned alive in their department, by accident, but would leave behind parents and friends who would be vindicated by the film's spirit; the actors would eat flowers and drink human blood and allow themselves to be buried alive and fall off the top of a mountain and would be close to a psychotic break – all for the sheer love of their art. Meanwhile each workday the director would rise at 4 a.m. to channel the necessary inspiration to ceaselessly improvise the scenes.

The general atmosphere of sexual obsession and infantile sadism, at one and the same time naïve and perverse, that traverses the theater of Arrabal, lent itself particularly well to the realization of whatever occurrence, extravaganza, or prank crossed Jodorowsky's mind to reappear in this first Latin American show of "panic cinema." The automatism of the sexually pathological subconscious was the only organizing principle of the project, at a far remove from the precise itinerary predetermined by the work's original script. *Fando y Lis* had neither structure nor global vision because necessity and coherence were not its abiding characteristics.

Jodorowsky justifiably believed in a phrase of [the Marquis de] Sade's wrenched out of context, "All excess is good," and wielded it as an aesthetic creed.[5] He prided himself on chaotic indeterminacy: "*Fando y Lis* could be the hell of Dante and Odysseus, the Apocalypse and a fairytale, could be the history of crime and an analysis of the unconscious, could be an adventure film, a critique of the vices of our society, a vision of the world post-nuclear war, an alchemical treaty, or an extended dream." But most certainly, yearning to be all of the aforementioned, the production proved to be none of the above, or only the product of a cluttered and furious pre-cinematographic imagination.

Poor Diana Mariscal, looking timidly into the camera, lets out horrible screeches, consuming a flower petal by petal against a backdrop of exploding bombs. The bearded, half-bald René Rebetez attempts to force snakes into the "pussy" of a grass doll. The faun-like Juan José Arreola and two older men throw themselves upon the girl's naked body. Bloated bourgeoisie delight in consuming syrup-steeped peaches as they castrate a resigned stallion-servant. Ten-month pregnant women appear as sexual objects. The Oedipal son pursues the maternal figure covered in feathers in a Felliniesque basement orgy. Upon reaching her, he spits in her face, in the hopes that she will cease to be a witch and become righteous, notwithstanding her heavily made-up appearance. The episodes of the film are punctuated with illustrations from the Divine Comedy and engravings of medieval alchemy. In an open-air festival, demonically possessed priests burn a piano as anonymous characters roll in the mud shouting that the happy mythic city of Tar does not exist. Delicate Sergio Klainer is chased by the nymphomaniac Erinyes until the all-powerful Father rises from the grave and possesses them all to shame the son for his latent homosexuality. Lis gives birth to live pigs, stand-ins for the feminine libido. She offers up her virginal body, reclining on a rubbish heap of cow skulls, and clamors from her wheelchair that Fando mustn't continue his solo descent into the labyrinthine crater. In a doll's hospital, Fando and Lis paint and deface their names on one another's bodies. A beggar of human blood drinks a full glass, leaving only the dregs for his small companion. Fando beats his tambourine, leaping puckish as an adolescent, stopping only to die with the twofold knowledge: nobody arrives to Tar and; satiating his sadomasochistic desires with Lis, he'd shortsightedly hastened her demise. With the rat bites and foot-sucking thus concluded on the screen, intertitles sign off with a flourish the film's mystical-erotic adventure: "And when his image was erased from the mirror, the word freedom appeared on the glass."

Yet if anything opposed and blocked freedom (of the imagination, of the tale) it was the film itself. All of this Sado-Maldorian paraphernalia and all of these invocations of inner liberty, of unattainable ideals, and the interchangeable victim-executioner love relationship, hung on a thin and listless weave of Freudian explanations.[6] *Fando y Lis* was a kaleidoscope of symbols and unusual provocations in appearance alone. With a pocket manual of psychoanalytic truisms, Jodorowsky would gamble that it would be enough to idly exceed all the traumas, inhibitions, and pathological deformations of Lis, of Fando, of the multitude of characters that they encountered on their journey to perfection, of the story, of the cinematic non-form, of the larger-than-life figure of Alejandro, of his delusional admirers and official bureaucrats who had the film banned for five years: *Nefando and Gis, Fango and Chis*, et cetera.

The overdetermined symbolism remains key for understanding the *Fando y Lis* phenomenon. The film's showing in the 1968 Acapulco Review created a formidable local scandal, resulted in the suspension of that annual festival, and demonstrated that, for "underdeveloped" spectators, the apparent disturbance of the senses was more scandalous than reality's objective ignominy. Scandal was no longer, as it had been in the Buñuelian years of 1929–1930, a form of aesthetic inquiry, but rather a successful platform of self-promotion within an emerging consumer society, where objects of cultural scandal would prove to be the most sought-after. But scandal would go out of style like fashion, the middle class would absorb in five years the terrible truth of having a subconscious and repressed desires, and the film would be released without further ado as the storm subsided.

Still, something was gained from the *Fando y Lis* case. Mexican cinema got its *Blood of a Poet* forty years late, its belated but persevering Cocteau. Neither film happening nor false surrealism nor New York underground, nor prefabricated delirium, nor naïve post-expressionism. Stripped of a true renovating force (Jodorowsky's role within Latin American cinema would be to evidence, with his Europeanizing "pygmy" avant-gardism, that [Hans Magnus] Enzenberger was correct to suppose that all of the avant-garde movements are as retrograde as the very conceit of an artistic avant-garde), devoid of an authentic questioning force, since the Freudian symbolic system only throws off decorative sparks, but never structures its images and figures as a dialectical discourse. Without hysteria or patronizing airs, *Fando y Lis* survives as an infuriating and melancholic soliloquy about the reciprocal destruction of lovers in search of a solipsistic utopia with a tempered beauty that could only guarantee it the irrational sensibility of an infantile fantasy.

And it will be precisely the exaggeration of this infantile fantasy, to the point of taking it to the realm of cretinism, and the absence of any constitutive romantic factor, derived even in some evanescent form from Arrabal's piece – the elements that will make its failure irremediable vis-à-vis the perspective of its own stated intentions – that will define *El Topo* (1970), Jodorowsky's second feature-length film, now in color and with a semi-independent millionaire's budget. Millionaire and semi-independent because the production will not depend on financing from the National Cinematographic Bank, but will pass over the latter and its petty rules, managing to fall back, for better or for worse, on the capital of Wall Street upon which in the final instance our cinematic industrial economy relies.

At the beginning of *El Topo*'s filming, Jodorowsky has seen his domestic cartoonish-theatrical stardom elevated to a third power, popularized courtesy of his budding cinematographic legend. With pleasure the joint violent rejection (the extremes meet) of the far cultural right (institutionalized hypocrisy, the film financiers who demand the expatriation of the director) and the far cultural left (the contempt and neglect of the representatives of the Mexican intelligentsia) – or better put, rejection and denouncement – are mobilized as supporters in reverse, becoming publicists-detractors of staggering promotional expediency. Jodorowsky will be, for three or four more years, the gravitational center of a "cult of ideas spectacle" in Mexico. All the cultural fashions, all the prestigious styles in vogue, all the imaginative audacities will constellate around him. The figure of this showman, capable of adapting with great fanfare [Friedrich] Nietzsche's *Thus Spoke Zarathustra* and of making the rarely accultured bourgeoisie (followed by the rising petty bourgeoise) flock to the theater to get spanked (*The Game that We All Play*), dwarfed the modest imaginative delusions of the majority of his film-generation peers. For better or for worse, Jodorowsky had wiped out the Mexican half-tone.

Cultural abuse, naïve by way of irresponsibility, mercantilist by way of narcissism, inconsistent by way of antonomasia, mystified on principle; cultural abuse has met its pluperfect match. A kind of trademark of the insolently prefabricated, a guarantee with a social reason to know that the provocation will only affect the most external wings of the ideological pyramid that crushes us, a surety of the scandal that enthrones childishness as an absolute value. In reality, any of the fertile ideas that make up *El Topo* – effectively treated, developed, deepened – would help a less exhibitionist filmmaker to build a halfway decent film. *And the lava ran over your mouth full of cobwebs and scorched your harmless forehead.* Free accumulation usurps the place of creative, inventive, perceptive, elective, restructuring capacity. And the curious thing is that the myth of modernity was the first to bolster this anachronizing anemia.

But, as [Hippolyte] Taine notes, nobody lives with impunity in a landscape. By dint of scratching all cultural fashions of his time and of all previously "accursed" periods, even without sincerely embracing anyone or ending up with some counterculture to challenge the very concept of art, Jodorowsky wound up believing that he had discovered – above and beyond the mix of disparate elements that his unconscious navigated – a supreme truth. Never dispensing with the pillage and his early affinities, Jodorowsky immersed himself completely in the discipline of yoga, in an emphatic and self-serving Orientalism that resulted in his feeling in possession of the absolute. A false order now aspired to sublimate the chaos of an unchecked imagination. The director of *El Topo* wrote, directed, and starred in his own production, regardless of Arrabal who would rebound to influence him powerfully by way of the latter's debut Tunisian film: *Viva la muerte* (*Long Live Death*) (1971).

Jodorowsky offered us, sans assistance from anyone, his truth, the truth, non-thought that synthesized all the irreconcilable theses and antitheses of the world, unfathomable knowledge, the symbol of complete resolution, the Nirvana of silence and immobility. Jodorowsky became priest (master) and acolyte (slave) at the same time, hierophant and hieroglyph to himself, revered guru and favorite disciple of his own mystical revelations. Occultism and esoterism discursively killed the little grace and spontaneity that redeemed *Fando y Lis*. The generic indeterminacy of that previous work was superseded; *El Topo* would be a delirious pop game, as if it were a prerequisite of his films, but above all else, there was the road to Damascus, the mysteries of Eleusis, and the humble renunciation of the former pleasures of sadism, before pushing them to their final limit. The path of perfection was so wide it could accommodate any excess. You could take a vow of chastity and smear blood on a woman's breast, you could profess to be ascetic and abandon yourself to the exorbitant spectacle, you could reject Judeo-Christian rites and slavishly praise all the upended liturgies; you could, in a word, be a vegetarian and eat animal – even human – meat daily. *El Topo*, consequently, would be a Buddhist western in its final determination and design.

The protagonist of *El Topo* is a bereaved gunman who had to defeat all, to save all regardless of who they were or why, in fierce duels and in nightmarish settings, against half a dozen invincible gunman no match for the skill, nothing spiritual, of Jodorowsky incarnate. Humor is out of the question. Arch-solemn philosophism sets the tone for the tasks of this trigger-happy Hercules, with a naked child always on his back, on the horse's rump or walking by his side, like a guardian angel and vigilant conscience during his successive trials in the desert – the first being to castrate Colonel David Silva who writhes like a gigantic toad on his luxurious bed and who perhaps is nothing more than God himself, but nonetheless is guilty of spearheading the massacre of a defenseless village, and the rape by bandits of a group of pedophile monks who granted immediately offer up their asses.

But El Topo will not realize the following adventures accompanied by the kid alone; rather he's joined by an Eve-Sancho Panza-Queen Bee assemblage – the Oedipal gunman (Juan José Gurrola), the perfectionist gunman (Víctor Fosado) who comes to a fiery end, and the hybrid gunman (made up of a man without legs climbing on a man without arms) – a composite rival whom the Zen gunfighter repeatedly seeks to liquidate on hanging bridges, in small ceremonial huts with a herd of goats, or on a horrendous field of decimated rabbits.

It is difficult to bear witness to chaos, especially when it feigns to be guided by a secret religiosity. The western action scenes read as having been filmed by a spineless Mariscal; the sadism displayed, shockingly "unhealthy," resembles the game of a backward adult who wants to scare the spectator by inciting them to imagine that *I am the big lion and you are the little lion, ergo, I tear off your arms and you shoot me and you do not kill me and so on to infinity,* or until all culminates in scenes of fanaticism in a neo-esoteric church in which an eye within a triangle is worshipped and the dazzling image of Jodorowsky, purified and shorn, amid deformed "dwarves" in the earth's depths, fornicates with a tender-hearted dwarf-woman. A heavenly intermediary, at the film's close, he will lead the disabled down the slope of the mountain to defeat; and the disappearance of the sacred Topo, fulminated by the light, will engender burial mounds of insects and fumes.

It is no longer a question of looting the Freudian symbology to attach all the sexual taboos that have fallen under their own weight per the pitiful *Fando y Lis.* It is about overwhelming us with the extravagance of an invertebrate imagination, even if the scope of its distorted worldview is reduced to so many fairground objects for target practice (how far we have come from Werner Herzog and *Even the Dwarves Started Small*); even if this moralizing Zen version of *The Wild Bunch* is made up of a cocktail of panic fables, each with its abstentionist moral that seems to have been conceived in the ass of a *Fellini-Satyricon* still debating its own fetal viscosity. Yet, if Zen Buddhism isn't a severe mental and moral discipline, it's nothing at all.

The indiscriminate mix of decadent western, comic book, teratological indulgence, misogynist vampirism, sexual psychopathy, and medieval surrealism has led to this explosive monstrosity. And Topo Gigio (Louie Mouse) emigrated to the West, feeling like a Warholian dictator of *freak* fashion.[7] From there he does not exit, nobody escapes.

NOTES

1. Translator's Note: Here and elsewhere, I occasionally broke up sentences when translating them into English. It's worth remarking, however, that the run-on affect in the Spanish neatly corresponds to the text's subject matter and both Jodorowsky's and Ayala Blanco's more general preoccupations with excess. Alternately, sometimes Ayala Blanco builds a cumulative argument by way of incomplete or fragmented sentences. Whenever possible, I preserved the affect.

2. TN: Within the Americas and Spain, the term "costumbrista" alludes to work that depicts local and regional customs, traditions, scenes, or types.

3. TN: Throughout I weighed the pros and cons of translating the text's outdated or overtly xenophobic, racist, or misogynist language (e.g. "Orientalist" or "dwarf") to its nearest English equivalent because the author's choice to deploy such language reflects not only the period in which the essay was written, but also contributes to Ayala Blanco's critique of Jodorowsky's efforts. At times, I opted to place certain terms in scare quotes.

4. TN: A section of the Secretaría de Relaciones Exteriores (Secretary of External Relations) called the Organismo de Promoción Internacional de Cultura (OPIC, Organism of the International Promotion of Culture) funded a theater in the "Casa de la Paz" ("House of Peace," Mexico City, Colonia Condesa, Cozumel 33). It was inaugurated

on March 24, 1965, with a work directed by Jodorowsky. In 1968, OPIC sponsored
the first Festival de Teatro Nuevo de Latinoamérica (Festival of Latin American New
Theater), timed to coincide with the 1968 Olympics.

5. TN: This quote likely corresponds to Sade's observation: "Everything is good when it's
    excessive."

6. TN: Ayala Blanco is referencing both Sade and Maldoror, the misanthropic anti-hero of
    Comte de Lautrémont's poetic novel written as a book-length prose poem, *Les Chants de
    Maldoror* (1868), with the neologism "sadomaldororiana."

7. TN: Topo Gigio was the protagonist of a children's puppet show on a 1960s Italian
    television show.

CHAPTER 4

One of Us: Corpo-reality and the Disabled Body in the Films of Alejandro Jodorowsky

Peter Sloane

Although thematically and stylistically eclectic – from the surrealism of *Fando y Lis* (1968), *El Topo*'s (1970) acid western and *The Holy Mountain*'s (1973) science fiction to the gothic horror of *Santa Sangre* (1989) – Alejandro Jodorowsky's visually, even viscerally, unsettling corpus is unified by an endeavor to reveal to both camera and audience the brute facticity of the human body in its myriad forms and malformations. His interest in corporeality finds expression in his films' recurrent macabre processions of eviscerated, sometimes crucified animals; the ritualistic denuding and frequent sexual violation of his subjects; as well as the repeated images of bloodied human corpses piled on wagons or strewn haphazardly about harrowing landscapes. Indeed, so aesthetically, ethically, and politically shocking are Jodorowsky's films that in 1968 a right-wing political group "ignited a riot during the Acapulco Film Festival in their efforts to prevent the showing" of his admittedly challenging first feature film.[1]

In some ways, these disturbing spectacles develop from his Antonin Artaud-inspired theatrical collaborations with Fernando Arrabal and Roland Topor, which resulted in their creation of the avant-garde *Mouvement Panique* in 1962. Enraptured by "Oriental" theater's "metaphysical tendencies" and frustrated with "Occidental" theater's growing dependence on text and its "psychological tendencies," Artaud envisaged the Theater of Cruelty, hypothesizing that the "fatigue of the organs" of perception, dulled by convention, "require intense and sudden shocks to revive our understanding."[2] Similarly, in the Mouvement Panique, the "unconscious mind and dreams are given free rein in an attempt to abolish all kinds of censorship and restriction."[3] As Josetxo Cerdán and Miguel Fernández Labayen note, for Jodorowsky this "free rein" takes the form of an "assault on middle-class 'good taste' [which] includes all types of extreme representations, of violence, sex, or human deformity."[4]

Yet, there is more than simple shock to Jodorowsky's confrontation with the conventions of film as form: in richly symbolic psycho-geographical spaces suffused with fluid syntheses of mysticism, magic, and disparate global religious practices, his seemingly morbid parade of anomalous, dis-animated, deconstructed bodies represents a gesture towards seeking out the ineffable element (life, perhaps, or the soul), which inheres *within*, but which recedes *from* the flesh-and-blood body.

Arguably to a greater degree than any other auteur, Jodorowsky's films exhibit a recurring fascination with the disfigured, deformed, or disabled body. In certain respects, unsurprisingly for a filmmaker so enamored with the allegorical mode, anomalous embodiment provides Jodorowsky with what David T. Mitchell and Sharon L. Snyder have influentially described as an "opportunistic metaphorical device." As they remark, although many "stories rely upon the potency of disability as a symbolic figure, they rarely take up disability as an experience of social or political dimensions."[5] Rosemarie Garland-Thomson similarly conceives the literary and filmic deployment of the non-normative, or in her term "extraordinary body," as "a concise trope for a wide range of human misery and corruption."[6] In these readings, as Lennard J. Davis summarizes, "disability is allegorical – it has to stand for something else – weakness, insecurity, bitterness, frailty, evil, innocence, etc. – and be the occasion for the conveyance of some moral truth – that people are good, can overcome, that we shouldn't discriminate or despair."[7] However, while exploiting the perceived symbolic resonance of the disabled body in his theologically inflected quest narratives, there is in Jodorowsky's films a considered positioning of disability as a material, existential, and social fact, one which challenges established conceptions of the filmic, the spectacular, and even the desirable. In this sense, he interrogates what Ato Quayson has called "aesthetic nervousness," a phenomenon which occurs when the disabled body intrudes into narratives, resulting from and in "the suspension, collapse, or general short-circuiting of the hitherto dominant protocols of representation."[8] Those "dominant protocols" involve, derive from, and reinforce embedded systemic sociocultural discriminations. While probing filmic probity, then, Jodorowsky instigates a critique of film's aesthetically exclusionary practices which works to obviate the narrative, visual, and social anxieties commonly associated with the disabled character.

Often accused of being gratuitously "grotesque" (one contemporary *New York Times* reviewer of *Fando y Lis* troublingly describes it as a "selection of freaks"), Jodorowsky composes a series of considered aesthetic and ethical provocations not simply to the sensibility of the cinema audience or the board of censors, but to the mechanical apparatus of the camera itself (1970). If, as he once remarked, "We have the language of the body and we need to do something together," this enigmatic "something" might take the form of a rehabilitative inclusive project which gives voice, or visibility, to bodies suppressed in the mainstream and employed for their transgressive appeal in arthouse or avant-garde film (*The Quietus*, 2015). Taking a disabilities studies approach, this chapter reads *Fando y Lis*, *El Topo*, *Holy Mountain*, and *Santa Sangre*, arguing that, like his visionary alter ego El Topo, Jodorowsky strives to dismantle the barriers erected by tradition (or perhaps "good taste") between the camera and the bodies which have come to be excluded from mainstream cinema and the cultural, social, and public spaces which it both constructs and (re)presents. By parading extraordinary bodies before a piece of technology which voraciously consumes violence, sex, war, famine, but which turns its own and therefore society's gaze from the actuality of both cognitive and somatic difference, Jodorowsky resituates the disabled body in a more brutal yet paradoxically more humanistic cinematic corpo-reality. Disability narratives often involve the search for a cure, one "which rehabilitates or fixes the deviance"; conversely, for Jodorowsky the disabled body acts as an agent *for* rather than subject *of* salvation.[9] Part of the strangeness of Jodorowsky's worlds is that they are not recognizably *our* worlds, but ideational prototypes for micro-utopian spaces of radical inclusivity which prove, ultimately, to be unsustainable either within or beyond the film frame.

I

That the body as material object is central to Jodorowsky's provocative cinematic vision becomes apparent in his first feature length film, *Fando y Lis*, in which the titular Fando literally carts his paraplegic wife's prone body around a post-apocalyptic landscape in a futile search for the mythical land of Tar. Necessarily, the narrative reinforces traditional conceptions of disability as inextricable from dependence, casting Lis as helpless and immobile and Fando as her altruistic caretaker. That her frame becomes a burdensome point of inert gravitational resistance to be hefted, dragged, and pushed over increasingly barren terrain also draws attention to the presence of the body, more so when, towards the film's end, Fando aggressively strips Lis before leaving her exposed and helpless (to which I return below). The use of nudity to foreground the innocence and vulnerability of the human body and by implication human subject plays a prevalent role in many of Jodorowsky's films: *El Topo* opens with a naked child (Brontis Jodorowsky), Hijo, exposed to the scorching elements in an inhospitable desert; *The Holy Mountain* begins with the charismatic Alchemist (Jodorowsky) disrobing and shaving the hair of two young women in an initiation ritual; *Santa Sangre* opens with Fenix (Axel Jodorowsky) naked, disoriented, nervous, and confined in a cell in a psychiatric unit. Each of these moments of nudity and the vulnerability of the undressed body is reinforced by the extravagant, institutional, or ritual dress of the scenes' other characters. But these instances of nakedness are de-eroticized, resistant to the dominant protocol of the male, or even female, gaze. If, as Fleming argues, his films "attempt to engineer a metaphysical encounter through the body and skin," rather than appearing gratuitously carnal, invitations for sensory or ocular pleasure, these unexpected opening images encourage not voyeuristic desire but empathetic concern, even care: Lis is a victim of repeated sexual abuse; Hijo a child seemingly mourning the loss of his mother; Fenix a patient in the care of an institution.[10] Paradoxically, then, these films' early introduction to the characters' nudity both establishes their corporeal economies while also demystifying the body and obviating traditional responses.

While displaying the body for the visual pleasure of the cinema audience, Jodorowsky also constructs scenarios in which the body is put very literally on display for the intra-diegetic gaze of the characters. In *The Holy Mountain*, The Thief (Horacio Salinas, with a marked resemblance to traditional Western representations of Jesus) daringly scales and enters the tower of The Alchemist before being initiated and taken as an apprentice. His and our first encounter in the tower is with The Written Woman (Zamira Saunders): naked, statuesque, adorned with symbols and jewelry, the camera moves from long shot into close-ups of her tattooed knees, buttocks in profile, stomach, vagina, breasts in profile, upper chest, and finally face in profile. She is rotated and divided by the camera into discrete areas of framed esoteric significance, the coded figure at once exposed yet undecipherable. The Written Woman's face remains affectless, expressionless, accepting without shame or accusation the gaze of the camera, The Thief as he approaches, and by extension the audience: focus is drawn not salaciously to the athletic anatomy, but cryptographically to the enigmatic glyphs inked into and under the skin. In her study of tattoos in the arts, Karin Beeler remarks that they represent "stories of desire, of trauma and violence, and of cultural preservation – stories that are intimately connected to the symbolic and physical or bodily aspects of the tattoo"; tattoos, she goes on, are "images and narratives of resistance and marginality" for numerous global cultures.[11] Indeed, The Written Woman is Black, and wears the traditional neck and arm rings of the South African Ndebele tribe. In this way the exposed body is simultaneously disinvested of the usually hidden mystery of its erotized somatic being but imbued with deeper significations associated with the mystical cutaneous symbolism. Jodorowsky may also be invoking the tradition of the "tattooed lady" – as he does with The Tattooed Woman (Thelma Tixou) in *Santa Sangre* – a popular circus performer in the early part of the twentieth century, part of the conventional "freak show" which features so often in his films.

Following a series of arcane rituals, The Thief is introduced to a group of deities representing the planets, each with its own archetypical association (Venus manufactures cosmetics, Mars weapons). We visit Jupiter's Art

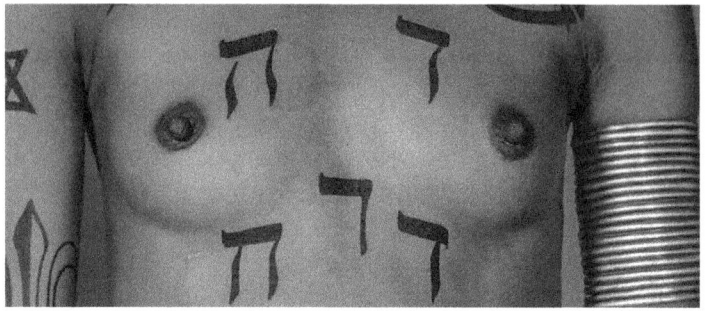

Figure 4.1 The tattooed chest of The Written Woman (Zamira Saunders)

Factory; in one scene artists daub the naked buttocks of models who then sit on blank paper in a kind of production line of Warholesque prints, or even parodic recreations of Yves Klein's *Anthropometry* (1961). The scene brings to mind Alain Robbe-Grillet's *Successive Slidings of Pleasure* (1974), in which Alice (Anicée Alvina), covers her body with red paint and repeatedly presses it against a white wall. Further inside the gallery we find a series of biomechanical installations; much like the camera frame does for The Written Woman, each contraption isolates and exposes to sight and touch those parts of the body which are usually covered, the bodies deconstructed, defamiliarized. With glee and growing arousal, we accompany two visitors as they interact with the displays: gently blowing a patch of pubic hair as the midsection writhes ambiguously, either in pleasure or discomfort, movement (perhaps escape) restricted by its apparatus; probing the crevice between buttocks; stroking limp penises abstracted from the bodies to which we assume they are attached. As with The Written Woman, the bodies are adorned, painted, but this time the target-like markings encourage eyes to dwell on and hands to explore hyper-sensitized erogenous zones. Each of the constrained bodies is also conventionally beautiful, muscular, athletic, filmic, lithe in motion as they respond to the rough haptic violations. The space resembles a museum of contemporary art, and we are unsure as to whether the fleshy sculptures are organic or mechanical, insensate synthetic facsimiles or (willingly or unwillingly) caged torsos. Regardless of ontology, the bodies featured are groped, molested, but this molestation is desensitized for character and viewer by the absence of faces and by implication subjects: the screens obscure responses, expressions of pleasure or discomfort, excitement or repulsion, and in so doing prevent empathy or recognition. The framing of the gallery facilitates a further degree of abstraction: naked is "nude" in the world of art. Perhaps Jodorowsky is commenting on the way certain contextual or cultural frames (film, gallery, museum) act to sanitize nudity, the erotic metamorphosing from an intimate private into a public aesthetic encounter.

The scene has echoes of a similar moment, or even moments, in *Fando y Lis*. Lis's journey from able bodied to disabled begins as she sits alone watching a puppet show. At the climax of his performance the puppeteer (Jodorowsky) cuts the strings from the limbs of the puppet, before helping Lis into the back-stage area where she is raped by a group of adults.[12] The cut strings foreshadow her later disability, the nerves severed (probably) psychosomatically between spine and legs, likely the result of this childhood trauma. Lis is carted around on what seems to be a mobile stage, an image reinforced by the presence of a gramophone and drum. Lis carries the embodied trauma of disability as well as the psychological trauma associated with intercourse; she has no desire to have sex with Fando. Frustrated and exhausted by their seemingly hopeless journey, Fando eventually strips Lis and leaves her exposed on her stage as three men approach, stroking her body as he directs: "touch her all over, don't be shy. The best of all is when you kiss her. Caress her using both hands." She becomes a kind of offering, on an alter/stage, to be consumed, spectated, touched, in an act of voyeuristic revenge by Fando for his own sexual frustra-tion. Clearly uncomfortable, the moment recreates and maps onto the original trauma of Lis's youthful assault behind the stage of the theater. As the pup-peteer passes her to her abusers, so Fando presents her to an uncannily similar group. In this way he is figured as the puppeteer, Lis, rather than the benefi-ciary of his benevolent kindness, the defenseless object of his anticipated but thwarted desires. Yet, like The Written Woman (though for different reasons) Lis remains affectless, radically dissociated from her own unfolding corporeal experience; it is as if her disability and dependence result in her transfiguration from self-directed subject to owned object, a removal of agency in which she becomes a victim complicit by acquiescence.

The intra-diegetic display of the disabled and/or powerless body is at the forefront of Jodorowsky's critical engagement with the exclusionary, exploit-ative, and discriminatory conventions not simply of cinema but of the society from which it arises, or which it reflects with all its contrived distortions and selective lacunae. In film, the disabled body occupies the paradoxical position of being radically excluded from view or spectacularly foregrounded as the center of carnivalistic performance, either purposefully (even conspicuously) hidden or displayed. But the terms under which the invisible body is granted temporary visibility are that its revelation takes place only within the contex-tualizing and containing frame of the freak show, offering protection from the fear that such malformed bodies might transgress boundaries of "taste" and impinge upon or disturb the unprepared witness beyond the show's permitted spatiotemporal parameters. In one of *El Topo*'s most moving scenes, El Topo, having awoken from his decades-long period of retreat, takes to the town with his dwarf caretaker/lover Mujercita (Jacqueline Luis) to try to earn money to excavate the mountain (like a mole) and connect it to the closest village via a tunnel. Their only way of earning money is to perform, actuating her physical difference as what Markotić describes as a "sight gag."[13] El Topo and Mujercita enact various mimed routines which exaggerate the discrepancy between his and her height, all the while exploiting the perceived oddity of their unconventional sexual relationship. After several street performances, they are asked whether they "want to make some money" and are invited to visit an exclusive club. Once inside, one of the patrons draws a revolver and tells them to undress, like "the wedding night": the pianist stops playing (in the same way that it might in a western when the mysterious stranger enters the saloon), all eyes turn to the couple, and Mujercita carefully removes El Topo's shirt before he gently undresses her to the raucous laughter of the patrons and prostitutes. Though clearly distressed, as the camera draws close to their faces in an instant of shared intimacy which emerges amid the hostile public spectacle, Mujercita reassures El Topo that "I Love you. They do not exist. There's nobody but you," before the camera retreats to reveal the semi-naked couple embracing framed by the cruelty of the clientele, many of whom are also naked but whose normative bodies arouse desire and not disgust. This moment of sensitivity in the face of callousness creates a deep bond between the embracing characters and empathetically between them and the viewer, who is invited to share not the exclusionary and cruel world of the club by participating in the mockery of bodily difference, but the caring and inclusive virtual micro-space established by Mujercita's forlorn words of encouragement.

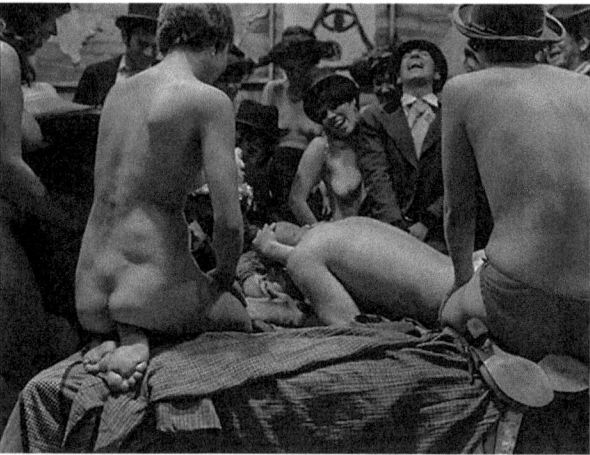

Figure 4.2 The humiliation of El Topo and Mujercita

Each of these scenarios involves bodies on display, vulnerable to sight and touch, unwanted physical attention, and each involves a powerlessness, a sense of being trapped which, it is implied, is a fundamental part of the human condition. Although, as Robert Neustadt suggests, for "Jodorowsky, we are imprisoned in our bodies because we consent to the illusion of our bodies as cage . . . the cage exists as a mental construct and depends completely on its prisoner's collusion," this "illusory" sense of self-constructed incarceration is not always the case, certainly for those characters whose bodies have been subjected to, even the motivation for, physical, emotional, or psychological violence.[14] Again, Neustadt's reading illustrates, on the one hand, an unwillingness to address or focus on the selectively invisible non-normative bodies in the films, and/or on the other, a reading of them as purely allegorical, peripheral.

II

Disability and bodily difference have a troubled history in film, the "dominant protocols" of which (borrowing Quayson's term), derive from the ableist society which produces and consumes a visual culture that has been historically enamored with the body beautiful, or at the very least "normal." Indeed, the opening text of Tod Browning's *Freaks* (1932) – a film which features a cast of actors drawn from the freak shows of the early part of the century, and focuses on the relationship between the beautiful trapeze artist Cleopatra (Olga Baclanova) and her dwarf lover Hans (Harry Earles) – says that "the love of beauty is a deep-seated urge [and] the revulsion with which we view the abnormal, the malformed and mutilated is the result of long conditioning" (1932). As Church remarks, "In normative society, freakery is premised on unequal viewing and social relations. A nondisabled audience retains the power to subject a non-normative body (traditionally, that of a person with disabilities) to the ableist gaze as entertaining spectacle, enjoying a mixture of shock, horror, wonder, and pity."[15] We return to the "sight gag," or the trope of "human wretchedness" that has come to typify mainstream film and literature's use of the non-normative body. These feelings provoked by the disabled body are either resistant to or immune from the scopophilia that Laura Mulvey influentially sees as endemic to mainstream cinema in which the (female) body is "coded for strong visual and erotic impact": in this understanding, the extraordinary body is inherently transgressive.[16] Even though in the avant-garde and "cult" cinema, non-normative bodies appear with greater frequency, as Church goes on, cult directors often "affectionately portrayed freaks as metaphors for social or psychic forces other than disability itself, implicitly using freakish physical difference to mark their films as more 'transgressive' than others."[17] *Freaks* might seem the archetypal example of this: it is a horror film merely by virtue of the presence of the "malformed and mutilated."[18] Indeed, El Topo's sincere and loving relationship with Mujercita acts as an echo of but counter to that between Cleopatra and Hans, in which she is involved in a plot to marry and kill him for his inheritance.

There have been periods during which film has been used to address the exclusion or intolerance of disability in society. In post-First World War Soviet cinema, for example, as Alexandre Sumpf writes, "Disabled veterans not only appeared in various fiction and non-fiction films, but in the interwar period cinema exclusively represented invalidity resulting from war and specifically the Great War."[19] This trend reoccurred in the slew of post-war U.S. films dealing with wounded and traumatized veterans reintegrating with a still insensitive society. John Huston's *Let There Be Light* (1946), funded by the U.S. War Department and one of four films made by Huston while he served in the Army Signal Corps, was intended to raise public awareness of and sympathy for victims of shell shock. However, due to the explicit portrayal of mental illness the film was banned by the U.S. authorities and not released until 1980. Such censorship is revealing about public and official attitudes to disability, reinforcing not simply the social exclusions that the film sought to highlight and address, but the suppression of cognitive and physical impairment on film. Perhaps most successfully, William Wyler directed Robert E. Sherwood's *The Best Years of Our Lives* (1946), which features Homer Parrish (Harold Russell) as a former promising young athlete who lost both hands in the war, and explores "uncomfortable social issues – such as joblessness, the housing shortage, and prejudice against the disabled – that were raised by the ongoing process of the reintegration of veterans."[20] Troublingly, the official trailer features only the able-bodied stars, advertising the more acceptable Myrna Loy and Dana Andrews. But these (frequently failed) experiments are exceptions: in general, and into the present, the disabled body in film is either excluded or used for primarily narrative or symbolic purposes, and rarely, returning to Mitchell and Snyder, with a concern for the lived experience of the disabled person or with the intention of encouraging more sympathetic societal attitudes to corporeal difference.

Jodorowsky, however, demonstrates an interest in the realities of being and becoming disabled from his first film. During the opening scenes, a young Fando plays a game with his father:

If you're a famous pianist and I cut
off your arm, then what will you do?

I'll become a famous painter.

And if I cut off the other one,
what will you do?

I'll become a famous dancer.

And if I cut off your legs,
then what?

Then I'll become a famous singer.

Of course, this is part of a game, one which ends with Fando telling his
father "You win." Yet, it also raises questions at the heart of Jodorowsky's
engagement with disability as a social and cinematic fact: what might happen
if *you* were to become disabled, or, as *Freaks* infamously has it, "one of us"?
Perhaps unavoidably, the game's rules are tempered by a functionalist ethos:
the defining question is "what will you *do?*" This scene inadvertently highlights
an ablest concern which is the implied rationale for discrimination – that
the disabled cannot *do* anything. As a result, the disabled are often excluded
from what Jean-Jacques Rousseau famously called the "social contract."
As Anita Silvers and Leslie Pickering Francis comment, "social contract
theory [. . .] stands between people with disabilities and justice," because those
with disabilities are deemed unable to "participate in cooperatively productive
activities."[21] This scene between young Fando and his ageing father also draws
our attention to the fact that being embodied renders us all susceptible to
age-related disability, because "Every life evolves into disability, making
it perhaps the essential characteristic of being human."[22] To have a body,
Jodorowsky suggests, is to occupy a precarious position always on the cusp of
acquired disability.

Jodorowsky's most prominent use of disability and deformity occurs in
El Topo, the "most frequently cited Latin American cult film," according to
Dolores Tierney, who argues that the "film's subcultural value relies on its
'otherness' to an Anglo or European mainstream" cinema, its foregrounding of
"preconceived notions of the 'other.'"[23] Again, one of the ways in which arthouse
film differentiates itself from the mainstream is by its inclusion of the non-
normative body. Although disabled characters appear throughout *El Topo*, it
becomes most prominent, powerful, and arguably transgressive in the mountain
enclave of inbreeding which results in a community in which disability is the
norm. After being shot by The Woman in Black (Paula Romo) when he gives up
his quest to become the greatest gunfighter, in a reversal of the (dis)abled (in)
dependent trope, seriously wounded El Topo is rescued by a group of disabled
characters (played by disabled people) who place him on a stretcher and carry
him to their mountain. He remains in meditation, or hibernation, or coma,
for decades until he is woken by a kiss from Mujercita, who has been caring
tenderly for his inert body since she was a child. El Topo is taken on a tour
of the vast mountainous cavern, and we see that the wretched, impoverished,
malnourished inhabitants sleep in discarded oil cans, in a scene which might
have come straight from a Beckett play. Yet, the scene lacks the dark humor of

Beckett, and instead presents a harrowing picture of the plight of the disabled, disfigured, deformed children and adults that constitute this community living on the hidden margins of society. Seemingly fantastic, the scene conveys with powerful symbolic resonance the reality of disabled life, which is predicated on various forms of exclusion from social spaces and insidious socioeconomic inequalities. As Mujercita tells El Topo in a way that is both literal (in their cave) and doubly figurative (in their bodies and as representatives of the marginalized), "we've been prisoners here for many years." El Topo is told that on the other side of the mountain's only exit, a hole in the peak, is a town, but that "they [the townspeople] won't help us get out [because] we are repulsive to them." Mujercita alights here on the fact that discrimination of the disabled or non-normative body operates not simply from a perception of use value but also from a visceral response based on appearances (the revulsion described in *Freaks*). After being shaved – in a reversal of *The Holy Mountain*'s initiation scene – he vows "I'll get money and I'll dig a tunnel" to connect the mountain to the village. Perhaps this is a foolhardy quest, given the brutality of the townsfolk, who abuse and slaughter slaves for entertainment. El Topo is also an outsider, in the sense that he is able bodied: his ambition represents a sincere desire to repay their kindness, but he has no real understanding of their plight, their reception, their history, or their lived experience. Yet, however misconceived or finally failed, this gesture towards reintroducing the excluded body into society is one of his project's most profound and characteristic, taking place both within the film frame and the cinema as microcosm of "real" society. One might interpret this single (pin)point of light (the mountain's aperture) in an otherwise dark chamber as a figuration both of the camera mechanism itself and the cinema screen in the darkened auditorium.

This idea of or desire for escape from incarceration reappears in *Santa Sangre*. In one flashback scene in the asylum, Fenix is introduced to his fellow patients, and four young men with Down syndrome are invited to welcome him; they approach and hug, caress his face, greet him with genuine kindness before the doctor leads them into the garden to join the rest of the patients and nurses in the garden, where they all play joyfully, tenderly. There are even suggested romances, two youngsters exchanging physical affection which clearly goes beyond platonic friendship. The institution is an asylum, but the majority of the patients seem to have Down syndrome, a condition which rarely appears on screen (with the exception of Antonio Naharro and Álvaro Pastor's 2009 *Yo, también*). Traditionally, the asylum has been used to contain the marginalized, a fact manifesting in film, as Markotić writes:

> literary and filmic representations of mentally and physically disabled people presume a normalcy that reinforces itself through medical and psychological regimes and, in some cases, incarceration and isolation.

These regimes constitute what disability activists call an "ableist" ideology, one that differentiates bodies by categories of able and less able,
visibility and invisibility, "handicapped" and "normal." The disabled
character thus represents a history of social, economic, and cultural
assumptions.[24]

In this instance, the institution and its doctors and nurses seem to care for –
and to treat with kindness – the patients. The scenes in the garden are almost
Edenic, free from discrimination, even hierarchy, beyond the uniforms worn
to distinguish one from another (able from disabled, normative from non-
normative, caretaker from cared-for). Shortly after, the doctor tells Fenix that
he and some of the others will be going to the cinema in the evening; they leave
the hospital under the care of a nurse and are introduced to the nightlife of
the city *as if* they were "normal" adults. They meet a pimp (Teo Jodorowsky),
who takes them under his wing: they are given cocaine, participate in dancing,
and finally have sex with a prostitute (Mary Aranza, implied and off screen).
In one of the film's most effective scenes, The Pimp carries a stereo and leads
the group through the streets in a merry dance sequence involving prostitutes,
transsexuals, vagrants, and disabled in a way which recalls but also subverts
and indicts the visually sublime Hollywood musicals of the mid-twentieth century. There are several ways of viewing this parade: we might see a parody of
classical Hollywood, the beauty and bodily grace of the iconicall filmic Astaire,
Rogers, or Kelly; or, we might suggest that Jodorowsky constructs a scenario in
which marginalized characters exist in a micro-utopian moment of acceptance,
where the social distinctions that facilitate various degrees of discrimination do not hold, and in which the non-normative and traditionally peripheral character occupies center stage not as "freak" but as equal. Although this
euphoric sequence promotes a sense of inclusivity, it is necessarily temporary,
the patients must return to their incarceration, the reality of their life enforced
by their corporeally coded difference.

Most remarkable in Jodorowsky's cinema, and his engagement with
disability, is the frequent use of composite bodies in a quasi-symbiotic
interdependence. The first gesture towards two people becoming one begins
in *Fando y Lis*. In the opening scenes as they enter the wasteland, Lis remarks
"What a misfortune to be paralyzed," to which Fando replies "It doesn't
matter if you're paralyzed, I'll take you everywhere." Fando cannot quite
know what his offer will involve. Over time he grows increasingly aggressive,
before in the final scenes he beats Lis to death in a moment of utter despair,
which he comes to regret. Her lifeless body is carried away, tellingly by a man
with a prosthetic leg, who places her on a white horse: this moment resembles
that in *El Topo* when he is lifted and carried away by the disabled. Fando is
not disabled, and the implication is that Lis had nothing to contribute to the

relationship, particularly in her unwillingness to have sex with Fando, and in this way, certainly before she is killed, she is figured as parasitic. A comparable but more equitable collaboration emerges in *The Holy Mountain*, when The Thief makes friends with The Crippled Man (Basilio González), who is legless and armless below the elbows. The two form a close bond, The Thief carrying The Crippled Man on his back, The Crippled Man acting as something of a guide. Their relationship supports Alessandra Santos's argument that "the message of *The Holy Mountain*, if any, is not only to question all beliefs and authority, but also to provide agency to the powerless."[25] Once again, The Thief is able bodied, and so his relationship with The Crippled Man is envisaged as largely asymmetrical: when The Thief scales and enters The Alchemist's tower, he cannot take his companion with him, and so the temporary union ends at a point which represents an insurmountable physical obstacle. *El Topo* perfects this trope of the composite body, as he seeks out the four master gunfighters in the desert wilderness. When he approaches the first master he is met by the master's companions, two disabled characters, one with legs but no arms, one with arms but no legs. The latter sits astride the former's shoulders, holding a lamp in one hand and a gun in the other, as if El Topo were confronted by a single watchman. Together they form a "normal" or complete body, and demonstrate a remarkable union, in one scene climbing a ladder together. The encounter offers a picture of a community which does not operate from the ideas of able and disabled; indeed, the master himself is blind, and his two disabled friends act as caretakers, guardians, protectors. In one scene the armless cripple shows astounding skill in combing and plaiting the hair of the second master with his feet, before neatly tying the plait with a bow (which

Figure 4.3 The gun master and his companions

seems to be referring again to *Freaks*, in which armless Frances O'Connor eats and drinks at a table with her feet with as much skill and grace as another might in the more conventional manner). Recognizing that The Master is more skilled, El Topo tricks him by digging a hole in the sand into which he blindly falls, before El Topo shoots him while his female companion kills the composite companion, in a brutal instance of violence in which the separated composite body is utterly defenseless. El Topo is visibly upset by their death, and tenderly lays the bodies side by side. This seems to be an important event in his development, a foreshadowing of his nascent care for the non-normative which comes to the fore after he is shot.

The composite body is most prevalent in *Santa Sangre*. The film takes its name from a religious sect, led by Fenix's mother Concha (Blanca Guerra). The sect worships a martyred child, who had her arms cut off and was raped and left to die on what is now the site of the church. Just as Lis's disability is foreshadowed by the cut strings, so Concha's is by the armless statue dedicated to the murdered child at her shrine. As a child, Fenix lives on a travelling circus with his father Orgo (Guy Stockwell), a knife thrower and ringmaster, and Concha, a trapeze artist. Orgo begins an affair with The Tattooed Woman, a highly eroticized, voluptuous, powerful, dominating figure. Concha confronts the pair before throwing acid on Orga's genitals (the scene echoes that early in *El Topo* when the Colonel is castrated), before he cuts off both her arms. Fenix is presumably taken to an institution, where we meet him, and from which he is rescued by his mother, who appears apparition-like outside his cell window. Concha and Fenix develop an odd relationship, in which she somehow takes control of his arms, which in effect become extensions of her body. We see them performing on stage in a dance show, dressing and eating as one body, even knitting, all without instruction or request, but as if they constituted a single organism. Their bond is reciprocal, in a way, Fenix still needing the love of his mother. Unfortunately, she retains a desire for revenge, and sets about killing her abusers with the aid of Fenix. Acting in union, forming a single entity, dexterous and seemingly telepathically connected, they represent perhaps the perfect example of Jodorowsky's figuration of the composite body. As we see, the trope develops from Fando assisting Lis, The Thief and Crippled Man collaborating despite their different abilities, the composite companion of The Master, to this instance of dual agency over the single body. Yet, like Lis, Concha is not played by a disabled actor. This is problematic for disability theorists and raises questions of the paradox of visibility and invisibility. As Lennard J. Davis writes, "media loves disability . . . People with disabilities are portrayed in the media as present, in the sense of ubiquitous, always marked as different, and yet rarely if ever played by actors with disabilities."[26] While advocating for the inclusion of the differently abled in his films, in the only two which feature disability in prominent roles, *Fando y Lis* and *Santa Sangre*, he does not cast disabled actors.

Unsettlingly, but inevitably, Jodorowsky's potentially positive disability narratives climax in brutality. Perhaps, as Susan Antebi remarks in a discussion
of the films of his Surrealist forebear Luis Buñuel, "violence surrounding the
representation of . . . disabled characters becomes part of a distinctly surrealist moral universe."[27] Antebi's suggestion that the Surrealist movement in
film simply adopted and exploited the extraordinary body for transgressive
purposes, the shock of making visible the traditionally invisible, is persistent.
Examples of this usage are undoubtedly present in Jodorowsky's films, in which
the disabled and deformed, though foregrounded, included, humanized, are
without exception killed by film's end. In *The Holy Mountain*, as the questers
undergo various rituals on the mountain, including ingesting psychoactive substances and boarding a sailboat, The Thief is reunited with The Crippled Man
in a hallucination. Although overjoyed to find himself back in the company of
his one-time companion he is encouraged to throw his friend over the boat's
side; reluctantly he agrees and tosses the defenseless and protesting Crippled
Man into the water to his certain death even after acknowledging that "he can't
swim." At the end of *Fando y Lis*, Fando kills his lover, brutally, apparently
because he could no longer bear the burden of her broken body which becomes
a symbol of their failure to find a better world. The final minutes of *El Topo*
are among the most harrowing on film: aided by Mujercita and his son Hijo, El
Topo manages to complete the tunnel connecting the hidden colony with the
town. Some hobble, others drag themselves along the floor, others are carried
by friends as they approach what they hope will be a new life. Predictably, given
the cruelty of the town, they are mercilessly executed by the townspeople in an
orgy of gunfire before El Topo slaughters them in retaliation and immolates
himself. The film's sympathies are obvious; they are not for the grotesque town
of greed and violence, slavery and brutality, but for the pitiable figures emerging into a social space from which they have been excluded and for which they
long to be included, accepted. The finale also implies caution, suggesting that
the public is unsympathetic towards and unprepared for the inclusion of the
extraordinary body. But this warning is not headed by Jodorowsky, whose films
have attracted much criticism for the way in which they confront the cinema
audience with a "selection of freaks."

Jodorowsky attempts to reconstruct corpo-cinematic reality, to offer to the
camera and audience a world in which the extraordinary body can occupy the
center frame, as opposed merely to the periphery of screen and/or society.
However, his micro-utopian ideational spaces are shown to be failed experiments in the cinematic rehabilitation of the disabled body. This failure gestures towards a series of sociocultural and artistic realties beyond the camera,
as Benjamin Fraser remarks:

The individual and social forces that construct and shape the presence of disability on film draw their power – whether seen as pernicious, progressive or neutral – from those forces that construct and shape the presence of disability off of film. In dismissing this on-screen presence – however problematic it may be – we risk dismissing the presence of disability in arguably less-artistic, but similarly socio-political, contexts off-screen.[28]

Filmic visibility or invisibility, as well as the manner of portrayal, the roles played, the treatment received on screen take their cue from the society which both gives rise to and consumes the spectacle. In centering the disabled body, Jodorowsky gestures towards a world in which the distinction between disabled and abled is less marked. His films act like El Topo's tunnel, a conduit between ableist society and the marginalized anomalously embodied sequestered beyond the film frame, beyond the public gaze. The choice we are presented with is, on the one hand, to see Jodorowsky's cinema as little more than transgressive, surrealist allegory which co-opts the disabled body into its symbolic economy, or, on the other hand, to view these works and their consistent exploration of the realities of disability as a comment on film's and society's rejection of somatic difference. These things are not incompatible or exclusive, of course, but readings which favor the former interpretation tend to overlook the latter, a fact marked by the frequent descriptions of deformity in his films as "grotesque," incidental as opposed to central. A reading which sees his engagement with extraordinary bodies as one concerned for the actuality of the lived experience of disability and with the ways in which film conspires to recreate and reinforce social exclusions leads to a more thoughtful understanding of his superficially simply shocking oeuvre. Indeed, such a reading might open more humanistic interpretations of the possibilities offered by his films.

NOTES

1. Jaime M. Pensado, "'To Assault with the Truth': The Revitalization of Conservative Militancy in Mexico During the Global Sixties," *The Americas*, vol. 70, no. 3 (January 2014), 499. Muristas, members of the "Movimiento Universitario de Renovadora Orientación (MURO), a university-based movement for the renewal of rightist principles" (Pensado, "'To Assault with the Truth,'" 490).
2. Antonin Artaud, *The Theatre and its Double*, trans. by Mary Caroline Richards (New York: Grove Weidenfeld, 1958), 44, 86.
3. J. Fernández, "'Minister of Horses': Samuel Beckett according to Fernando Arrabal," *Journal of Beckett Studies*, vol. 24, no. 2 (2015), 229.
4. Josetxo Cerdán and Miguel Fernández Labayen, "Arty Exploitation, Cool Cult, and the Cinema of Alejandro Jodorowsky" in *Latsploitation, Exploitation Cinemas, and Latin America*, ed. Victoria Ruétalo and Dolores Tierney (New York: Routledge, 2019), 110.

5. David T. Mitchell and Sharon L. Snyder, *Narrative Prosthesis: Disability and the Dependencies of Discourse* (Ann Arbor: The University of Michigan Press, 2000), 48.
6. Rosemarie Garland-Thomson, *Extraordinary Bodies: Figuring Physical Disability in American Culture and Literature* (New York: Columbia University Press, 1997), 84.
7. Lennard J. Davis, "The Ghettoization of Disability: Paradoxes of Visibility and Invisibility in Cinema" in *Culture – Theory – Disability: Encounters between Disability Studies and Cultural Studies*, ed. Anne Waldschmidt et al. (Transcript Verlag, 2017), 44.
8. Ato Quayson, *Aesthetic Nervousness: Disability and the Crisis of Representation* (New York: Columbia University Press, 2007), 15, 26.
9. Mitchell and Snyder, *Narrative Prosthesis*, 53.
10. David H. Fleming, *Unbecoming Cinema* (Bristol: Intellect, 2017), 102–103.
11. Karin Beeler, *Tattoos, Desire and Violence: Marks of Resistance in Literature, Film, and Television* (London: McFarland and Company, 2006), 3–4.
12. Many of the scenes also feature dismembered dolls, symbolic of Lis's broken childhood, but they are also reminiscent of the works of Kati Horna, a Mexican Surrealist artist who worked closely with Jodorowsky during his work in the theater, becoming his official photographer.
13. Nicole Markotić, "Punching Up The Story: Disability and Film," *Revue Canadienne d'Études Cinématographiques/Canadian Journal of Film Studies*, vol. 17, no. 1 (2008), 2.
14. Robert Neustadt, "Alejandro Jodorowsky: Reiterating Chaos, Rattling the Cage of Representation," *Chasqui*, vol. 26, no. 1, Chasqui: revista de literatura latinoamericana (1997), 63.
15. D. Church, "Freakery, Cult Films, and the Problem of Ambivalence" *Journal of Film and Video*, vol. 63, no. 1 (2011), 3.
16. Laura Mulvey, "Visual Pleasure and Narrative Cinema" in *Feminism and Film Theory*, ed. Constance Penley (New York: Routledge, 1988), 62.
17. Church, "Freakery," 7.
18. Herzog would return to disability in two very moving documentaries: *Handicapped Future* (1971) and *Land of Silence and Darkness* (1971).
19. Alexandre Sumpf, "War Disabled on Screen: Remembering and Forgetting the Great War in the Russian and Soviet Cinema, 1914–1940," *First World War Studies*, vol. 6, no. 1 (2015), 75.
20. David A. Gerber, "Heroes and Misfits: The Troubled Social Reintegration of Disabled Veterans in *The Best Years of Our Lives*," *American Quarterly*, vol. 46, no. 4 (1994), 554.
21. Anita Silvers and Leslie Pickering Francis, "Justice through Trust: Disability and the 'Outlier Problem' in Social Contract Theory," *Ethics*, vol. 116, no. 1 (2005), 41.
22. Garland-Thomson, *Extraordinary Bodies*, 524.
23. Dolores Tierney, "Mapping Cult Cinema in Latin American Film Cultures," *Cinema Journal*, vol. 54, no. 1 (2014), 131.
24. Markotić, "Punching Up The Story," 7.
25 Alessandra Santos, *The Holy Mountain* (New York: Columbia University Press, 2017), 2.
26. Davis, "The Ghettoization of Disability," 39.
27. Susan Antebi, "Landscapes of Children: Picturing Disability in Buñuel's *Los Olvidados* (1950)," in *Cultures of Representation: Disability in World Cinema Contexts*, ed. Benjamin Fraser (New York: Columbia University Press, 2016), 81.
28. Benjamin Fraser, "Introduction: Disability Studies, World Cinema and the Cognitive Code of Reality," in *Cultures of Representation: Disability in World Cinema Contexts* (New York: Columbia University Press, 2016), 8.

CHAPTER 5

Prophets and Sinners in the 1970s Films of Alejandro Jodorowsky

Naomi Lindstrom

In the cinematic universe of Alejandro Jodorowsky, audiences encounter characters who resemble, to varying extents, the biblical prophets. In addition, traditional features of prophetic discourse, such as denunciations of sinful communities and descriptions of the consequences of misconduct, may be found uttered as dialogue or performed as actions. Some of the characters in the Jodoverse (a term used here for this creator's vast production in various media) appear to be trustworthy bearers of divine messages, while others are portrayed as false or inadequate prophets. Beyond creating such fictional beings, Jodorowsky often appears to cast himself, as director, in a prophetic role. Like a prophet, he addresses his people, consisting of the movie-going public, illustrating scenes that are in some ways the cinematic equivalent of prophetic discourse.

There is virtually unanimous agreement among viewers of Jodorowsky's films that this director has drawn a great range of elements from multiple religious traditions and fused them in his work. Between them, his two 1970s films on philosophical and spiritual themes, *El Topo* (1970) and *The Holy Mountain* (1973), exhibit features of divination by Tarot, the thought of George Ivanovich Gurdjieff, alchemy, Taoism, asceticism, and Buddhism, as well as the New Age outlook that suffuses all of Jodorowsky's endeavors. Allusions to the Hebrew Bible and the New Testament also appear with frequency. Ariana Huberman, who has researched Jewish mysticism in Jodorowsky's oeuvre, asserts that "some of the most predominant sources of the supernatural in his work are Jewish life, Jewish mysticism, Kabbalah, and Jewish popular beliefs."[1]

Viewers often perceive the films as overloaded with too many disparate references and symbols to discern a coherent pattern. As George Melnyk puts it, referring only to one of the traditions that Jodorowsky mines, "The abundance of biblical symbolism can be overwhelming."[2] Jeremy Guida, who judges Jodorowsky's work to be overrated, also finds the director's reliance on a large and eclectic repertory of allusions dizzying; he raises the suspicion that "among the possibilities is that Jodorowsky is throwing random symbols together."[3] Jodorowsky skeptics such as Guida view *El Topo* and *The Holy Mountain* as "without a clear significance,"[4] while Josetxo Cerdán and Miguel Fernández Labayen characterize the director as working in the exploitation genre and employing religious references in an "anarchic" manner rather than to build up meaning.[5] D. H. Fleming views Jodorowsky as creating his films "nihilistically,"[6] with no clear conceptual framework.

It is possible to acknowledge that the director's films sometimes border on chaos and yet to find significant connections among their elements. Ben Cobb assumes such a stance when he states: "At first glance, the complex mass of his symbolism can seem tortured and confused, but there is very often an inner coherence";[7] similarly, Robert Neustadt describes Jodorowsky as artfully generating an effect of chaos and confusion while developing his ideas.[8] The present analysis follows the path taken by Cobb and Neustadt, tracing a conceptual pattern in films that at moments appear to verge on incoherence.

In this chapter I argue that, amid the wild profusion of references, icons, and symbols, one current of thought in particular may be traced throughout Jodorowsky's films of the 1970s: the prophetic mode that arises in Judaism and extends into Christianity. While Jodorowsky has established himself as a universal creative figure, he is from a Jewish family, although as Huberman observes he has a conflicted relation with his origins.[9] He grew up in the predominantly Catholic society of Chile. His films and his writing reveal a familiarity with and awareness of the prophetic current in both traditions. To give a particularly overt example, desert-dwelling characters known as "maestros del revolver" ("gun masters") in *El Topo* are identified as "PROFETAS" ("PROPHETS") by an intertitle bearing this single word. As will be discussed below, several Jodorowsky characters exhibit at least selected features of a prophet.

My analysis will show that Jodorowsky's films from the 1970s are more firmly rooted in the prophetic tradition, and are more judgmental, than might at first appear to be the case. They rely on concepts of sin, punishment, and repentance that are not only clearly identifiable and consistent but, in some instances, surprisingly conventional, or possibly even retrograde, for a creative figure widely perceived as an icon of the 1960s–1970s counterculture.

This chapter centers primarily on *El Topo* and *The Holy Mountain*, the two Jodorowsky films in which prophetic themes are most prominent. The director's adaptation of *Dune*, Frank Herbert's novel of 1965,[10] would have focused upon a prophetic leader; however, after intensive pre-production during 1975–1976, the undertaking was discontinued for financial reasons. Devotes of both Herbert and Jodorowsky have preserved documentation of the planning that went into the project. Especially useful is the 2013 documentary *Jodorowsky's Dune*, directed by Frank Pavich. Pavich reconstructs the plan for the film by using the storyboards for the project and interviews with Jodorowsky and his collaborators or, as he calls them, his "spiritual warriors." While it is obviously impossible to analyze a film that was never made, this unfulfilled project will be discussed briefly.

For the current chapter, I adapt the concept of the prophet that has been established by students of the biblical figures recognized as such in Judaism and Christianity. Abraham Joshua Heschel begins his classic study of 1962, *The Prophets*, with a useful general characterization, "What Manner of Man is the Prophet?"[11] This scholar emphasizes that the primary mission of the prophet is not to predict the future, but rather to denounce the sins of the people and move them to repent and repair their relations with the divinity, who has entrusted His emissary with privileged information. Heschel observes that prophets exhibit common personality traits, such as an extremely low tolerance for even everyday human misconduct: "To us injustice is injurious to the welfare of the people: to the prophets it is a deathblow to existence: to us, an episode; to them a catastrophe, a threat to the world."[12] Even seemingly trivial offenses, such as smug satisfaction with one's religious observances, provoke harsh prophetic wrath. Heschel observes that while the prophet unleashes rough harangues and invective, "behind his austerity is love and compassion."[13]

In his 1996 *The Burden of Prophecy*, Albert Cook provides a general description of prophetic speech. This researcher, who grounds his analysis in speech act theory, notes that the utterances of prophets "are aimed at getting the Israelites to change heart and change their ways."[14] He also makes the point that prophets emerge during "stressful" periods when human behavior has fallen far short of divine expectations.[15]

As a creative figure, Jodorowsky adapts this tradition with notable freedom. He ranges well beyond the prophetic books of the Bible to draw upon other episodes involving prophets, especially Moses, and such widely-known narratives as the foretold destruction of Sodom and Gomorrah.

AN ABUNDANCE OF PROPHETS

In both *El Topo* and *The Holy Mountain*, various characters possess features typical of prophets. In *El Topo*, the most salient of these is the titular protagonist, although secondary characters also display prophetic traits. Melnyk characterizes the film as having "a plot that is imitative of the kind one would find in the then innovative spaghetti western genre," though with many deviations from its conventions.[16] During the first half of *El Topo*, the protagonist has the appearance and violent behavior of a Wild West outlaw, roaming over a desert landscape and gunning down numerous adversaries. At the same time, El Topo believes that he has a special connection with divinity. He is not shy about identifying himself with Moses, considered in Judaism to be the greatest of all prophets, and recreates two of this figure's best-known miracles. During a desert trek, El Topo uses a log to turn bitter water sweet[17] while summarizing the original episode from Exodus.[18] Later, after praying loudly to God, he obtains water from a rock, modernizing Moses's miracle[19] by shooting the stone rather than striking it with a rod.

Though able to perform miracles, the gunslinging Topo lacks the moral attributes that would qualify him as the prophet he aspires to be. Arrogant to an extreme, he flaunts his special powers; when one of his opponents asks who he is to mete out justice, he replies without hesitation "I am God" ("Soy Dios"). He is not concerned with persuading evildoers to repent and avert divine punishment; rather, as a denizen of the hyper-individualistic Wild West, he applies frontier justice. While prophets should harbor compassion, El Topo at times shows cruelty towards the objects of his wrath, in one case castrating a local dictator in front of his troops. He allows himself to be led astray by a beautiful, bloodthirsty woman who persuades him to abandon his small son and earn her love by winning gun duels. While El Topo at times succeeds in righting wrongs, he does so through violence and trickery rather than through the prophet's methods of teaching, exhortation, and spiritual guidance.

In the second part of the film, a regenerated Topo makes a greater effort to carry out a Moses-like mission. He has spent many years maintained in suspended animation by a colony of disabled people trapped inside a mountain cavern. The protagonist awakens, undergoes a ritual rebirth, and attempts to serve as a liberator and spiritual leader. His first words upon reawakening are "I am not a god" ("No soy un dios"), reversing his earlier assertion and showing that he has overcome his arrogance. The new Topo exhibits altruistic behavior and seeks to guide his helpless followers. Naomi Lindstrom, interpreting the second half of *El Topo* as an apocalyptic narrative, correlates the reborn Topo and his band of mountain dwellers with the army of good in the great final battle against the forces of evil, and indeed they possess an angelic purity.[20]

However much improved he may be, El Topo is still not worthy of the mantle of a prophet. Moses enjoys a close prophetic relation with the divinity and envisions and realizes a great project that will continue to unfold over generations. El Topo is lacking in both these areas; he is not in regular contact with a source of supernatural guidance and fails to plan ahead, indisputably a serious failing for a prophet. After he carves an exit from the mountain where his followers are trapped, the inhabitants rush out and pour into the nearby town, a cesspool of wickedness, where they are promptly gunned down by the men and women of the ruling class. Seeing his work as liberator come to nothing, El Topo fatally shoots the bourgeois townsfolk and detonates explosives before self-immolating.

The destruction of the town is a departure from the prophetic model in which wicked communities risk annihilation by the divinity. El Topo, having earlier renounced violence, destroyed his weapon, and sought to become a prophetic leader, now reverts to his earlier habit of dispensing his own personal brand of retribution. Powering through grave wounds to mow down the townspeople, the enraged gunman appears driven by a desire for revenge. Such an approach is unsuited to prophets, whose goal is to lead the people to repent and reconcile with God rather than to take the law into their own hands. A fundamental part of the prophets' mission is to alert listeners to the future consequences of their misdeeds; Moses's numerous warnings to both Egyptians and Hebrews are among the best known in the Bible. In contrast, El Topo never cautions the citizens that their wickedness may doom them. His inadequacy in the prophetic role appears to be the motive for his subsequent suicide by fire. This act appears successful as a form of self-purification, since the last image of *El Topo* shows his grave serving as home to a flourishing, productive beehive. At the film's end, the protagonist is another example in Jodorowsky's gallery of would-be or incomplete prophets.

The characters in *El Topo* who seem closest to achieving the prophetic ideal are not the protagonist but the four "maestros del revolver" or "gun masters" with whom the protagonist fights duels. As noted above, the intertitle "PROFETAS"[21] appears during this sequence of linked episodes. In a complication, the audience sees the word only halfway through this narrative thread, after El Topo has already found and killed two of the four masters. This timing suggests that only the last two masters fully deserve to be called prophets, while the first two are less worthy of the appellation.

To what degree do the masters resemble prophets? All four are receiving revelations of supernatural origin, since they have acquired considerable knowledge of El Topo and his failings before he drops in on them. They all possess an inner discipline that the protagonist lacks. Living in isolation in the desert, they dedicate themselves to meditation and self-transformation. They are like prophets in their extreme sensitivity to sin, which they immediately detect in El Topo. The second master delivers a harsh prophetic diatribe against El Topo, inveighing against the absence of love behind even his seemingly altruistic deeds: "You don't love, you break, you murder, and nobody loves you. Because when you think you are giving, really you are taking" ["Tú no amas, tú rompes, tú asesinas y nadie te ama. Porque cuando crees que das, en realidad estás tomando"]. The second master's mother also exhibits prophetic characteristics, denouncing El Topo's past and warning him of the future. She has been reading the outlaw's fortune and intones in a deep, trance-like voice: "You are falling. You will fall even further" ["Vas cayendo. Caerás todavía"], before unleashing upon him a stinging rebuke that is a modern equivalent of prophetic invective.

At the same time, the masters reveal other traits not typical of a prophet. This is most true of the first two masters, who are given to vanity, pride, and ostentation. The first boasts that he has learned to take bullets without serious injury; he demonstrates this feat, appearing less like a recipient of divine revelation than like one of the circus performers who abound in the Jodoverse. The second flaunts his extreme dexterity and marksmanship. These two also indulge in luxuries that are out of keeping with the severe nature of the prophet. The first lives with two servants in a tower near an oasis, while the second owns such high-status possessions as a fur coat and a male lion which, in several shots, is glimpsed pacing near the human characters. The first two masters represent a form of spiritual leadership that is still poorly developed, but will appear in more evolved form in El Topo's interactions with their later counterparts.

The third and fourth masters, who appear following the word "PROFE-TAS," are solitary and self-effacing. Cobb observes the progression towards simplicity in the successive masters' abodes and worldly goods: "Each Master's surroundings and possessions are less than the Master before . . . The First Master lived in a tall tower, the Second Master in a wagon, the Third Master in a lean-to. The Fourth Master has only a pole in the desert and a sheet covering his body."[22] This critic points that the fourth master takes austerity to such an extreme that he lacks even a source of water.[23] The two final masters draw little attention to their own exceptional abilities. They focus instead upon the protagonist, seeking to dissuade him from his brutal, impulsive approach to life. The third master strives to be a moral teacher to the outlaw. He exhorts El Topo to give priority to his heart, though the lesson goes unheeded as his student shortly afterward kills him. The fourth master is the one who comes closest to fulfilling the prophetic ideal. His appearance corresponds to the popular image of a prophet: a gnarled, wild-haired man who bears the signs of a lengthy stay in the wilderness. This purified visionary is the only master whom El Topo cannot defeat and the only one who succeeds in bringing him to the realization that he is on the wrong path. Following this last encounter, El Topo repents. He visits the graves of his victims, prays while reciting Psalms, and destroys his gun.

While in *El Topo* prophetic or pseudo-prophetic traits are distributed among several figures, in *The Holy Mountain* they are assigned primarily to a spiritual leader known as the Alchemist. The Alchemist is a fictional character played by Jodorowsky, but not in the same sense that he acts the part of El Topo. The director-actor incarnates El Topo as a flawed, tormented human being who often behaves badly and misjudges situations. In contrast, the Alchemist is represented as an ideal to which to aspire: flawless in his behavior, correct in his assessments, and never caught off guard by events. While El Topo is laconic, the Alchemist eloquently imparts his teachings to his followers and, by extension, to the viewing audience.

The Alchemist is closely aligned with the real-world Alejandro Jodorowsky. At the film's end, this spiritual leader breaks the fourth wall; he orders the camera to pull back, revealing the crew and equipment, then blurs the actor/director distinction by addressing viewers. Guida criticizes the tendency of Jodorowsky admirers to "conflate the characters he played with Jodorowsky the man," implying that the director benefits unfairly from the "charismatic religious authority" ascribed to his fictional entities.[24] Charisma aside, there is good reason to associate the Alchemist with the director; the character expounds tenets central to Jodorowsky's outlook, such as the need to constantly transform the self. As Cobb puts it, "Jodorowsky plays Alchemist as both actor and director."[25] Given these considerations, I here consider the Alchemist a fictional character who functions as a spokesman for and a highly idealized version of the director.

How much of a prophet is the Alchemist? Like every other entity created by Jodorowsky, the character is difficult to identify because he fuses features of several traditions. In the film's opening sequence, he performs a purification ceremony that turns two garishly sexualized young women into spiritual seekers. The audience next encounters him inside a high tower that materializes in the outskirts of Mexico City. Little is revealed about him other than that he wears flowing garments, his movements are extremely precise, he has an effortless mastery of Asian martial arts, and he is well versed in multiple arcane systems. Fleming categorizes the Alchemist as a psychedelic guru: "Reflecting the LSD-culture of the time, the Alchemist (Jodorowsky) who opens and guides the freeform cinematic 'trip' finds strong parallels in Castaneda's 'Don Juan' character as well as [Timothy] Leary's conception of the psychoanalytic/ psychedelic guru/guide."[26] This characterization is excessively simple. The Alchemist does indeed lead his disciples through a hallucinogenic ceremony, but it is only one of many exercises that they carry out under his spiritual guidance. A more complex and learned concept of self-renovation is involved than Leary's exhortation to "tune in, turn on, drop out."

What most clearly qualifies the Alchemist as a prophet is his mission of transforming fallen human beings into spiritually enlightened ones, as would a prophet seeking to lead a wayward community to repent. His disciples are degenerate beings whom he recruits in an effort to reform them. However, his methods diverge from those of a biblical prophet. Rather than chastise his listeners for their sins, he attracts them as his followers by appealing to their greed and ambition. He promises gold to The Thief and tells the seven capitalists that the pilgrimage to the Holy Mountain will bring immortality, one thing that they can never purchase. Once they have accepted his leadership, he guides them away from their previous wickedness.

In the following part of this chapter, I move away from the discussion of characters who to various degrees resemble prophets. Instead, Jodorowsky, as the creator of the films, functions as a prophet. Admirers often view him in this role; Cobb, for example, observes that "Following the adulation received by *El Topo* from both the cultural intelligentsia and the hip spiritual elite, Jodorowsky had emerged as some kind of arcane prophet."[27] Jodorowsky at moments characterizes himself as similar to a prophet, not as a human being but as in his role as creator. In the documentary *Jodorowsky's Dune*, he says that during the elaborate pre-production of *Dune* "I was like a prophet. I was enlightened."[28] Here I posit that certain scenes from his films serve as the functional equivalent of prophetic harangues or invectives directed against particular forms of misconduct. The extreme asperity and even coarseness of Jodorowsky's satire is a continuation of the prophets' practice of castigating their listeners with bitter reproaches.

COMMUNITIES OF SINNERS

Like all prophets, Jodorowsky emphasizes certain sins over others when he excoriates the errant ways of humankind. To see which forms of iniquity he most condemns, I examine episodes in *El Topo* and *The Holy Mountain* featuring communities whose sole function in their respective films is to exemplify deplorable behavior. These episodes reveal that in Jodorowsky's universe, the most reprehensible categories of misconduct are not always the ones that might be expected, given the director's fame as an experimental countercultural artist.

Both *El Topo* and *The Holy Mountain* feature scenes set in communities that resemble the wicked cities and towns described in a variety of biblical narratives. The most emblematic cases are Sodom and Gomorrah, which prove irredeemable, and Nineveh, which repents and averts destruction. In creating modern equivalents of these iniquitous cities, Jodorowsky delivers, through his characteristically bitter mockery, severe moral judgments upon characters' conduct.

In the latter half of *El Topo*, such a corrupt community inhabits a frontier town. This outpost, known only as "el Gran Pueblo," appears at moments to be in the U.S. Southwest and at other times in a desert region of Mexico.[29] Whatever its nationality, the settlement is beyond doubt one of the most unceasingly evil communities ever portrayed on film. The outwardly prim citizens, while displaying fanatical devotion to a strange new form of worship, spend most of their time indulging in behaviors that combine debauchery with cruelty. El Topo is an outsider to the town, but as a would-be Moses to the colony of disabled outcasts, he visits, condemns, and destroys it.

In portraying the wicked town, Jodorowsky links the bourgeois citizens' sexuality to their callous disregard for others' well-being. The townspeople release their pent-up desires upon a population of indigenous and, in one case, Afro-descendant slaves. In a scene set in a beauty parlor, townswomen harass a slave with unwanted sexual overtures. The salon customers' acting out of sexual desire crosses the line into injustice and cruelty when the women sexually assault the slave, then accuse him of rape to enjoy seeing him lynched. For this scene Jodorowsky cast older actresses who are shown coarsely flaunting their bodies while wearing only lingerie, slippers, and gaudy makeup and jewelry. (The portrayal of the sexual desire of older women as ludicrous, repulsive, and dangerous might well be considered ageist and sexist by today's standards.) This episode also reveals the somewhat ascetic outlook on sexuality that is one of the surprisingly conservative features of both *El Topo* and *The Holy Mountain*.

The town's menfolk are equally abhorrent in their pleasures. Their principal diversion is inflicting gratuitous pain upon the slaves. Their sadism is manifested in some exceptionally gruesome sequences. One of the most disturbing is set at a rodeo where human slaves are used in lieu of cattle. After watching branding irons being heated, the audience sees a close-up of a slave's contorted face and hears his screams, followed immediately by a close shot, filling almost the entire screen, of a brand being applied to flesh. In line with the town's pervasive hypocrisy, the superficially proper male citizens maintain a secret underground room that has features of both a brothel and a frenetic orgy.

Among the more dated features of *El Topo* is its perpetuation of the widespread idea that same-sex attraction and the blurring of gender lines are forms of sinful decadence. Such an outlook is most overtly expressed in a scene set in the sheriff's office and jail. The sheriff and his deputy are revealed as same-sex lovers who, after kissing and cuddling one another, are preparing to anally penetrate male prisoners when the scene abruptly ends. During this episode, brief shots of a table allow viewers to spot gargantuan servings of meat; in the work of the vegetarian Jodorowsky, carnivorous gluttony is a certain sign of depravity. In a scene set in the town's corrupt church, the camera pans over the frenzied congregation, showing varying degrees of cross-dressing among the males. Men in female garb appear also in the above-mentioned orgy scene. Such allusions to sex between men and porous gender boundaries link the wicked town with Sodom and Gomorrah as they appear in the popular imagination.

In trying to understand these seemingly conservative elements, one should remember that *El Topo* was conceptualized and shot at the end of the 1960s, when the gay liberation movement was in its early days and there was little effort to avoid sexual and gender stereotypes. In addition, it is helpful to remember Estevão Garcia and Sylvie Debs's astute observation about Jodorowsky's history as a theater director and actor during the 1960s, from which they derive clues to his general outlook. They note that while Jodorowsky favored avant-garde works, he remained completely distant from the socially committed artistic movements of the 1960s.[30] He appears to have upheld innovation and experimentation as the highest values in art and to have given relatively scant importance to promoting a consistently progressive social outlook.

Religious hypocrisy also figures in Jodorowsky's list of most heinous sins. The town's ruling class is in thrall to a bizarre cult featuring faked miracles, the Eye of Providence, cross-dressing, and an obsession with guns. For all the weird-ness of the sect, as Cobb observes, Jodorowsky is mocking "the church in general" and especially participants' striving to "advance their own social status"[31] by performing extreme piety. Through his usual implacable satire, Jodorowsky castigates the conspicuous display of religious devotion and status-seeking that afflicts congregations. In so doing, he places his work in the prophetic vein; as Heschel points out, ostentatious and self-seeking religious observance is among the human failings most despised by prophets. In this scholar's words: "The prophet knew that religion could distort what the Lord demanded of man, that priests themselves had committed perjury by bearing false witness, condoning violence, tolerating hatred, calling for ceremonies instead of bursting forth with wrath and indignation at cruelty, deceit, idolatry, and violence."[32]

As well as lust, greed, and indifference to human suffering, the town's dom-inant population exemplifies more seemingly frivolous sins such as vanity and sumptuosity. The women wear heavy, gaudy jewelry and furs and the men are often seen in impressive suits of thick fabric despite the desert climate. The embellished, tailored dress of the townsfolk contrasts with the simple robes of the reborn Topo and the worn, baggy clothing of his oppressed followers. In Jodorowsky's films, characters who are spiritually pure or undergoing purifi-cation are typically shown in flowing or shapeless garments, while a number of evil characters favor more form-fitting clothing that gives them a vainer or more flirtatious appearance. (These observations apply only to scenes in which the actors are clothed; both good and evil characters appear nude or nearly naked in Jodorowsky's work.)

The loosely organized plot of *The Holy Mountain*, most of which follows a quest to reach a mountain peak believed to confer immortality, also portrays prosperous cities of iniquity. As noted above, The Alchemist leads a group out of a debased state into enlightenment. His followers consist of The Thief, a drifter who is often on screen but has extremely little dialogue, and seven powerful deal-makers and industrialists, each identified with a planet. One by one, the seven introduce themselves by means of fictitious promotional short films or infomercials. These movers and shakers are heard in voiceover touting their life and career accomplishments while the images on screen corroborate their boastful assertions. While they are proud of what they have achieved, what viewers see is a hyperbolic display of greed, vanity, debauchery, and callousness. Each entrepreneur has attracted a little village of supporters and sycophants who bond through their enthusiasm for capitalistic exploitation. For example, Pluto, hosting a lavish banquet, unveils his plan to house factory workers in coffins. His entourage appears delighted with both the project and the promotional event, which features erotic decorations and performances. The banquet fare consists solely of alcohol and the generous servings of meat that, as noted above, signal moral decay in Jodorowsky's oeuvre. As in *El Topo*, the spectacular display of sexuality appears to be a symptom of ethical deficiencies in general. The community illustrates both sexual and economic voracity and a callous willingness to profit from the mistreatment of laborers.

The Alchemist summons these exemplars of greed and undertakes to transform them, in his phrase, from excrement into gold, although they initially believe themselves to be pursuing immortality. As Garcia and Debs observe, one of the first steps is to leave the corrupt city and head to rural areas, in line with the traditional belief that country living promotes virtue.[33] The process of self-refashioning is eclectic, including among other measures burning money and effigies of the old self, therapeutic pantomime, native healing practices, a hallucinogen, and a symbolic rebirth. It culminates in a purification ritual, head-shaving, that occurs with some frequency in the Jodoverse. The disciples' mettle is tested when they reach their destination, Lotus Island, and stumble into a modern, globalized version of the biblical cities of the plain. Lotus Island is the correct location of the sacred mountain, yet its name contains a cautionary allusion to the eroded minds of the lotus eaters of Greek mythology. The travelers have scarcely set foot on the island when they are waylaid by a barker representing the Pantheon Bar. Shouting "Come, come, come! I have everything. Food, drink, beds, baths, men, women!" he seeks to degrade the pilgrims into hedonistic tourists.

At the beginning of this scene, the Pantheon Bar is portrayed as a perennial bacchanal. Guests in ostentatious costumes carouse, seek sexual partners, and crudely devour a roasted pig. The bar's loud rock music and the revelers' dance moves identify it as a parody of wealthy, globe-trotting hippies. As the scene continues, the pilgrims pass by a succession of predatory vendors hawking illusory and unethical delights. Jodorowsky is often viewed as an icon of the 1960s/1970s counterculture. Yet his depiction of the Pantheon Bar constitutes a pitiless lampoon of the hip scene. Its salesmen and clientele exemplify not only such timeless individual sins as lust, vanity, hypocrisy, and gluttony but also more modern, society-wide harms such as U.S. cultural imperialism (a duplicitous poet wears an Uncle Sam hat) and hyper-commercialized tourism.

Although Jodorowsky famously appealed to a tripped-out viewing public and Fleming calls *The Holy Mountain* "a piece of philosophical cinema constituting part of the LSD-film subgenre or movement,"[34] this episode includes a condemnation of facile reliance on mind-altering drugs to achieve a sense of illumination and growth. A dissipated vendor glibly claims that "The philosophical stone of the alchemists was LSD!" and "The Book of the Dead was a trip!" attempting to reduce all arcane systems of thought to drugs for purchase. Like other evil characters in Jodorowsky's universe, the psychedelic huckster abuses a slave, in this case a beautiful adolescent boy whom he force-feeds drugs. It should be noted that *The Holy Mountain* does not condemn psychedelic drugs as such, since The Alchemist leads his followers to an indigenous woman who administers an organic hallucinogen. The pilgrims reach their hard-won enlightenment by enduring the grueling effects of the natural drug accompanied by a demanding course of ritual exercises. Consequently, they reject the purveyor's simplistic, consumeristic version of the psychedelic experience, signaled by pills that resemble brightly colored candy.

In this episode, the corrupt community at the Pantheon Bar is not subjected to punishment, as occurs in *El Topo* and numerous biblical narratives, but rejected. Strengthened by the transformative process through which the Alchemist has led them, the pilgrims resist the temptations of the vendors. They also remain unimpressed with a strongman who illustrates the sins of pride and vanity with his muscle-flexing poses, vociferous boasts, and super-human but meaningless feats. One of the travelers assumes the role of an irate prophet to verbally castigate the false poet, but in other instances they simply observe with evident disgust the corruption of the Pantheon Bar before resuming their journey to the holy mountain.

As notable as the sins that Jodorowsky highlights are the ones that he does not denounce, especially those having to do with humankind's relation to the other species and to Earth. Jodorowsky gives little importance to the idea that human beings should preserve the well-being of other sentient life forms. To note just the most extreme incidents of harm to animals, an entire colony of rabbits dies on screen *El Topo*; *The Holy Mountain* features numerous crucified lambs on display; in the latter film, lizards elaborately costumed as Aztec/Mexica warriors and toads dressed and armored as Spanish conquistadores are blown to bits before the eyes of the viewers.

The treatment of animals in Jodorowsky's 1970s films did not receive much critical examination in the initial reviews, though it was occasionally denounced by such contemporaries as T. E. D. Klein. In a 1974 *New York Times* essay "They Kill Animals and They Call It Art," Klein cited Jodorowsky as a prime example of the misconduct described in his title.[35] In recent times, an increasing number of viewers see this aspect of the films as a moral failing rather than simply a technique used for shock value, and an internet search for "Jodorowsky animal abuse" leads to numerous detailed discussions. Guida, who can hardly be considered a defender of Jodorowsky, offers a valuable clue to this troubling issue when he states "By contemporary standards, [*El Topo* and *The Holy Mountain*] are . . . extraordinarily violent."[36] The reference to "contemporary standards" should serve as a reminder that concepts of what is acceptable have shifted greatly over the past five decades. It was not until 1975 that Peter Singer's *Animal Liberation* established "speciesism" as an ethical failing.[37]

AN UNREALIZED WORK OF PROPHECY

While Jodorowsky was never able to shoot his adaptation of *Dune*, all the evidence that has been collected about it indicates that it would have further developed his prophetic mode.[38] What appears to be Jodorowsky's script for *Dune* is available online, though the director has disputed its authenticity.[39] However, the most reliable source of information about the project is the earlier-mentioned *Jodorowsky's Dune*. Despite its title, this 2013 documentary does not offer any actual footage from Jodorowsky's *Dune*, most likely because there is nothing to be found. Instead, it reconstructs to some extent the intended visual style of the film by showing and at times animating images from the storyboards. Interviews with the voluble Jodorowsky and several other people with knowledge of the pre-production give further clues to this creator's vision for *Dune*.

Jodorowsky is insistent about the prophetic nature of his project. Almost at the outset, the director's face appears on screen as he asserts: "My ambition with *Dune* was immense. So what I wanted was to create a prophet" ["Mi ambición con *Dune* fue tremenda. Entonces lo que yo quise fue crear un profeta"]. Subsequently, Jodorowsky states that the special-effects virtuoso Douglas Turnbull was spiritually inadequate to collaborate on "a film who was a prophet."[40] Unsurprisingly, he also characterizes himself as a prophet.

In his remarks in the documentary, Jodorowsky gives importance to two characters: Paul Atreides, who of course is central to the novel, and the loathsome Baron Vladimir Harkonnen. As the many readers of *Dune* know, in Herbert's novel Paul sees into the future and sways the thought of his listeners; he resembles, at various times, a prophet and a messiah. Jodorowsky had cast his son Brontis as Paul and made some modifications to the character, subjecting the then-young actor to rigorous training in mixed martial arts. In *Jodorowsky's Dune*, the director describes his version of Paul, which commingles the features of a prophet and a messiah with mastery of martial arts and a New Age expanded consciousness, resulting in a hybrid "superior person."

If Paul is one of Jodorowsky's eclectic prophets, Baron Harkonnen was to be one of the characters through whom the director mocks and denounces various sins. As in *El Topo* and *The Holy Mountain*, gluttony signals the presence of wickedness in general. For this role, Jodorowsky cast Orson Welles; discussing his choice, Jodorowsky remarks that the iconic actor-director was at that time infamous for his seemingly limitless eating and drinking. *Jodorowsky's Dune* shows a sketch of the obese Baron holding in his mouth a piece of meat; as noted, the director's shorthand note for degeneracy.

The prophetic nature of the project for *Dune* is asserted categorically by Clément Pelissier. In his admiring essay "From Filmmaker to Prophet," this critic states that Jodorowsky's unrealized film would have been fully in this tradition: "the dream of adapting Herbert's novel arose from a philosophy that Hollywood would find terrifying: that of the prophetic film."[41] He subsequently refers to Jodorowsky as "our filmmaker prophet."[42] Although Pelissier's main argument is that Jodorowsky was functioning as a prophet in his attempt to bring *Dune* to the screen, he observes that the director exercises other forms of teaching and leadership as well, calling him also "A leader of men, a chieftain or a 'guru.'"[43] By providing multiple characterizations of Jodorowsky's role, Pelissier recognizes the hybrid nature of the prophet in the universe that the director has created.

All available evidence indicates that Jodorowsky was preparing to make another film that would have drawn heavily, though by no means exclusively, on prophetic conventions. Not only was the protagonist envisioned largely in the prophetic mold, but the villain appears to have been designed to exemplify the sins considered most reprehensible in the Jodoverse.

CONCLUSION

The concept of creating or becoming a twentieth-century prophet is an important aspect of Jodorowsky's filmmaking of the 1970s. Many of his fictitious characters exhibit or strive for features of the prophet. The director is uninhibited about assuming for himself the prophetic mantle, with bitterly satirical scenes from *El Topo* and *The Holy Mountain* serving as the cinematic equivalent of scathing prophetic harangues and diatribes. The unrealized *Dune* appears to have been designed to continue this pattern.

At the same time, amid this abundance of figures with prophetic features or aspirations, there is not one who could be considered exclusively and completely a prophet. Some of the characters that Jodorowsky constructs could be classified as inadequate prophets who are not evolved enough or do not have enough supernatural guidance to fulfill their missions. El Topo, even after undergoing a regenerative transformation, is unable to measure up to the Moses-like role to which he aspires. Of the four gun masters, the first two have flaws, such as vanity and self-absorption, that impede them from exercising prophetic leadership.

Cultural eclecticism is a hallmark of Jodorowsky's films, and the prophets he creates, whether faulty or successful in their missions, are invariably hybrid beings. In this director's cinematic universe, a character with strong prophetic qualities is likely also to have studied Asian martial arts and philosophy. The most thoroughly evolved of the prophetic leaders, The Alchemist, has a superb mastery of Asian combat techniques. As the plot unfolds, audiences discover that this idealized character possesses a seemingly boundless knowledge of various arcane systems of thought. Jodorowsky's statements about the central character of *Dune* make it clear that his intention was to make Paul Atreides another prophet skilled in martial arts and with a broad knowledge of spiritual matters.

Beyond assigning prophetic features to the characters that he invents, Jodorowsky as director assumes the role of the prophet. This tendency is most visible when he invents fictitious communities for the purpose of satirizing human misconduct. The filmmaker's exceptionally rough, often repugnant mockery becomes a modern equivalent of the bitter reproaches that prophets unleash against the inhabitants of the wicked cities to which God has sent them.

Features of the prophet and of prophetic expression appear throughout the films that Jodorowsky realized in the 1970s. However, none of the fictional characters in these films exemplifies purely the figure of the prophet, and neither does the director. Instead, the concept of the prophet is made capacious enough to include other traditions, ranging from martial arts through arcane systems of thought to messianism.

NOTES

1. Ariana Huberman, "Beyond Exotic: Jewish Mysticism and the Supernatural in the Works of Alejandro Jodorowsky" in *Latin American Jewish Cultural Production*, ed. David William Foster (Nashville: Vanderbilt University Press, 2009), 45.
2. George Melnyk, "The Transcontinental Cinema of Alejandro Jodorowsky," *Film International* (Enschede, Sweden), vol. 16, no. 4 (2018), 62.
3. Jeremy Guida, "Producing and Explaining Charisma: A Case Study of the Films of Alejandro Jodorowsky," *Journal of the American Academy of Religion*, vol. 83, no. 2 (2015), 544.
4. Guida, "Producing and Explaining Charisma," 546.
5. Josetxo Cerdán and Miguel Fernández Labayen, "Arty Exploitation, Cool Cult, and the Cinema of Alejandro Jodorowsky," in *Carsploitation, Exploitation Cinemas, and Latin America*, eds. Victoris Ruétalo and Dolores Tierney (New York: Routledge, 2009), 107.
6. D. H. Fleming, "The Pill-Films of Alejandro Jodorowsky," in *Cinemas, Identities, and Beyond*, eds. Ruby Cheung and Fleming (Newcastle upon Tyne: Cambridge Scholars, 2009), 183.
7. Ben Cobb, *Anarchy and Alchemy: The Films of Alejandro Jodorowsky* (London: Creation Books, 2007), 126.
8. Robert Neustadt, "Alejandro Jodorowsky: Reiterating Chaos, Rattling the Cage of Representation," *Chasqui*, vol. 26, no. 1 (1997), 56–74.
9. Huberman, "Beyond Exotic," 42.

10. Frank Herbert, *Dune* (New York: Ace, 2005); original 1965.
11. Abraham Joshua Heschel, *The Prophets* (New York: Harper Perennial Classics, 2001), 3–31; original 1962.
12. Ibid., 4.
13. Ibid., 6.
14. Albert Cook, *The Burden of Prophecy: Poetic Utterance in the Prophets of the Old Testament* (Edwardsville: Southern Illinois University Press, 1996), 8.
15. Cook, *Burden of Prophecy*, 8.
16. Melnyk, "Transcontinental Cinema of Alejandro Jodorowsky," 60.
17. Jodorowsky, *El Topo: A Book of the Film* (New York: Putnam, 1971), 34–35.
18. Exodus 15.22–26. The biblical passages cited in this chapter correspond to The Jewish Publication Society, *JPS Hebrew-English Tanakh*, 2nd ed. (Philadelphia, PA: The Jewish Publication Society, 2003).
19. Exodus 17.6.
20. Naomi Lindstrom, "La expresión profética y apocalíptica en la producción de Alejandro Jodorowsky," *Chasqui*, vol. 42, no. 2 (2013), 129.
21. Jodorowsky, *El Topo*, 57:55.
22. Cobb, *Anarchy and Alchemy*, 96.
23. Ibid., 97.
24. Guida, "Producing and Explaining Charisma," 550.
25. Cobb, *Anarchy and Alchemy*, 125.
26. Fleming, "Pill-Films of Alejandro Jodorowsky," 187.
27. Cobb, *Anarchy and Alchemy*, 127.
28. Jodorowsky in Pavich, *Jodorowsky's Dune*, 40:56.
29. Cerdán and Fernández Labayen in their "Arty Exploitation" discuss *El Topo* as a film set in Mexico, but recognize the ambiguity of the frontier town by referring to it as a "border village," 107.
30. Estevão Garcia and Sylvie Debs, "Le Mexique d'Alejandro Jodorowsky dans *La montagne Sacrée*," *Cinémas d'Amérique Latine*, no. 20 (2012), 10.
31. Cobb, *Anarchy and Alchemy*, 106.
32. Heschel, *The Prophets*, 13.
33. Garcia and Debs, "Le Mexique d'Alejandro Jodorowsky," 21.
34. Fleming, "Pill-Films of Alejandro Jodorowsky," 187.
35. T. E. D. Klein, "They Kill Animals and They Call It Art," *The New York Times*, June 13, 1974, https://www.nytimes.com/1974/01/13/archives/they-kill-animals-and-they-call-it-art-more-and-more-directors-are.html
36. Guida, "Producing and Explaining Charisma," 540.
37. Peter Singer, *Animal Liberation: A New Ethics for Our Treatment of Animals* (New York: HarperCollins), 1975.
38. While Frank Herbert is today thought of as the author of six *Dune* novels or *Dune Chronicles*, at the time Jodorowsky was developing his version only the 1965 *Dune* and its 1969 sequel *Dune Messiah* had been published. Jodorowsky appears to have been adapting only the first of the *Dune* novels.
39. "Jodorowsky's Dune Uncovered," unverified script published on *Dune Behind the Scenes*, https://www.duneinfo.com/unseen/jodorowskys-dune-uncovered (accessed June 7, 2021).
40. Jodorowsky in Pavich, *Jodorowsky's Dune*.
41. Clément Pelissier, "From Filmmaker to Prophet," in *The Seven Lives of Alejandro Jodorowsky*, eds. Vincent Bernière and Nicolas Tellop (Los Angeles: Humanoids, 2020), 63.
42. Pelissier, "From Filmmaker to Prophet," 65.
43. Ibid., 63.

CHAPTER 6

H. P. Blavatsky and Alejandro Jodorowsky: The Influence of the Russian Orthodox Church and Theosophy on Psychomagic in *El Topo* and *The Holy Mountain*

Peter Scott Lederer

INTRODUCTION

Helena Petrovna Blavatsky influenced the New Age movement. The emergence of organizations such as her Theosophical Society (founded 1875) reinforced the importance of esoteric study. *Theosophy* is a combination of the Greek "Theos" and "Sophia," and literally translates as "God's Wisdom."[1] It is a synthesis of a range of sources including Victorian scientific theories, Neoplatonism, and Buddhism. It appealed to the upper classes, feminists, and scientists of the late nineteenth and early twentieth centuries. Blavatsky's idea was that there is one eternal source that binds humanity. Theosophists interpret how nature, divinity, and humanity interact with each other. Their intentions are to more fully understand this through wisdom-seeking.

Blavatsky was faced with severe criticism from both scientists and religious figures. However, her intentions were merely to communicate the wisdom she received from the sages of the past and to contest Victorian concepts of Christianity in order to advance a true understanding of the hidden world. Her "mediumship," like Jodorowsky's psychomagic, has been greatly misunderstood. Like her guru masters in Tibet had taught her, she argued that "spiritualism" was not mere witchcraft or otherworldly and that the "supernatural" was not beyond nature.

Blavatsky was born in the Russian Empire in Yekaterinoslav (present-day Ukraine). Her familiarity with spirituality was first communicated through the Russian Orthodox Church. With the publication of *The Secret Doctrine: The Synthesis of Science, Religion, and Philosophy* (1888), she made Theosophy and its unconventional hermeneutic reading of ancient symbols, particularly the cross, accessible to those who misunderstood her teachings. Although born in Chile, and a Jew, Jodorowsky has ancestral roots similar to Blavatsky's. The symbolism of the Orthodox Church informs his films and his performance-therapy he calls "psychomagic." Jodorowsky's parents were from Yekaterino-slav, where the symbolism of Christianity was everywhere: "symbolism was the initial principle of the Christian cult, real objects were allocated with [a] supernatural sense."² All such symbols hold a "secret value": the temple itself "is a real connection of the earth and sky, material and spiritual, unity of the terrestrial and transcendental beginning of life. The symbol itself is the special sign representing sensual or spiritual reality which is understood not as such, but in [a] wider more general sense."³ Behind every symbol is a diverse cultural story and explanation, "riddles" that "need to be solved."⁴ With this in mind, it is understandable why Jodorowsky praised "great devotees of magic, like Éliphas Lévi, Aleister Crowley, or Corneille-Agrippe" who "asserted that the human being has two bodies – one physical and the other light (also called the energetic body or soul) [. . .] The body of light forms part of the unpronounce-able name of God. The purpose of those magicians was to develop or wake up this body of electricity, integrating it into daily consciousness."⁵

Jodorowsky's films and psychomagic are shaped by these origins, Theoso-phy, and the symbology of these beliefs. In this chapter, I utilize a comparative methodology to argue how *El Topo* (1970) and *The Holy Mountain* (1973) bor-row Blavatsky's concepts. Theosophy's influence on these works has not been considered. The assumptions critics have regarding the Tarot, Blavatsky's spiritualism, and Jodorowsky's unconventional views are interrogated. Tarot readings, Theosophy, and psychomagic are all arguably creative arts therapies: types of treatment that explain how an individual's relationship to a creative work is valuable in wisdom-seeking and the healing process. I then detail how Theosophy and the Orthodox Church developed around the use of symbols to first understand Blavatsky's and Jodorowsky's thinking, followed by an analysis of scenes from *El Topo* and *The Holy Mountain*.

THEOSOPHY

In 1886, William Q. Judge, co-founder of the Theosophical Society, confirmed: "in symbology, the symbol is only right when it fitly represents all the ideas meant to be conveyed, and in all its parts is consistent with the whole, as well as being also in conformity to tradition and the rules of the ancients."⁶ There is an important spiritual journey involved in interpreting symbols; their study and interpretation form the single significant element in the education of students of Theosophy, who do not confuse them with meaningless glyphs, superstition, or general concepts of magic. The obliteration of Western

Christian dogma was also a main concern for these "spiritualists"; Éliphas Lévi, an important influence on Blavatsky, stressed this point. Arthur Edward Waite's 1922 preface to Lévi's *The History of Magic: Including a Clear and Precise Exposition of its Procedures, its Rites, and its Mysteries* (1860) affirms some primary concepts that anticipate Blavatsky's, and also Jodorowsky's, teachings. Lévi's book, Waite argues, "offers the 'negation of dogma.'"[7] Lévi dispelled myths of magic and other "alleged phenomena" but "still held to his general philosophy of the subject, being the persistence of a secret tradition from remote times and surviving at the present day (1) in the tenets of Kabalism and (2) in the pictorial symbols of the Tarot [sic]."[8] The Western Church in modern times has "lost the [Kabbalistic] keys of knowledge, and [. . .] mistakes everywhere the sign for the thing signified."[9] Lévi, Blavatsky, and Jodorowsky conduct Theosophic "magic" on a higher plain through rethinking the symbols the modern Church has obscured.

In *Isis Unveiled* (1877), Blavatsky writes:

we ought, perhaps, to explain the ancient use of allegory and symbology. The truth in the former was left to be deduced . . . Hence the rejoinder of Jesus when his disciples interrogated him because he spoke to the multitude in parables. 'To you,' said he, 'it is given to know the mysteries of the Kingdom of Heaven, but to them it is not given.'[10]

There are reasons to hide truths behind symbols. It was never the intentions of Theosophists to conceal what they knew but to inspire the search for these hidden meanings; that they remained half-buried and involved some digging was the test for wisdom-seekers. As Blavatsky stresses,

[she] does not even give the *keys* to [ancient symbolism], but merely opens a few of the hitherto secret drawers [. . .] Its chief attempt is to show, that however divergent the respective doctrines and systems of old may *seem* on their external or objective side, the agreement between all becomes perfect, so soon as the esoteric or *inner* side of these beliefs and their symbology are examined and a careful comparison made [. . .] Its doctrines and sciences [. . .] represent a complete and unbroken system; and that he who is brave and persevering enough, ready to crush the *animal* in himself, and forgetting the human *self*, sacrifices it to his Higher Ego, can always find his way to become initiated into these mysteries.[11]

Theosophy is dependent on the spiritual leaders of the past. For her readers, and the public that distrusted her, Blavatsky repeats that she is only a communicator of this wisdom: "I have here made only a nosegay of culled flowers, and have brought nothing of my own but the string that ties them."[12] This, in combination with understanding how symbols initiate self-awareness, can be understood further through analyzing the iconography of the Eastern Orthodox Church and the use of the Tarot.

ICONOGRAPHY, THE RUSSIAN ORTHODOX CHURCH, AND THE TAROT

Russian Orthodox Church iconography informs Blavatsky's and Jodorowsky's interpretation of symbols. Church icons guided the creation of the Tarot (Figure 6.1) and are embedded in *El Topo and The Holy Mountain*. In 988, Russia accepted Orthodoxy from the Byzantine Empire, adopting "already developed canons and symbols, both religious and secular."[13] After the fall of Byzantium, Russia became the center of Orthodoxy. Christian symbols in the Empire and the surrounding countries it influenced became increasingly significant: these consisted not only of "difficult theological designs, but also ordinary elements of life": "the cross was minted on coins, decorated [with] an imperial diadem, [and] put on merchant letters and private letters."[14] Furthermore, the coat of arms of modern Russia – a two-headed eagle with Monomakh's cap and a scepter – is "a Christian symbol of power."[15] Most importantly, the Russian Orthodoxy refused Papal authority.

Figure 6.1 "Le Chariot" from Jean Dodal's deck, eighteenth century

The Orthodox Church is enveloped in mystical symbolism: mosaics and paintings on the walls and ceilings of the Church present persons in the icons for worshippers to experience authentic encounters. Unlike the structures of Western Roman Catholic churches, whose Gothic designs reach towards heaven, the design of the Byzantine Empire influenced Eastern Orthodox churches, bringing the divine down to earth. Sacred mysteries become familiar through the iconography in these churches. These symbols were not idols to be worshipped but permitted a greater spiritual understanding to unfold. They were not merely aesthetic objects but, like symbols, directed one's attention towards something else. This is replicated in the Tarot and emulated in Jodorowsky's works. Furthermore,

> the symbolics in [the] architecture of an Orthodox church are difficult and many-sided. [They] express what directly cannot be represented – [they are] the terrestrial embodiment of the heavenly, spiritual, non hand-made, sacral. Unlike Catholic temples built according to the art style dominating during construction, the Orthodox churches are built according to Orthodoxy symbolics.[16]

The fundamental experience is that God is with us, and that through the contemplation of icons, we can experience this intra-cosmic deity more fully. The first mention of icons can be found in Exodus 25.2–9, when God commands Moses to make an icon. Moses makes carved images of these. In Christianity, the icon connects worshippers directly with the body of Christ; it is the incarnation of God that is at its basis. This is in the New Testament when Philip says, "Lord, show us the Father" and Jesus replies: "he that hath seen me hath seen the Father."[17] The "image," then, is the icon. This need for icons in the Orthodox Church is reinforced in the Nicene Creed: "I believe in one God, the Father Almighty, Creator of heaven and earth, of all things visible and invisible."[18] The language within the walls of Orthodox buildings is that "of architectural forms": within these forms are symbols that house the idea of God, "a univers[al] symbol of the terrestrial (profane) and sacral world of touching."[19]

This is important for understanding Jodorowsky's syncretic, Theosophic understanding of the Tarot. Most experts on the Tarot do not conceive it as a complete structure. Jodorowsky, on the other hand, organizes it as if it were a temple: "In all traditions, the temple summarizes the creation of the universe, as a divine unit that has exploded into pieces."[20] Jodorowsky insists that, like Osiris, who was imprisoned in a chest and dismembered and cast into the ocean, the chest of the Tarot is meant to be restored by the reader (Isis, the soul) "in a sacred quest" to resuscitate the God "not in an immaterial dimension but in the material world."[21] This is the esoteric mission of the Tarot, Theosophy, and the

Figure 6.2 Jodorowsky holding "Le Soleil" and "Le Toille" from the Camoin-Jodorowsky Tarot de Marseille deck/Jodorowsky Films (2018) "Why I never found Love? Tarot Reading by Alejandro Jodorowsky for Christophe" [Video]. YouTube. https://www.youtube.com/watch?v=EUDtIrp_Xzg

iconography of the Orthodox Church: "cathedrals behave like mirrors," notes Jodorowsky, and "the Tarot of Marseille, a Judeo-Christian creation, indicates to us in The World ([Tarot card] XXI) that we should use it like a mirror."[22]

Tarot cards probably originated in fifteenth-century Italy, but Jodorowsky argues they appeared around 1000 CE, when it was possible to see "a church, a synagogue, and a mosque cohabitating."[23] They are "shaped by each era's culture and the needs of individual users. This is partly why these decks can be so puzzling to outsiders, as most of them reference allegories or events familiar to people many centuries ago."[24] In fact, "before the [eighteenth] century, the imagery on these cards was accessible to a much broader population."[25] Jodorowsky discovered the cards in a closet when he was seven: "I found a small rectangular metal box. My heart began beating faster. Something told me I was about to receive an important revelation. I opened it. Residing inside was a Tarot card called 'The Chariot.'"[26] Having "studied and memorised the seventy-eight Arcana of the Tarot of Marseille," he pledged to become a reader and turn his readings into a "kind of synthetic psychoanalysis" he called "tarology."[27]

Over the course of his life, Jodorowsky would collect more than 1,000 decks: "alchemical, Rosicrucian, kabbalistic, gypsy, Egyptian, astrological, mythological, Masonic, sexual, and so forth."[28] Given the deck created by Arthur Edward Waite, he realized that "these Arcana only act as stimulants of the intellect": "[t]he term *Arcanum* is derived from the Latin *arcanum*, which means 'secret'"; the Tarot is used "not as entertainment but as a game charged with an inexplicit meaning that we must gradually uncover."[29] The seventy-eight Arcana of the Tarot are divided into two principle groups: the twenty-two

Arcana known as the "Major" and the fifty-six Arcana called "Minor." Whereas the Major cards explore more universal aspects or human traits, the Minor are more specific and particular, meant to explore the personal areas of daily life. Both of these features correspond to Jodorowsky's performance-based therapy, which emulates how the Tarot directs people "to a hidden meaning, a mystery defying rationality, and appears appropriate to us to the extent that we are using [it] not as entertainment but as a game charged with an inexplicit meaning that we must gradually uncover."[30]

In 1997, Jodorowsky accomplished restoring the Tarot cards to their popular seventeenth-century design. Their colors and symbols were carefully reproduced to allow more significant readings. Jodorowsky insists that other Tarot decks fail to properly represent their symbols' original intentions: "I'm a purist."[31] For Jodorowsky, the Tarot is a sacred game: "a point of reference, of reflection, of divination."[32] David Colman suggests "Jodorowsky's philosophy of the tarot [. . .] is flexible and even slippery."[33] This, however, is precisely because the subjective experiences of readers and their clients are fluid and dynamic. Combined with Theosophy, it becomes apparent how the Tarot becomes critical for analyzing Jodorowsky's work.

EL TOPO

El Topo is a violent, surreal western fused with mystical Eastern overtones. The film is considered a "head trip" or "psychedelic western" by some critics.[34] It enjoyed success at midnight screenings following its premiere in New York City after it followed a film produced by John Lennon. It has been routinely "contextualized" as the film that initiated the midnight movie phenomenon and "the socio-historical scenario in which such cultural phenomenon appeared."[35] It "captured the countercultural imagination" and the event was called a "midnight mass."[36] Blood and spectacle in *El Topo* are necessities. Jodorowsky's inclusion of strange, crude objects and cruel, outlandish behavior, though, has psychotherapeutic intentions. He notes the importance of unusual acts to "ancient black magic," which sometimes "employed charms made of revolting products, such as fecal matter, parts of human cadavers, and animal poison," considering each substance an "impure" or "rare" ingredient necessary for a "certain effectiveness."[37] It was the energy invested in gathering such items which helped to create the "magic" rather than the products themselves: "[t]o heal or solve a problem we need an iron will. The tireless battle to fulfil a goal that seems impossible develops our vital energy. Medieval sorcerers understood this very well when creating formulatory that proposed to perform impossible acts."[38] It is with this knowledge that critics should approach a bizarre and graphic film like *El Topo*.

Its aesthetics have been described as emphasizing the "striking contrasts between rich earth tones and explosions of bloody red."[39] Alessandra Santos labels the main elements of *El Topo*: "spirituality, visual and topical transgressions that include humour, blood baths, dead animals, religious cults, disabled bodies, lesbian sex, rape and self-immolation."[40] The protagonist's claims to Godhood and the heavy religious symbolism throughout the film, however, evolve from Eastern mysticism and anticipate the psychomagic Jodorowsky would later develop and practice.

After discovering a town in which everyone has been killed, El Topo ("the Mole") – a lone gunslinger dressed entirely in black (Jodorowsky) – hunts down the murderers. He then decides to leave his son Hijo (Jodorowsky's real son) with monks and rides off with a woman, Mara (Mara Lorenzio), a slave kept by the gang's leader. He embarks on a mission to kill four warrior masters to prove to her that he is the greatest warrior. Each master represents a certain ideology. El Topo is able to defeat all four in separate duels. He, however, is severely injured in a manner replicating stigmata when a female version of his own self (Paula Romo) defeats him in a gun battle. Mara rides off with this new master-warrior woman. The Mole is rescued by a group of mutant cave-dwellers and awakens many years later underground. He manages to find an exit from the cave and escapes with his dwarf wife (Jacqueline Luis), but he is determined to help the others and performs in a nearby town to raise money. Hijo then reappears as a young monk and reunites with his father, only to despise him for his act of abandonment. He, though, agrees to help El Topo rescue the cave-dwellers. After the mutants are freed, the townspeople, who follow an extreme cult religion, massacre them. El Topo shoots down the townspeople and then immolates himself after he is mortally wounded. After giving birth, his wife makes a grave for him and rides off with Hijo. The symbols in the film are overwhelming, so only a few here are examined.

In the opening shot, a pole rises out of the sand. El Topo rides up to it on a black horse. He is carrying a black umbrella with his naked son behind him. El Topo takes out a stuffed toy bear and a photo of the boy's mother from a leather pouch. He speaks to Hijo: "Today you are seven years old. Now you are a man. Bury your mother's picture." The boy buries the bear and picture, but only half-way: they are half-buried, half-hidden, half-forgotten. The two ride off.

Jodorowsky offers viewers an explanation of the symbolism in this opening scene: "[w]hen a man buries a pole in the sand, he automatically creates a sundial and begins to mark time. To begin marking time is to begin creating a culture."[41] The protagonist, though, is a variation of the first Tarot card, The Fool. The Fool is also the zeroth card: "The Fool has a name, but he does not have a number. It is the sole Major Arcana card not to be defined numerically [. . .] the Major Arcana all include a cartouche on top in which their number is inscribed. This cartouche is empty in the case of the Fool."[42] It is possible

Figure 6.3 El Topo and his son on horseback

to gather a fair idea of the mystery in Jodorowsky's symbols if his own concepts of the Tarot's numerology are first considered: "[i]n traditional numerology [. . .] I discovered that the number 1 was claimed as the first odd, active, male number representing the Father, the unit, and number 2 was the first even number, one that was passive and female, representing the Mother and multiplicity."[43] Jodorowsky chooses not to "exalt" the male image, however, and his Tarot readings also do not; instead, he merely associates the number 1 with "activity."[44] Furthermore, Jodorowsky's process of reading the Tarot is progressive; it adds rather than subtracts: "it describes a process of advancement and growth by one degree after the next."[45]

Associating the Mole in *El Topo* with the Fool card, and following from a numerology-based reading, one should proceed to Blavatsky's understanding of the evolution of symbology. Blavatsky provides a useful example of an illustration. Imagine:

a plain disk, [circle]. The second in the archaic symbol shows a disk with a point in it, [circle with a dot] – the first differentiation in the periodical manifestations of the ever-eternal Nature, sexless and infinite [. . .] potential Space within abstract Space. In its third stage the point is transformed into a diameter, [circle with a line]'.[46]

When this line is crossed by a second one (a circle with a cross), it now becomes the Mundane Cross: "the sign of the origin of human Life."[47] Blavatsky continues: "[w]hen the circumference disappears and leaves only the [cross], it is a sign that the fall of man into matter is accomplished [. . .]

The cross within a circle symbolizes pure Pantheism; when the cross is left uninscribed, it becomes phallic."⁴⁸

Theosophy and psychomagic do not direct readers or their clients to be passive but rather to engage in how symbols work. Thus, the pole is not merely a phallic symbol but an esoteric one inspiring reawakening. In combination with the child, it becomes this Theosophic representation of the fallen man and his quest to heal. In *El Topo*, the number o is the natural, unimpeded desert landscape in which the protagonist, the number 1, suddenly appears. The Mole becomes the dark point upon this empty disc and must abandon his son – with whom he becomes 2, a passive number symbolizing duality – to fulfill his destiny. The cross's two lines signify the point where humanity's suffering is located; the tragedy of existence must be embraced to allow transformation to occur. Theosophist Arthur M. Coon offers an extension of Blavatsky's explanation of the evolution of the circle and dot. Quoting the mystic Manly P. Hall, he identifies the symbolism of the dot as "the first departure from things as they normally are. It is the first illusion of the self, the first limitation of space."⁴⁹ It is a "sacred island, is the beginning of existence, whether that of a universe or man," symbolizing "the cause" and the "line [. . .] is the symbol of the dot in growth or motion."⁵⁰

Jodorowsky's explanation for the umbrella is more mysterious: "[s]trange to carry an umbrella in the desert where it never rains! Perhaps El Topo is waiting for the rain to come forth from his body and collect it in the black chalice: the umbrella."⁵¹ When El Topo ties the umbrella to the pole, Jodorowsky explains that this "black chalice, the cup, becomes fused with the pole," it is a "marriage between that which exists face down waiting to be nourished from the ground: the umbrella; and that which exists growing upward waiting to be nourished by the sun and the sky: the pole."⁵²

The scene, though, is vital for understanding psychomagic's need to associate biography with symbol. Jodorowsky named his son after a family from the town where he was born: "The father of the family, a baker, always allowed his children to play with any toy they wanted. My father forbade me to play with war toys. He was a pacifist. And since all toys symbolize war, I could never play. But the Brontis children could play. They were free."⁵³ Jodorowsky routinely finds the root of people's problems is in their "family terrain."⁵⁴ He assists them in uncovering and then reburying their past:

[i]n the practice of the kosher Hebrew diet, when instruments that were in contact with dairy products come into contact with the flesh of an animal, making them impure, the instruments are buried in the earth for a certain number of days. At the end of this time, the instruments are extracted: the earth has purified them. Inspired by this, I have recommended many time to consultants [patients] to bury objects, such as clothes of photographs, to free themselves from past sufferings.⁵⁵

Thus, the burying of the photo is the beginning of careful, instructional but constructive guidance. The black umbrella represents the nourishment gained from retrieving and extinguishing negative memories; the fatalistic tone of the entire film emphasizes how this is therapeutically advantageous. This usage of symbols and trauma can be appreciated more fully during the scenes in the town of crazed cult followers when the most iconic esoteric symbol is revealed: the Eye of Providence.

The church followers in the town are depraved and misled by their religious leaders. They commit atrocities upon Blacks and cave mutants. The Eye of Providence is their symbol. It seems odd that Jodorowsky places this symbol in a disturbing sequence, but the context must be understood: he sees the distorted extremism associated with any symbol or school of thought, and allowing such ideas to become inflexible and dogmatic, horrifying. Its employment here can also be compared with the gross misuse of the image of Christ by the centurion shop owners in *The Holy Mountain* later.

Theosophy recognizes the Eye of Providence as the all-seeing eye of an omniscient and omnipresent God. Eye iconography has been associated in many different cultures and religions. In Catholicism, the triangle with the eye is the symbol of the Holy Trinity. It later became a Masonic symbol. Coon expresses the significance of this threefold pattern to the Theosophical Seal, explaining how it represents a triangle relationship: "God-man-religion."[56] The "first geometric figure" is "the universal gauge or measure of every creative act, whether that act pertains to the world of things or the world of consciousness."[57] This threefold image is also a progression from the pole in the beginning of the film and the dot in the circle. However, it is grossly misused by the church leaders, much as "the Cross in Christianity has descended from

Figure 6.4 Church leaders and their religious symbol, the Eye of Providence

a symbol into a mere glyph: its significance is lost, and it remains a reminder, a banner."⁵⁸ This criticism of the misuse of religion and symbols is more intensive in Jodorowsky's next film.

THE HOLY MOUNTAIN

The Holy Mountain's criticisms of Christianity echo Blavatsky's. Blavatsky railed against scientists, academics, and clergy, setting her up as a new spiritual authority arguing to replace outmoded religious doctrine and contest Victorian authoritarianism. Part of her polemic was the West's misunderstanding of Christ. Christianity, in this impure form, is such that,

> having rejected the doctrine of emanations and replaced them with direct, conscious creations of angels and the rest out of *nothing*, [it] now finds itself hopelessly stranded between Supernaturalism, or miracle, and materialism. An *extra*-cosmic god is fatal to philosophy, an *intra*-cosmic Deity – i.e. Spirit and matter inseparable from each other – is a philosophical necessity.⁵⁹

This is deeply rooted in Jodorowsky's critique of the Church in *The Holy Mountain*, which Santos argues "dismantles all idols and icons, including all forms of religious and mystical beliefs."⁶⁰ Santos calls Jodorowsky's work "interdisciplinary."⁶¹ However, she does not associate this word with the complex Theosophic elements in his films, and instead uses the term in the customary sense to describe Jodorowsky's "multidisciplinary artistic background and exploratory filmic style [. . .] especially the influence of theatre and comic books, but also ranging from cabaret dancers to elaborate sculpture, and collaboration with recognised artists and musicians."⁶² Whereas Santos is correct to suggest that *The Holy Mountain*'s "proposal is to destroy all idolatry, whether religious, political or even the cult of celebrity Hollywood created,"⁶³ there is much more here to interrogate in an interdisciplinary manner, which requires exploring the Theosophic elements of the film.

Blavatsky's and Jodorowsky's knowledge of symbols, like the Eastern Orthodox Church's understanding of icons, permits the real intra-cosmic deity discovered in meditation and contemplation to arise. It is this intra-cosmic deity that is at the heart of *The Holy Mountain*'s plot as much as its Tarot-inspired protagonist. The film is about a messianic character (Horacio Salinas) who meets a mystical guru and alchemist (Jodorowsky) who teaches him the renunciation of worldly possessions. He and seven others, each who represents a planet, are guided by the master on a pilgrimage to the Holy Mountain, where they hope to achieve absolute enlightenment and become immortals.

In the beginning of the film, a Christ figure, referred to as The Thief, awakens from a drunken stupor, his face covered in flies. This Christ-like character is also a play on the Fool card of the Tarot but more so here. This is apparent when the camera pans left, where two Tarot cards (The Fool) are shown. It pulls back to a wider shot and an armless and legless man (Basilio González), represented by the Five of Swords card, helps The Thief to his feet. Santos identifies the cards as representing innocence and potential.[64]

Figure 6.5 The Crippled Man rescues The Thief

The Thief, like El Topo, represents The Fool's "original boundless energy, total freedom, madness, disorder, chaos."[65] What is his destiny? Jodorowsky gives readers an example of a reading of the Fool card (the Alpha of the Major Arcana) when it is placed beside another card, such as The World (The Omega): these are "the two points between which all possibilities are deployed."[66] The Alpha and The Omega, of course, are the first and last letters of the Greek alphabet and together represent the beginning and the end, a title for Jesus, emphasizing His divine unity with God. The symbols A and Ω are often placed on Jesus's right and left side in paintings, replacing the Orthodox Christogram. In *The Holy Mountain*, The Fool becomes "a perpetual beginning and The World an infinite culmination."[67] He is "the archetype of initial energy" and it is "the archetype of realization."[68] He is headed towards "the oval of the World."[69]

There is a certain madness accompanying a Tarot card as complicated as The Fool, which is emphasized by The Thief's madding screams later when he awakens and realizes he has been turned into a god but is still lost. Most of all, however, he "represents liberation, a flight (material, emotional, intellectual, or sexual)."[70] Jodorowsky says The Fool is "a pilgrim making his way to a sacred site [. . .] If we choose the most elevated interpretation, we shall see The Fool as an individual detached from all needs and complexes and judgments, unbound by any taboos because he has abandoned all demand."[71]

The Thief and the armless/legless man wander through the Central American town to a carnival, where they join the "Great Toad and Chameleon Circus" troupe, surely Jodorowsky's absurdist mystical cabaret. Violent imagery is again required to provoke deeper mystical transcendence that escapes exoteric Christianity. In this bizarre scene Jodorowsky condemns the Spanish crimes against the ancient culture. Chameleons are dressed up as the indigenous Aztecs and the toads as the Spanish invaders on a giant pyramid set, where they eventually explode in a blood bath. As Patrick Nash explains,

> Toads are the Spanish, who have pillaged and destroyed the land the lizards (aka the indigenous people of the land) have spent centuries developing. The scene is intensely violent and graphic, but at the core is the harsh truth of colonialism, in that, for too long, there has been a myth built around the intentions behind the colonization of the Americas, with the Spanish and other immigrants depicted as "saviours" to the people of the region, rather than the horrible, destructive force they actually were.[72]

Whereas these post-colonial tropes are usually noted, critics have missed the Theosophic metaphor here. The Spanish conquistadors are viciously critiqued by Jodorowsky as eradicating the indigenous peoples under the guise of Christian righteousness. Blavatsky challenged the misuse of power by both scientists and the clergy. She condemned the Church fathers as distorters of monotheism. The ecclesiastic authority had corrupted Christianity, and England and the Americas were pseudo-Christian countries. She argued that in the Russian Orthodox Church, however, the purer ideal of Jesus was preserved. Similarly, Blavatsky believed she was upholding true, esoteric Christianity with Theosophy: exoteric Christianity was fraudulent.

Santos explains that "*The Holy Mountain* is a parody of the sacred" and "functions as a critique of the hypocrisy of the Church when The Thief, after working for the animal circus, encounters a tourist shop with a 'Christs for Sale' sign."[73] He is captured by several brutish, obese men dressed like Roman centurions. They throw him in a potato cellar after getting him drunk, where he awakens surrounded by plaster models replicated from his mold while he was passed out (Figure 6.6). True Christianity has disintegrated into a commercial product to be consumed by the masses. Jodorowsky's message is Theosophic: a new system must be rebuilt based on the wisdom of the ages, displacing an old system dependent on religious authoritarianism and the distorted interpretations of the teachings of Jesus.

When The Thief meets The Guru/Alchemist, he is told he is "excrement" and that he can change himself into gold and taught how the Tarot can help him "create the soul." This initiates his quest to the Holy Mountain. Blavatsky,

Figure 6.6 The Thief awakens in horror

Jodorowsky, and other Russian mystics often went on pilgrimages. Blavatsky explains this Eastern tradition:

> there are several documents in the St. Petersburg Imperial Libraries to show that, even so late as the days when Freemasonry and Secret Societies of Mystics flourished without hindrance in Russia, namely at the end of the last and the beginning of the present century, more than one Russian Mystic travelled to Tibet via the Ural Mountains in search of knowledge and initiation in the unknown crypts of Central Asia. And more than one returned years later, with a rich stone of information such as could never have been given him anywhere in Europe.[74]

The other initiates follow to assist The Thief on his voyage but succumb to the corruptions of the world: power, greed, and sex. These symbols, however, have less to do with the fictional story and more to do with the greater real mystical journey Jodorowsky compels the audience to begin, which The Alchemist reveals at the film's end:

> I promised you the great secret and I will not disappoint you. Is this the end of our adventure? Nothing has an end. We came in search of the secret of immortality. To be like Gods. And here we are . . . mortals. More human than ever. If we have not obtained immortality, at least we have obtained reality. We began in a fairytale and we came to life! But is this life reality? No. It is a film. Zoom back camera. We are images, dreams, photographs. We must not stay here! Prisoners! We shall break the illusion. This is Maya. Goodbye to the Holy Mountain. Real life awaits us.

The Alchemist breaks the fourth wall and directly looks at the camera as it pulls back and reveals the complete set of cameras, lights, and crew. One critic describes this as Jodorowsky "showing us the folly of Savior-worship as a concept, as any powerful person can fall victim to corruption on their journey to enlightenment, even Jesus."[75] The moment, though, is a clear Theosophic lifting of the veil, underlining that people should "believe in no Magic which transcends the scope and capacity of the human mind, nor in "miracle," whether divine or diabolical."[76] Humans must develop new sensibilities and perceptions.

The shock of breaking the fictional frame, in combination with the use of the Tarot symbols, is Jodorowsky's filmic use of psychomagic. It is precisely this world of symbols and their (re)production that Jodorowsky's therapy stresses as relevant for overcoming trauma and reaching the pinnacle of enlightenment. Psychomagic is built on first identifying the patient's "family tree." It is neither "magical" nor "supernatural" but understands that symbols lead to fuller and more complete wisdom. Jodorowsky and Blavatsky's messages are not superstitious but psychological. Psychomagicians, then, are psychotherapists in the sense that they use symbols as a way for their clients to raise self-awareness.

CONCLUSION

Jodorowsky's psychomagic does not depart from the symbolism and arguments embedded in Theosophy, the Tarot, the icons of the Orthodox Church, and his films. How a person reacts to metaphor points towards spiritual growth: "[t]he unconscious is capable of accepting symbolic or metaphoric fulfilment: a photograph of someone can represent the actual person or a part can represent the whole."[77] Jodorowsky's therapy echoes Blavatsky's Theosophy in bringing readers and their clients to the realization that they are their own masters, unlike the supernatural witchery or charlatanry critics have accused the two of promoting:

> For a primitive therapy to function, the witch doctor, supported by the spiritual superstitions of the patient, must maintain a mystery, present himself as the possessor of superhuman powers obtained through a secret initiation and relying on divine and supernatural allies to being about a cure. The remedies they provide are mysterious to their clients, and the actions they recommend are intended to be performed without knowing why. In [p]sychomagic, to the contrary, we need the individual's understanding instead of the superstitious beliefs. The patient should know the reasons for each of his actions. The psychomagician makes the transition from witch doctor to adviser. Using psychomagic prescriptions, the patient becomes his [or her] own healer.[78]

Jodorowsky's films should not be criticized for their assumed pretentiousness. Symbols are psychotherapeutic; they heal and lead people to greater wisdom and understanding: "the objects that surround us and accompany us form part of the language of the unconscious."[79] Theosophy, the Tarot, psychomagic, and Jodorowsky's films recognize that "spiritualism" is not "supernatural" but permits individuals a way to release that which has long been hidden; they bring to the surface what people have long repressed. They are not "mystical" but practical and subjective therapeutic lessons that rely on the experiences of clients and audiences. Thus, the artistic and therapeutic paths are unified. Jodorowsky still performs Tarot readings every day in the cafés of Paris, offering "magical" solutions to all those who seek his advice.

NOTES

1. "Theosophy" (Oxford: Oxford University Press, 2012).
2. Liliya R. Akhmetova, Elmira U. Abdulkadyrova, and Irina M. Maiorova, "Semiotics and Symbolism in the Orthodox Church Architecture," *International Journal of Humanities and Cultural Studies* (August 2016), 182.
3. Ibid., 182.
4. Ibid., 183.
5. Alejandro Jodorowsky, *Manual of Psychomagic: The Practice of Shamanic Psychotherapy*, (Rochester, VT: Inner Traditions, 2009), 11–12.
6. William Q. Judge, "Theosophical Symbols," *Theosophical Articles*, vol. 1 (1886), 1.
7. Arthur Edward Waite, preface, in Éliphas Lévi, *The History of Magic* (London: William Rider & Son, 1922), xx.
8. Ibid., xviii.
9. Ibid., xx.
10. Helena Petrovna Blavatsky, *Isis Unveiled: A Master-Key to the Mysteries of Ancient and Modern Science and Theology* (Los Angeles, CA: The Theosophy Company, 1877), 272.
11. Helena Petrovna Blavatsky, "The Babel of Modern Thought," *Lucifer*, vol. vii, no. 41 (January 1891), 94.
12. Helena Petrovna Blavatsky, *The Secret Doctrine: The Synthesis of Science, Religion, and Philosophy*, 3rd ed. (London: The Theosophical Publishing House, 1893), 30, Gutenberg.org.
13. Akhmetova et al., 182.
14. Ibid., 182.
15. Ibid., 182.
16. Ibid., 181.
17. John 14.8–9, *The Bible*, King James Version (Grand Rapids, MI: Zondervan, 1983).
18. "Catholic Church, Byzantine-Ruthenian Rite: The Creed," 1.
19. Akhmetova et al., 181.
20. Alejandro Jodorowsky, *The Way of Tarot: The Spiritual Teacher in the Cards* (Rochester, VT: Destiny Books, 2009), 17.
21. Ibid.
22. Ibid.
23. Ibid., 11.

24. Hunter Oatman-Stanford, "Tarot Mythology: The Surprising Origins of the World's Most Misunderstood Cards," *Collectors Weekly*, 18 (2014): par. 2.
25. Ibid.
26. Jodorowsky, *The Way of Tarot*, 7.
27. Jodorowsky, *Manual of Psychomagic*, 1.
28. Jodorowsky, *The Way of Tarot*, 9.
29. Ibid., 22.
30. Ibid.
31. David Colman, "When the Tarot Trumps All," *The New York Times*, November 11, 2011, par. 5.
32. Ibid., 12.
33. Ibid., 14.
34. Alessandro Santos, *The Holy Mountain* (London: Wallflower Press, 2017), 22.
35. Ibid., 55.
36. J. Hoberman and Jonathan Rosenbaum, *Midnight Movies* (New York: Harper & Row, 1983), 94.
37. Jodorowsky, *Manual of Psychomagic*, 7.
38. Ibid., 7.
39. Jim Hemphil, "DVD Playback. Review of the Films of Alejandro Jodorowsky," *American Cinematographer*, vol. 88, no. 6 (2007), 12.
40. Santos, *The Holy Mountain*, 21–22.
41. Alejandro Jodorowsky, *El Topo: A Book of the Film* (New York: Putnam, 1971), 1.
42. Jodorowsky, *The Way of Tarot*, 22.
43. Ibid., 20.
44. Ibid.
45. Ibid., 25.
46. Blavatsky, *The Secret Doctrine*, 33.
47. Ibid.
48. Ibid.
49. Arthur M. Coon, *The Theosophical Seal: A Study for the Student and Non-Student* (India: The Theosophical Publishing House, 1958), 15.
50. Ibid.
51. Jodorowsky, *El Topo: A Book of the Film*, 1.
52. Ibid., 2.
53. Ibid., 8.
54. Jodorowsky, *Manual of Psychomagic*, 12.
55. Ibid., 8.
56. Coon, *The Theosophical Seal*, 101.
57. Ibid.
58. H. T. Edge, "The Universal Mystery-Language and Its Interpretation: III," *The Theosophical Forum* (March 1936), par. 5. www.Theosophy.org
59. Blavatsky, *The Secret Doctrine*, 45.
60. Santos, *The Holy Mountain*, 85.
61. Ibid., 65.
62. Ibid.
63. Ibid., 10.
64. Ibid., 71.
65. Ibid., 85.
66. Jodorowsky, *The Way of Tarot*, 26.
67. Ibid.

68. Ibid., 38.
69. Ibid., 26.
70. Ibid., 87.
71. Ibid., 85.
72. Patrick Nash, "Hidden Gem: Alejandro Jodorowsky's *The Holy Mountain* is Dazzling, Astounding, and Groundbreaking," *Hollywood Insider*, (March 16, 2021), par. 11. www. Hollywoodinsider.com
73. Santos, *The Holy Mountain*, 82.
74. Blavatsky, *The Secret Doctrine*, 19.
75. Nash, "Hidden Gem," par. 17.
76. Blavatsky, *Isis Unveiled*, 6.
77. Jodorowsky, *Manual of Psychomagic*, 3.
78. Jodorowsky, *Psychomagic: The Transformative Power of Shamanic* (Rochester, VT: Inner Traditions, 2004), ix.
79. Ibid., viii.

CHAPTER 7

Dionysus Resuscitated: Alejandro Jodorowsky and the Aesthetics of Intoxication

Florian Zappe

> For there to be art, for there to be any aesthetic activity and observation, one physiological prerequisite is indispensable: *intoxication*.
>
> Friedrich Nietzsche

The larger part of Alejandro Jodorowsky's cinematic oeuvre is surrounded by an aura of being idiosyncratically cryptic up to the point of utter incomprehensibility. In order to come to terms with the epistemological challenges presented by his work, the interpretative gateways that have been used to find access to his films relied on two major pillars: critics have either approached them through various theories on avant-garde art, highlighting the sociocultural function of the anti-organic aesthetics of Jodorowsky's works, or they have tried to decipher them by scrutinizing their spiritual content, mostly in context with the countercultures of the 1960s and 1970s and their interest in "New Age" spirituality.

This chapter wants to offer an alternative route of accessing Jodorowsky's cinema by proposing a reading of his films – my points of references will be the so-called "cult classics" *El Topo* (1970) and *The Holy Mountain* (1973) as well as his "comeback film" *Santa Sangre* (1989) – through the lens of Dionysian aesthetics, specifically in its Nietzschean rendering. Admittedly, this may not seem to be a completely untrodden path as critics have occasionally identified a kinship between Nietzsche's and Jodorowsky's work. Ben Cobb has written about the role of *Thus Spoke Zarathustra* – a book that Jodorowsky also had adapted for the stage in the 1950s – as "the single most valuable source for both the character of El Topo and the story of his journey."[1] Johan Faerber remarked that the rebellious ethos of the *Mouvement Panic*, the theater and performance art group Jodorowsky founded in collaboration with Roland

Topor and Fernando Arrabal in Paris in the early 1960s, was fueled by a "hatred of culture in the sense that Nietzsche once gave to the term – that is, as the resolute and relentless taming of death culture against all of life's powers" and marked by a "hyperbolized concern that becomes absolutely Dionysian[.]"[2] But given that Jodorowsky carried much of this artistic vigor over into his work in cinema, it seems surprising that he has never been explicitly discussed as a Dionysian filmmaker.

First formulated in *The Birth of Tragedy* and then developed further, Nietzsche associates certain characteristics – chaos, ritual, inebriation, ecstasy, irrationality, madness, rebirth, etc. – with Dionysian art. These elements define an "aesthetics of intoxication" which holds the potential for the transcendence of conventional(ized) subjectivity. By reading Jodorowsky through Nietzsche, this chapter will show that he not only shares the philosopher's understanding of art as a nontheistic and immanent metaphysical realm but also his aesthetico-philosophical axioms. I will argue that his transgressive cinema can be understood as a modern resuscitation of the aesthetics of intoxication which attempts to make the Dionysian nexus of aesthetic experience and transcendence productive for a twentieth-century context.

THE AESTHETICS OF INTOXICATION

Associating Jodorowsky's cinema with states of intoxication has a long tradition in the sparse body of literature on his work. Although the filmmaker's personal experiences with drugs are – probably to the surprise and disappointment of some of his devotees – limited to moderate experimentation,[3] *El Topo* and *The Holy Mountain* especially are widely regarded as prime examples of what David H. Fleming has defined as "unbecoming 'head cinema': a type of drug film targeted at US 'head audiences' (cult filmgoers with a preference for watching films high on marijuana or drugs such as LSD)."[4] The compatibility of the films' aesthetics with the experiential needs of the substance-savvy countercultural audiences of the early 1970s is a well-known and often retold part of the Jodorowsky myth and has certainly contributed to his status as one of the figureheads of psychedelic cinema,[5] going as far as enthroning him as "the only authentically countercultural filmmaker."[6] But to follow that cliché by encapsulating his "pill films"[7] in the rebellious zeitgeist of this period would be too narrow a perspective. They undoubtedly stand in a longer line of tradition in Western art and thought that identifies inebriation as an aesthetic paradigm and that finds its most influential philosophical manifestation in Friedrich Nietzsche's writings.

Jason Ciaccio has argued that the "idea of an 'aesthetics of intoxication' seems to be nearly synonymous with Nietzsche's work" as the theme "runs like a curious thread through the labyrinth of [the philosopher's] evolving thought."[8] The allegorical heart at the center of this philosophical idea is the figure of Dionysus that accompanied Nietzsche from his first book *The Birth of Tragedy from the Spirit of Music* (*Die Geburt der Tragödie aus dem Geiste der Musik*), published in 1872, until his psychological breakdown in Turin in January 1889 when the philosopher – on the brink of delusion – adopted this persona and signed several of his last notes (the so-called *Wahnzettel*) with the Greek god's name. Throughout the various stages of his philosophical productivity, the concept of the Dionysian and of Dionysus has been an ever-present yet "highly ambiguous and fluid one"[9] that evolved from an object of philological study towards an essential element in Nietzsche's theory of art. His first engagement with these ideas in *The Birth of Tragedy*, published when Nietzsche was still a professor of classical philology at the University of Basel, still had a distinct historical perspective, yet without asserting a claim for "pursu[ing] historical accuracy."[10] The book is equally a contribution to the study of Hellenic culture and the genesis of the tragedy in the context of the Attic *Dionysia* as it is a commentary by proxy on the state of the arts in his contemporary times (especially on the role of Richard Wagner whom Nietzsche still idolized at that time). Since the categories established in *The Birth of Tragedy* are by now part of the canon of aesthetic theory, and since in any case it is not possible to recapitulate Nietzsche's complex argument in detail in the context of this chapter, I just want to highlight some central aspects that will prove, in what follows, essential for the understanding of the kinship between his and Jodorowsky's metaphysics of art.[11]

According to Nietzsche, the ancient Greeks attributed the quasi-metaphysical power to overcome the despair caused by the realization of existential contingency to the realm of art: "Art alone can re-direct those repulsive thoughts about the terrible or absurd nature of existence into representations with which man can live."[12] The driving forces behind artistic practices are two dialectical principles that Nietzsche refers to as "artistic drives,"[13] the Apollonian (sometimes also translated as Apollinian or Apolline) and the Dionysian (or Dionysiac), embodied by the respective deities. While Apollo is associated with structure, stability, representation, and rational subjectivity, Dionysus, the god of wine,[14] dance and festivities, invokes notions of ecstasy, drunkenness, fluidity, affect, and the transgression of culturally predefined notions of subjectivity "to the point of complete self-forgetting."[15] This not only involves the idea of temporal liberation from social norms and constraints during the period of (physiological and/or psychological) intoxication but is also linked to the symbolic "cycle of death and rebirth,"[16] which holds the potential for more enduring experiences of (self-)transformation. In that, it is vital to Nietzsche's philosophy of individuality.

The philosopher's engagement with Dionysus in his first book marks the starting point for what Ciaccio has identified as the preoccupation of Nietzschean thought with intoxication, although the term itself remains "a signifier with an ever-shifting set of signifieds: he employs it as a trope to address such a varied set of concerns about modernity that the concept takes on a depth of metaphoricity as multivalent as his idea of the body itself."[17] In *The Birth of Tragedy*, Nietzsche makes a distinction between "the separate art-worlds of *dream* and *intoxication*[,] an opposition [. . .] which corresponds to that between the Apolline and the Dionysiac"[18] that is linked to both, aesthetic form as well as experience. The "dream-images" of Apollonian art are, even if their content may be speculative or mythological, marked by *"semblance"*[19] to the world and the aesthetic experience accordingly defined by epistemological coherence as Jessica Wood points out: "The individual under the spell of Apollo encounters a world of phenomena, and comforting images; identity is also experienced as individual, and one perceives oneself as a being distinct and bordered off from other beings."[20] While the Apollonian aesthetic – as an aesthetic of harmonious meaning-making – affirms the subject's situatedness in and understanding of the world, the Dionysian drive aims for the opposite:

> Under the influence of the Dionysian the individual reaches a state resembling intoxication, triggered by narcotics or the approach of spring. Dionysus sweeps aside Apollo's comforting illusions, and reveals the primordial undercurrent of existence beyond the world of phenomena. The principle of individuation collapses, and man, now relieved of his status as an individual, experiences unity with the primordial oneness.[21]

While this early exploration of the Apollo-Dionysus-dyad is still rooted in a historical treatise on the origins of Greek tragedy, Nietzsche's later writings provide a broader understanding of the concepts – especially of Dionysian intoxication which has to be understood as a state of stimulation not as narcotization – in the context of a universal philosophy of art. In section eight of the chapter "Raids of an Untimely Man" in his *Twilight of the Idols, Or, How to Philosophize with the Hammer* (*Götzen-Dämmerung, oder, Wie man mit dem Hammer philosophiert*), entitled "Towards a psychology of the artist," Nietzsche defines intoxication as an essential precondition of any relevant artistic practice and creativity:

> Intoxication must already have heightened the sensitivity of the whole machine: otherwise, no art will be forthcoming. All kinds of intoxication, as different as their causes may be, have this power: above all, the intoxication of sexual excitement, that oldest and most primordial form

of intoxication. Likewise the intoxication that follows all great cravings, all strong emotions; the intoxication of the festival, of the competition, of daredevilry, of victory, of every extreme commotion; the intoxication of cruelty; the intoxication of destruction; intoxication due to certain meteorological influences, such as the intoxication of spring; or under the influence of narcotics; finally, the intoxication of the will, the intoxication of an overloaded and swollen will.[22]

Here, Nietzsche points to the ambiguity of intoxication in a radically affirmative way by embracing the pleasurable origins of the altered states the subject can experience (desire, spring fever, substance induced stimulation, etc.) as well as the darker ones such as violence and cruelty which equally uproot the individual via the experience of suffering – a central component of Dionysian transformation.

He continues to distinguish between an Apollonian and a Dionysian form of intoxication. The former is primarily visual as it "keeps the eye excited" whereas the latter is more affective and visceral as "the whole system of emotions is excited and intensified: so it vents all its means of expression at once and brings out the power of representing, imitating, transfiguring, transforming, every sort of mimicry and acting, all at once."[23] In that, Dionysus becomes the transhistorical avatar of the transgressive artist who mobilizes the entire affective apparatus of aesthetic strategies in order to produce a potentially transformative, wholistic and intoxicating *Gesamtkunstwerk*.

APOLLO, DIONYSUS, AND CINEMA

Although Nietzsche's death in 1900 predates the evolution of film from a medium of technological spectacle towards the predominant artform of the twentieth century, his categories are applicable. If we accept Nietzsche's claim that Apollonian intoxication is primarily directed at influencing "the power of vision,"[24] it seems to suggest itself to label Apollo the god of cinema, but such an attribution would ignore that that film, in its ability to evoke manifold affects in an individual, is also intoxicative in a Dionysian sense. In order to distinguish between Apollonian and Dionysian forms of cinema, we must take into account the effects cinema can have on the subjectivity of its viewers.

Félix Guattari reflects on cinema's role in the process of subjectivation of the individual in his essay "Cinemachines." "Cinematographic performance," he claims, "affects subjectivity. It affects the personological individuation of enunciation and develops a very particular mode of conscience."[25] The "cinemachines" of commercial cinema are agents of power that use the specific qualities of the medium to inscribe the hegemonial social imaginary that Guattari defines as capitalist, Oedipal-familialist, racist, conformist, etc., into the individual (and vice versa). Mainstream industry films, he suggests, will unavoidably produce as well as reproduce hegemonial subjectivities, not because they function as simplistic propaganda pieces advocating specific ideological positions but because they fulfill the stabilizing role of Apollonian art (establishing individuation and situatedness by providing coherent meaning): "When it is exploited by capitalist [. . .] powers to mould the collective imaginary," Guattari states, "cinema topples over to the side of meaning."[26] These Apollonian "cinemachines" may be dream-machines in the sense that they evoke excitement, suspense or entertainment but aesthetically their products remain entrapped in the long (and enduring) dominance of a cinematic paradigm that stresses scenic realism, verisimilitude, identification, spatiotemporal coherence and narrative linearity and is, as one critic framed it, "conservative at best, reactionary at worst, attempting always to recuperate with ameliorative closure whatever problems and divisions it creates."[27]

Dionysian cinema, on the contrary, denies its audiences this soothing closure by undermining established epistemological patterns and thereby evoking affective reactions that cannot be integrated into the dominant social imaginary and the subjectivities it produces and upholds. It is that kind of cinema that throws sand in the gears of the commercial "cinemachines" and their smooth processes of meaning-making by overwhelming, confusing, challenging, arousing, shocking, maybe even repelling the audience by mobilizing the weaponry of disturbing aesthetics against the stifling conventionality, predictability, and unimaginativeness of the film industry's conservative standards.

DIONYSIA AT MIDNIGHT VS. THE A(N)ESTHETICS OF HOLLYWOOD

That Jodorowsky and his art are surrounded by a quasi-religious aura has been noted repeatedly. In an article that discusses the origin and dynamics of the filmmaker's cult-leader like charisma, Jeremy Guida stresses that his films not only offer an eccentric engagement with a broad spectrum of religious doctrines and symbols on the diegetic level but also that certain practices of reception of these films have a structural similarity to religious service. This is especially true for *El Topo*, the film that is widely credited to mark the beginning of the midnight movie phenomenon that emerged at Ben Barenholtz's Elgin Theater in New York in the early 1970s. In any case, it was among the first "cult" films in this context around which a ritualistic practice of reception emerged that subverted the traditional cinema situation (which is, in essence, modeled on the bourgeois theater and its passive mode of reception). The unusual screening time gave the entire event a matins-like aura, the consumption of drugs was (at least) tolerated, audiences interacted with the action on the screen, and watching the film repeatedly became a standard for the nascent devotee audiences. Guida asserts that "the unique setting and viewing practices associated with the midnight screenings contributed to [Jodorowsky's] charismatic authority" and judges a contemporary newspaper review that compared this particular mode of reception to an orgiastic rite as "appropriate, considering the Dionysian and sometimes religious associations with such practices."[28] He does not not elaborate further on this observation but certainly highlighted an important connection.

For Nietzsche, the orgiastic is "that element out of which Dionysian art grows."[29] The nexus between the two ideas is rooted in the Dionysian festivities of ancient Greece which he describes as "festivals of universal release and redemption and days of transfiguration" where "for the first time the tearing-apart of the *principium individuationis* becomes an artistic phenomenon."[30] These events aimed at, as Wood phrases it, "a (temporary) abandonment of the structures of society and an embrace of a wilder and more basic mode of existence"[31] and demanded a physical retreat from the environment of everyday life (the polis), the consumption of stimulating substances, and the suspension of libidinal restraints as necessary prerequisites for this ritualistic experience. In this light, we may understand the midnight movie screenings as subcultural *Dionysia*, set in the sanctuary of a non-quotidian heterotopic space. The cinema hall, in this context, functioned not as a temple of Apollonian escapism in form of Hollywood's reassuring a(n)estetics. It rather provided a site of Dionysian intensity where the intoxicative interplay of ceremony, substance use, alternative aesthetics, sexual expressiveness, and insurgent aggression gave birth to a significant cultural phenomenon with a focus on the "interconnectedness of elusive details intrinsic as well as alien to the films that enables allegorical and political interpretations that position themselves outside the realm of normalcy."[32]

In its resistance to be incorporated into the dominant sociocultural imaginary (essentially that of the white middle-class), the midnight movie circuit – heavily drawing on the cultural capital of provocation and shock – constituted a ritualistic space of Dionysian counter-cinema that offered its cultists the possibility of a euphoric and life-affirming engagement with non-normative styles, themes, and subject positions on the level of aesthetic experience and beyond: "Whether feelings of *communitas*, or the rupture of profane time, or dense ritual experience, the unique set of practices associated with screening these films at midnight produce some degree of religious affect."[33] This mode of perception had thus similar transformative ramifications as the ancient *Dionysia* which, in Nietzsche's understanding, "forge[d] a bond between human beings" who "expresse[d] their membership of a higher more ideal community."[34]

El Topo marked the beginning of the collective cultural experience of the midnight movies and Jodorowsky also provided a second contribution to the phenomenon with the *The Holy Mountain*. *Santa Sangre*, on the other hand, was produced years after the heyday of the cult. The three films are certainly different in terms of their content and their cinematic style but they share, as I will show in the following, some distinctly Dionysian qualities.

JODOROWSKY'S CINEMA OF INTOXICATION

We have seen that Nietzsche's understanding of Dionysian intoxication exceeds a mere pharmacological definition. The term gains a holistic meaning within his philosophy of art, referring equally to the psychological predisposition of the artist, the content and aesthetics of the artwork, and the transformative impact on the subjectivities of the audience during the reception of the artwork. Jodorowsky's maxim according to which cinema should function not only like but *as* a psychedelic drug expresses a similar understanding of intoxication as an aesthetic paradigm that aims for a similar transformative effect.[35] "With every new picture," Jodorowsky once stated, "I must change myself, I must kill myself, and I must be born. And then the audiences, the audiences who go to the movies, must be assassinated, killed, destroyed, and they must leave the theatre as new people."[36]

El Topo can be seen as a paramount example of an artwork born out as well as evocative of the various facets of intoxication Nietzsche has deemed essential for Dionysian art. The visual vocabulary of the film depicts sexual ecstasy, excessive violence, and destructive impulses in highly stylized yet unobstructed and graphic images that aim at confrontation. Yal Sadat has compared Jodorowsky's aesthetic approach to that of a fellow Dionysian artist: Antonin Artaud. Drawing on Artaud's "Theater of Cruelty," Sadat identifies Jodorowsky as a representative of a "cinema of cruelty" that "aims to destroy the viewer's cultural points of reference and to shatter their moral compass, forcing them to mourn the generic notions they're familiar with."[37]

While it is certainly true that *El Topo*'s style does not lend itself to evoke the soothing cinematic experience associated with Apollonian cinema, the enduring myth that the film, as one critic phrased it, "cannot be narrated or told, let alone analysed,"[38] is a popular misconception that may be a cornerstone of the mystique surrounding Jodorowsky but does not hold up to closer examination. While it is certainly true that his films, in their rejection of mimetic representation and traditional plotlines, bear a close kinship to the disruptive artworks of the modernist avant-gardes, they *are* narrative and even follow one of the oldest formulas in the history of storytelling. Robert Neustadt has remarked that almost all of Jodorowsky's works, regardless of the medium of expression (be it film, literature, theater, or comics), deal with a quest narrative, "an initiatic search for self in a world gone haywire."[39] Structurally, these stories often follow the form of an ancient epos and present their content in a series of vignettes and episodes in which the intellectual, cultural, and spiritual traditions of the "Western" as well as the "Eastern" world are reworked and reassembled in a way that aims at a deterritorialization of hegemonial culture in a Deleuzean sense.[40]

At the heart of the Jodorowskian search-for-self story is a distinctly Dionysian motif – the cycle of death and rebirth – which features prominently in all three films discussed in this chapter. In *El Topo*, it provides the structuring principle of the film's narrative. It starts with the image of the protagonist (the gunman El Topo) and his son on a horse in a desert, shortly before the two complete an initiation rite in which the son has to symbolically bury his childhood in the form of a teddy bear and a photograph of his mother in order to enter the realm of "manhood," which the film presents as a world of archaic violence and chauvinism (Jodorowsky is certainly far from being a feminist filmmaker[41]). Towards the end of film, the director returns to this initial image. After El Topo has killed himself in an act of self-immolation, we see the son, now a grown-up man, sitting on a horse, together with his deceased father's lover and their child. They look down at El Topo's grave and ride off into the open desert. In spite of their tacky primordial pseudo-Oedipal symbolism these two scenes framing the film's narrative indicate that a cycle has closed.

Before being confronted by his son towards the end of the film, the protagonist himself has undergone several metamorphoses. The first of these transformations occurs when El Topo adopts the role of avenger of the massacre in the frontier town at the beginning of the film. The next occurs with the series of duels against the four gun masters in the desert, instigated by the Lady Macbeth-like character Mara, which become decisive events in El Topo's "becomings."[42] The fact that the four gun masters are associated with eclectic attributes of mythological and spiritual origin makes it obvious that El Topo, on his search for a self, has progressed into the realm of metaphysics. These "last man standing" confrontations are, however, not to be understood as metaphorical struggles with specific religious teachings but rather with the idea of religious metaphysics in general. As Robert Ebert has aptly observed,

> Jodorowsky lifts his symbols and mythologies from everywhere: Christianity, Zen, discount-store black magic, you name it. He makes not the slightest attempt to use them so they sort out into a single logical significance. Instead, they're employed in a shifting, prismatic way, casting their light on each other instead of on the film's conclusion. The effect resembles Eliot's *The Waste Land*, and especially Eliot's notion of shoring up fragments of mythology against the ruins of the post-Christian era.[43]

El Topo breaks under the realization of the end of traditional metaphysics and denounces both God and violence when he destroys his gun, before he is "stigmatized" with gunshots by the nameless woman dressed in black who leaves him to die in the desert. This symbolic and almost physical death leads to the protagonist's next reincarnation as the messianic leader of the community of outcasts who have saved his life. But also this stage of his mystical quest for a self fails and leads to a further excess of violence.

Fleming has noted that *El Topo* is "Nietzschean in its intense embrace and expression of suffering and rage, as well as the eponymous protagonist's [. . .] ongoing desire to flee the filthy and corrupt world of men."[44] While the ascetic desire of withdrawing from the world is rather a Zarathustrian motif, the acceptance and, to some extent, celebration of suffering is clearly Dionysian. "He who is richest in fullness of life," Nietzsche writes in *The Gay Science* (*Die fröhliche Wissenschaft*):

> the Dionysian god and man, can allow himself not only the sight of what is terrible and questionable but also the terrible deed and every luxury of destruction, decomposition, negation; in his case, what is evil, nonsensical, and ugly almost seems acceptable because of an overflow in procreating, fertilizing forces capable of turning any desert into bountiful farmland.[45]

On the diegetic level of his film, Jodorowsky may not offer his protagonist any philosophical or spiritual salvation from the metaphysical void he is facing – the desert remains the desert. But the film itself, in its fundamentally affirmation of the potentials of the "evil, nonsensical and [the] ugly," which of course involves raging violence as an antithesis to any idea of moral or rational order, undoubtedly follows a Dionysian ethos and consciously uses these elements to trigger a defamiliarizing and therefore potentially transformative affect in the spectator.

The Holy Mountain takes up the motif of the mystical quest again, but the Dionysian character of the film is not, at least not to the same extent, defined by violence, suffering, and destruction but rather presented in flamboyant, multicolored images that are drowning in iconoclastic and esoteric symbolism. An elaborate, meditative soundtrack combining an orchestral score, pop tunes, and Eastern spiritual chants adds to the atmosphere of detachment from the rational world.

We face a different kind of protagonist in this film. The thief is no revenant of El Topo. His Christ-like physical appearance does not indicate the dormant violence of a mysterious gunslinger but rather of a peaceful pilgrim. What he has in common with the protagonist of Jodorowsky's debut is the Zarathustrian impulse to retreat from a morally corrupt world. Particularly significant in this context is his presence during a massacre executed by soldiers that takes place during a quasi-Dionysian festival in what seems to be a South American town – an interesting detail considering that the film's release more or less coincided with Augusto Pinochet's *coup d'état* in Chile, Jodorowsky's native country.

Like *El Topo*, *The Holy Mountain* draws heavily from a variety of spiritual traditions and symbols, but it puts more emphasis on the ritualistic and the orgiastic. It is "ostensibly a spiritual film that is almost entirely about bodies and flesh, and as we will soon discover, employs corporeal bodies, affective performance, intensive movements, dynamic rhythms and abject bodily forces to make felt what it is a body is capable of thinking and doing."[46] The central character who orchestrates that complex interplay between bodies and minds is The Alchemist, played by Jodorowsky, a cult leader who guides his disciples (including The Thief) through a series of rites to overcome their individualities and to prepare them for a pilgrimage to the eponymous holy mountain where they would learn about the secret of immortality. The famous meta-reflective scene in which The Alchemist breaks the fourth wall and abandons the border between the diegetic and the nondiegetic worlds by revealing to his disciples that they themselves are characters in a film, merely "images, dreams, photographs," has deep philosophical implications. The Alchemist's declaration at the end of the film – "If we have not obtained immortality, we have won reality [. . .] Goodbye to the Holy Mountain! Real life awaits us!" – is a Nietzschean denunciation of transcendental metaphysics in favor of a radical immanent worldview.

Santa Sangre is often discussed as Jodorowsky's contribution to horror cinema, but this is certainly a misnomer as this film, like the director's entire oeuvre, defies the industry's definition of genre. In terms of the comprehensibility of the narrative, it may be more traditional than *El Topo* and *The Holy Mountain* but it is certainly not less Dionysian when it comes to its themes and aesthetics. This starts with the protagonist's first name, Fenix, which is the Spanish translation of Phoenix, the mythological bird representing the cycle of death and rebirth. He is the child of the heterotopic space of the circus, traditionally a realm of the ritualized subversion and suspension of social norms and values. It is a world full of Dionysian commotion and suffering, of performative violence (the knife-thrower in the circus ring) and actual (the knife-thrower mutilating his wife), sexual energy, and eccentric rituals (the burlesque burial ceremony for the deceased circus elephant). Throughout the film, Jodorowsky presents numerous variations of the familiar symbolic and narrative tropes that do not have to be listed here. But there is one scene in *Santa Sangre* that has no equivalent in the other two films as it explicitly exposes the kinship between the cinematic experience to the drug experience. The adult Fenix, a heavily traumatized patient in a mental asylum, is, along with a group of fellow inmates, allowed to visit the cinema.

Before they enter, a caricature of a Latin American drug dealer seduces the group to the consumption of cocaine by arguing that "this stuff" – he refers to cinema – constitutes a potential health risk. In spite of its blatancy, this analogy reflects on Jodorowsky's understanding of film as a stimulant.

Dionysian intoxication, understood in its broadest possible philosophical meaning, is the prerequisite for this aesthetic experience as Nietzsche has shown in his metaphysics of art formulated in the context of late nineteenth-century modernity. Jodorowsky, his *confrére*, has successfully resuscitated this idea in the cultural moment of late twentieth-century postmodernism.

NOTES

1. Ben Cobb, *Anarchy and Alchemy. The Films of Alejandro Jodorowsky* (London: Creation Books, 2007), 72.
2. Johan Faerber, "Endless Theater," in *The Seven Lives of Alejandro Jodorowsky*, eds. Vincent Bernière and Nicolas Tellop (Los Angeles, CA: Humanoids, 2020), 22–23.
3. In a 2014 conversation with Rhett Jones, Jodorowsky expressed a reluctant attitude towards drug-taking. He claimed to have consumed marijuana for "a year or two" mainly for image reasons while selling *El Topo* to audiences and distributors and to have moderately experimented with LSD and magic mushrooms before realizing that exuberant consumption would "burn [his] brain" (Rhett Jones, "Alejandro Jodorowsky on Reality, Bad Dads and the Right Amount of Drugs," http://animalnewyork.com/alejandro-jodorowsky-reality-bad-dads-right-amount-drugs/ [accessed December 9, 2021]).
4. David H. Fleming, *Unbecoming Cinema: Unsettling Encounters with Ethical Event Films* (Bristol and Chicago: Intellect, 2017), 102.
5. David Church has made an insightful attempt to define psychedelic film as a genre: David Church, "The Doors of Reception: Notes Toward a Psychedelic Film Investigation," https://www.sensesofcinema.com/2018/feature-articles/the-doors-of-reception-notes-toward-a-psychedelic-film-investigation/ (accessed November 23, 2021).
6. Yal Sadat, "Cinema of Cruelty," in *The Seven Lives of Alejandro Jodorowsky*, eds. Vincent Bernière and Nicolas Tellop (Los Angeles, CA: Humanoids, 2020), 42.
7. Fleming, *Unbecoming Cinema*, 102.
8. Jason Ciaccio, "Between Intoxication and Narcosis: Nietzsche's Pharmacology of Modernity," *Modernism/modernity*, vol. 25, no.1 (2018), 115.
9. Jessica Wood, *Portraits of the Artist. Dionysian Creativity in Selected Works by Gabriele D'Annunzio and Thomas Mann* (New York: Peter Lang, 2017), 53.
10. Ibid., 52.
11. For a comprehensive synopsis of Nietzsche's arguments in *The Birth of Tragedy*, I recommend: Andrew Cooper, *The Tragedy of Philosophy. Kant's Critique of Judgement and the Project of Aesthetics* (Albany: State University of New York Press, 2016), 133–160; Robert R. Williams, *Tragedy, Recognition and the Death of God. Studies in Hegel and Nietzsche* (Oxford: Oxford University Press, 2012), 143–158; Wood, *Portraits of the Artist*, 65–73.
12. Friedrich Nietzsche, *The Birth of Tragedy and Other Writings*, trans. by Ronald Speirs (Cambridge: Cambridge University Press, 1999), 40.
13. Ibid., 59.

14. Wood pointed out that in the pantheon of Greek mythology, Dionysus was initially not the god of wine but "merely a deity of certain plants and vegetation, among which the vine featured most prominently" (Wood, *Portraits of the Artist*, 53).
15. Nietzsche, *The Birth of Tragedy*, 17.
16. Douglas Burnham, "Dionysiac," in *Understanding Nietzsche, Understanding Modernism*, eds. Brian Pines and Douglas Burnham (London: Bloomsbury Academic, 2019), 296. (For more on the connection between Dionysus and the motifs of death and resurrection, please see Wood, *Portraits of the Artist*, 55.)
17. Ciaccio, "Between Intoxication and Narcosis,"116.
18. Nietzsche, *The Birth of Tragedy*, 14–15, emphases in the original.
19. Ibid., 15, emphasis in the original.
20. Wood, *Portraits of the Artist*, 65–66.
21. Ibid., 66.
22. Friedrich Nietzsche, *Twilight of the Idols, Or, How to Philosophize with the Hammer*, trans. by Richard Polt (Indianapolis, IN: Hackett Publishing Company, 1997), 55.
23. Ibid., 56.
24. Ibid.
25. Félix Guattari, "Cinemachines," in *Chaosophy. Texts and Interviews 1972–1977*, trans. by David L. Sweet, Jarred Becker, and Taylor Adkins (Los Angeles, CA: Semiotext(e), 2009), 264.
26. Ibid., 242.
27. Robert Phillip Kolker, "On Certain Tendencies in American Film Criticism," *American Quarterly*, vol. 38, no. 2 (Summer 1986), 331.
28. Jeremy Guida, "Media Review: Producing and Explaining Charisma: A Case Study of the Films of Alejandro Jodorowsky," *Journal of the American Academy of Religion*, vol. 83, no. 2 (June 2015), 546.
29. Nietzsche, *Twilight of the Idols*, 90.
30. Nietzsche, *The Birth of Tragedy*, 20–21.
31. Wood, *Portraits of the Artist*, 131.
32. Ernest Mathijs and Jamie Sexton, *Cult Cinema: An Introduction* (Malden, MA: Wiley-Blackwell, 2011), 15.
33. Guida, "Media Review: Producing and Explaining Charisma," 547, emphasis in the original.
34. Nietzsche, *The Birth of Tragedy*, 120.
35. "I ask of film what most North Americans ask of psychedelic drugs." Alejandro Jodorowsky, *El Topo: The Book of the Film* (New York: Douglas Book Corporation, 1971), 97.
36. Jodorowsky qtd. in Guida, "Media Review: Producing and Explaining Charisma," 539.
37. Sadat, "Cinema of Cruelty," 42.
38. Ángel S. Harguindey qtd. in Antonio Lázaro-Reboll, "Alejandro Jodorowsky and *El Topo*," in *The Routledge Companion to Cult Cinema*, eds. Ernest Mathijs and Jamie Sexton (London: Routledge, 2019), 427.
39. Robert Neustadt, "Alejandro Jodorowsky: Reiterating Chaos, Rattling the Cage of Representation," *Chasqui*, vol. 26, no. 1 (May 1997), 56.
40. See Fleming, *Unbecoming Cinema*, 117.
41. In 2019, the Museo del Barrio in New York called off a retrospective on Jodorowsky's work over a controversy regarding an interview the director gave in 1972 in which he had claimed that he actually raped actress Mara Lorenzio in a scene in *El Topo*. This was never confirmed and Jodorowsky later claimed that the statement was merely "surrealist publicitiy" capitalizing on the shock value of the claim. ("Alejandro Jodorowsky Speaks

Out After El Museo Del Barrio Calls Off Retrospective," *Artforum*, https://www.artforum.com/news/alejandro-jodorowsky-speaks-out-after-el-museo-del-barrio-calls-off-retrospective-78538 [accessed January 21, 2022]).

42. Fleming, *Unbecoming Cinema*, 118.
43. Robert Ebert, "El Topo," https://www.rogerebert.com/reviews/el-topo-1972 (accessed January 15, 2022).
44. Fleming, *Unbecoming Cinema*, 104.
45. Friedrich Nietzsche, *The Gay Science*, trans. By Josefine Nauckhoff (Cambridge: Cambridge University Press, 2001), 234–235.
46. Fleming, *Unbecoming Cinema*, 123.

CHAPTER 8

The Music in *The Holy Mountain*: A Jodorowskian Sound Machine

Daniel Escoto

Famously following up the midnight movie pioneer *El Topo* (1969), Alexandro Jodorowsky's *The Holy Mountain* (*La montaña sagrada*, 1972) is the modern fable of an ensemble of great sinners questing for spiritual enlightenment. The film's music, created by the multifaceted director himself alongside international jazz star Don Cherry (1936–1995) and musician, director, and arranger Roger Frangipane (1944–2020), plays a seminal – not to mention complex – role in the storytelling. However, in spite of the soundtrack's own appeal, it is repeatedly taken for granted by viewers and critics who are perhaps engrossed in the film's other characteristics, such as its highly allegorical imagery, its reception, its countercultural relevance, and its cult status.[1]

Perhaps the most attractive trait of the music "at first listening" is its undeniable eclecticism. Amid the selection there is raga, chamber music, psychedelic rock, jazz, and orchestral arrangements with affinities ranging from Georges Delerue's work for French cinema to the peplum subgenre. The exuberance and recurring grandeur of the score frequently goes hand in hand with the monumentality of the film's visual concept. Its spectrum encompasses both experimental sound and the more conventional music associated with a large-scale Hollywood production. Occasionally, the latter contrasts with Jodorowsky's eccentric *mise-en-scène*. These disparities sometimes enhance the film's sardonic sense of humor.

In this chapter, I intend to dissect the music in *The Holy Mountain*. This exercise might be of service to weigh its stated polyvalent place in the film's narrative and aesthetic discourse.[2]

***

First, some words about the soundtrack's history. By 1970, Jodorowsky had just completed his second full-length *El Topo* and was searching for distribution.

Serendipitously, John Lennon and Yoko Ono offered a midnight slot at the close of their film festival at the Elgin Theater in New York. That opportunity ignited the film's cult following. Allen Klein, famed pop music impresario and Lennon's manager at the time, would then approach Jodorowsky to produce his next feature.

The new project drew inspiration from fantasy novel *Le Mont Analogue* (*Mount Analogue: A Novel of Symbolically Authentic Non-Euclidean Adventure in Mountain Climbing*), left unfinished by French pataphysical author René Daumal, a disciple of George Gurdjieff. Other sources were "mountain myths" from diverse world cultures, like the Mount Carmel epitomized by sixteenth-century mystic St. John of the Cross. Additionally, Jodorowsky had recently manifested his interest in filming a transcendent experience for the actors and himself, so another influence for the script, along with his own yoga and Zen trainings, was the novel "ARICA Method" of Bolivian guru Óscar Ichazo, which promised enlightenment in forty days after an intensive mixture of mind-opening techniques (including lysergic experimentation). The director was attracted by this spiritual concoction apparently not because of its promised "express" effectiveness but because of its dubiousness.[3] This primary skepticism might be one of the primary roots of the film's satirical tone which we will deal with further on.

Jodorowsky engaged himself directly in the composition of the project's music as he did with the direction, production, writing, scenery and production design, costume design (together with Nicky Nichols), editing, and acting.[4] He demanded for *The Holy Mountain* "another kind of music – something that wasn't entertainment, something that wasn't a show, something that went to the soul, something profound,"[5] so he reached out to Cherry, who in past years had transitioned from free jazz to the concept of "organic music," a spiritual pan-ethnic, environmentalist community-minded artistic enterprise. According to musician and record label manager Andy Votel,

> when first encountering jazz trumpeter and composer Don Cherry alongside his artist wife Moki Cherry in New York, the director was particularly struck by the young family's lifestyle which involved recycling the city's discarded items; clothes, furniture, even musical instruments (. . .) The earthy persona of Cherry on both a creative and philosophical level not only appealed to Jodorowsky's personality and experience buy also drew stylistic parallels with the dystopian backdrop and commentary against greed and social engineering of *The Holy Mountain*.[6]

The recording sessions were held in early 1973 at A&R Recording, Record Plant, Sear Sound, Bell Sound, and additional editing at Electric Lady, all of them studios in New York. Cherry was joined by members of avant-garde ensemble the Jazz Composer's Orchestra, with which he had previously collaborated. Sequences from the footage were screened at the sessions so the musicians would play under Cherry's direction but with significant room for improvisation.[7] Multi-instrumentalist Christer Bóten recalls: "Jodorowsky was very enthusiastic about the music and very pleasant to all of us, his personality was powerful. I still have visions of him drumming his fingers on Don's back while we were playing. His methods of communication were unorthodox but the passion was there and he spoke in more theatrical terms."[8]

However, Jodorowsky would require other sonorities beyond the music provided by Cherry and the Jazz Composer's Orchestra. In order to nuance the plot's various episodes and the distinct characters presented, he was interested in including bits of diverse musical styles. Along came, from Yoko Ono's *Approximately Infinite Universe* album personnel, Ronald Frangipane, who took charge of the orchestral and rock bits needed in the score.[9] There is also credit for musician Henry West, Jodorowsky's long-time collaborator in music matters, who acted as advisor.[10]

***

Two young, blonde women, wearing a version of Marilyn Monroe's iconic white ivory dress, wait upon their knees. A black-cladded figure (Jodorowsky), his face hidden under a black hat of enormous proportions, fastidiously executes steps: he removes their makeup and nails, strips them naked by tearing their dresses, shaves their heads, and finally embraces them. This liturgy is followed by a succession of close-ups to collage-reliquaries of the occult, cluttered with eyes, pearls, snakes. Above all this, main credits roll.

Very much like the initial sequence of *Fando y Lis* (1967), in which we witness the female main character conscientiously eating a whole flower, her chewing almost unbearably loud, the sound of air raid sirens and bombings in the background, and the initial sequence of *El Topo*, with the protagonist playing the flute after making his naked son bury a picture of his mother and a teddy bear, abruptly ending the boy's childhood, *The Holy Mountain*'s opening ritualistic, vehement sight/sound images both welcome and confront the viewer, setting a tone for the cinematic experience that will follow. Becoming to this shock spectacle of what we infer is some kind of purification, powerful music colors the sequence: a Tibetan Tantric chant for Buddha which starts at a moderate volume and crescendos to an utmost level of intensity and intricacy of the guttural male voices. At the same time, a hypnotic sense is provided by the drone and the intermittency of the cymbals and percussion vessels.[11] The clash contained in a ceremony of apparently indistinguishable origin, one of a Western icon (Marilyn) and a non-Western invocation, kicks off the film's images-music-storytelling interweaving.

Immediately after credits, The Thief (Horacio Salinas) – a bearded Christ-like or prophet-like figure – begins his symbol-fueled journey in a desertic wasteland. A gimbri (typical lute from the Gnawas of Morocco), perhaps evocative of an indeterminate biblical setting, plucks away an insistent rhythmic tune while he lies drunkenly asleep, pissed and covered with flies; then he is lapidated by a crowd of little boys. A flute solo sweetly accompanies a crippled Dwarf (Basilio González) who sympathizes with The Thief and offers him a joint of marijuana; the compassionate tune is picked up by a whole orchestra of grand, melodramatic scale – not unlike George Delerue's Baroque-inspired theme for *Le Mépris* (1963, Jean-Luc Godard) – while both characters wander off stoned, gleeful, and indifferent through a modern Latin American city (Mexico City) otherwise overcome with trucks carrying murdered corpses, grenadiers fusillading youngsters (while smirking tourists take photographs), and marching with crucified lambs while oblivious aristos kneel in the streets in a praying manner.[12] Thief and Dwarf meet a particular circus troupe (now ironical ragtime plays in the background) which fits with this crude, cynical cityscape. The troupe presents a blood-spattered reenactment of the Conquest of Mexico with toads and chameleons attired as Spaniards and Aztecs. The performance is first driven not by Mexican but by Andean music with charango (lute) and quenas (flutes), soon eclipsed by a generic Nazi-esque march with a German male chorus (simply repeating "Ein, zwei, drei, vier!") which in turn cross-fades with dissonant, uncanny chords by the stirring orchestral strings of the faux Baroque overture that started the city sequence.[13]

One strikingly different orchestral arrangement – a march which evokes the brassy, martial soundtrack for a sword-and-sandal picture – illustrates yet another vignette in this dystopia: centurion-dressed men selling crucifixes and Sacred Hearts to tourists.[14] The mood changes with a light, psychedelic tune, its rhythm set by handclapping, while the centurions invite The Thief to a drinking binge. He then passes out and a sort of abstract, electroacoustic variation of the chanting that starts the film, heavily distorted, sounds from a distance while the centurion-merchants take a cast of him to fabricate hundreds of Jesuses. It is as if this musical repetition suggested that the non-Western spiritual purgation of the opening sequence is turning into its obverse: a nightmarish merchandising to which The Thief awakens in terror, lost among infinite reproductions of himself: refractions of his ego. High-pitched male screaming, with chaotic jazz percussions in background, climaxes the music while he proceeds to whip the centurions and destroy the reproductions (like Christ at the temple), except one (his true Self?). The sound nightmare finishes abruptly in absolute silence while The Thief, at the end of this trance, lovingly holds this double in his arms, and another Baroque-inspired dramatic string arrangement fades in, bridging to the next sequence. References to Christianity continue to appear: now we see a group of prostitutes – several adult and teen women, one girl, a chimpanzee (Chucho-Chucho) – attend church and immediately after, in front of the façade, search for callers. At the musical piece's climax, an old man offers his glass eye as payment for the girl. The prostitutes encounter The Thief carrying his effigy, accompanied by The Dwarf; at first they laugh at him but then they follow him.

Leader and acolytes pass by a decaying church. We can see the courtyard through the fence, where there is yet another nod to Mexico's then-recent 1968 and perhaps 1971 violence: grenadiers (casks and anti-gas masks on) dancing tenderly with working-class men of different ages to diegetic music; a band with marimba plays the popular Mexican waltz "Alejandra," composed by Enrique Mora Andrade and premiered in 1907 during Porfirio Díaz's dictatorship. The redolent waltz is still heard when The Thief wanders through the decaying building and finds a bishop lying in bed with a human-scale crucifix.[15]

Then melancholic jazz, with Cherry's distinct trumpet playing, signifies spiritual nostalgia in a new ego detachment ritual: The Thief proceeds to eat his double-figure's face and then lets it fly off to the skies with the help of red and blue balloons, like an Ascension.

Later on, a high-pitched buzz builds tension as The Thief undertakes an ascent of his own: riding a gigantic hook, he is lifted up to the top of a red tower in the city and enters a circular opening that leads into a tunnel. The buzz evolves into a music trance featuring chanting and Indian tabla (hand drums), similar in intensity to the initial Marilyns sequence and the Christ-destruction sequence. This track follows our protagonist walking through a gallery painted with the colors of the rainbow. The same spiritual master who purified the Marilyns, now dressed in white, awaits. Besides him is a woman (Ramona Saunders) with the writing of different spiritual traditions tattooed on her nude body. The chanting and drumming gain momentum as The Thief wrestles with the master – commonly known as The Alchemist. After, The Thief is defeated and starts a learning process ushered by The Alchemist and The Written Woman. Soft bells from the music punctuate when his chakras are touched.

A tender tune with distorted piano and strings plays concurrently as The Thief makes ablutions in a pool. This music's strings become dissonant and afflicted: The Alchemist submits The Thief and his excrement to an intensive alchemic process in an athanor as The Written Woman mimics playing with a stylized cello. The teaching process continues in a mirror hall, The Thief dressed in a brown version of The Alchemist's robe.

Another hall, illustrated by modern versions of Tarot's Major Arcana, is introduced by new music, also from Indian tradition: tabla, a bowed instrument called the dilruba (both famously featured in The Beatles' "Within Without You"), and a sarangi (another string instrument). The mentoring continues in a special chamber where The Thief and The Alchemist are surrounded by wax figures of the nine big sinners. A solemn toll announces the first of seven vignettes with the stories of each of them: Fon (Juan Ferrara) from Venus.

Fon's world deals with beauty, comfort, and cosmetology, and the music that characterizes him expresses this in a silky, chilly, violin-based easy-listening tune set against the factory sustained by his female workers'/concubines' labor. Next, a mocking circus-like upbeat march ironizes the enamored women fighting over him. The march abruptly stops and the easy-listening melody continues while a new sequence in a radically different tone begins: Fon lies sensually with a new woman in the factory, who in a rapture fills her mouth with beads.

Another toll introduces Isla (Adriana Page) from the planet Mars. Sensuous jazz is heard as she awakens from a placid slumber, besides two female lovers, all three naked. This voluptuosity and insouciant spirit in the music combines with the imagery of the "luminous" part of her world: a reproduction of a detail with the ladies' nipples in the emblematic painting *Gabrielle d'Estrées et une de ses soeurs* (*Gabrielle d'Estrées and One of Her Sisters*) (Fontaineblue School, 1594), Isla's own purple dandy attire and necktie, her fluffy pet dogs, a flock of black geese, a one-legged female herald (who mimics blowing a large trumpet at the same time Don Cherry's trumpet is heard), and a group of pretty boys, Isla's secretaries, who erotically cavort among each other in a sort of play pen.[16] Her "shadowy" side is the production of murderous mass weapons of all kinds, and it is musicalized in a contrasting, maniacal way. At the end of this segment, we listen to bits of an energetic blues rock piece (which reminds us of Janis Joplin's 1971 hit "Move Over") while arms "needed for the young generation's marches and sit-ins" are shown: "psychedelic shotguns," "rock and roll weapons" (literally, electric guitars and platform shoes tied to rifles), and "grenade necklaces." "Mystical weapons for Buddhists, Jews and Christians" (pistols with Buddhas, menorahs, and crucifixes) are also portrayed.

The third toll, and we are immediately transported to the world of Klen from Jupiter. One funereal tune guides us across his icy, sumptuous mansion; a jazzed-up variation of the gloomy tune illustrates Klen picking up his mistress and both doing drugs and having sex in his limo; then too when they visit his art factory. Some works are printed with human buttocks; there are installations with interactive live genitalia and other body parts (overt parodies of Yves Klein's 1962 *Anthropometries* and Nouveau Réalisme).[17] Klen's star object is a "love machine": a contraption with its own electronical mating sounds (which bring to mind those belonging to electroacoustic, concrete music, and the popularization of synthesizers testified by Wendy Carlos's successful 1968's *Switched-On Bach* album). The machine wails, hoots, whistles, screeches, and moans until it reaches an orgasm by the mistress's manipulation, even giving birth to a baby machine celebrated by a happy, victorious, naïve electronic tune.

At the next toll: Sel (Valerie Jodorowsky) from Saturn. Just like Isla's and Klen's segments, shifting music pieces stress out the contrasting light/dark facets of the character. At first presented in the guise of a shrieking clown professionally devoted to children, her music is a lively circus march. Then a calmer bit, still from the circus world – featuring a barrel organ, is heard while she takes off her colorful costume, wig and makeup. Once devoid of her entertainer persona, her new attire, hairdo, and countenance transforms her into a silver-screen diva from the 1940s, a reminder of Joan Crawford (or perhaps Eva Perón in her Victory roll era), melancholy and severe, owner of a factory of war toys crafted by old people that enables the government to condition younglings. The music, accordingly, is dark (Jean Sibelius's well-known Valse Triste Op. 44, No. 1). Sel's strategy of world dominance is presented: for example, if Peru is the next military target, toy native vampires are produced that can only be killed by a white cross, as well as a laxative branded *Lima Perú*, and a comic book that presents a Peruvian villain. This vignette is illustrated by a fragment of a quena version of huayno (an Andean popular song for dancing), "Valicha," composed in 1945 by Miguel Ángel Hurtado Delgado from Peru, then by a military fanfare evoking the world of Marvel's and DC Comics's superheroes. Sinister electroacoustics resume the segment, which ends with naked children armed with bows, like corrupted Cupids, being prepared to hate and kill.

At the fifth toll: Berg (Nicky Nichols) from the planet Uranus. The joyful belly-dancing song "Shimmering Breeze" was chosen to musicalize this character, awakened out of his beauty sleep by his wife, a stout lady who goes from tickling him to spanking him to stripping for him, showing a green-dyed pubis. The couple adoringly watch and bottle-feed their baby, an impressive cobra, while gentle melodic music, punctuated by rattling sounds, plays along.[18] An electronic naïve tune à la Jean-Jacques Perrey is heard while Berg unwrinkles his wife's pompous gala suite. She lulls the cobra with a twisted, salacious version, in mispronounced Spanish, of the folk nursery song "Duerme, negrito, duerme" (originally from the Venezuela-Colombia border and popularized by Atahualpa Yupanqui): "Sleep, little black one, I'll eat your tushy" ["Duerme, negrita, te voy a comer tu colita"]. Just like in the other planet vignettes, the character's other self is revealed: actually Berg is an important financial adviser, and a puffed-up military anthem rolls as he and his wife enter into a sumptuous hall to meet the president. *Danzón* – a lush and parsimonious partner dance from Cuba and Mexico – music sounds and the couple, escorted by hunks, stroll through a park and is served cake.

The sixth toll: Axon (Richard Rutowsky), Neptunian Chief-of-Police. His first sequence shows a ceremonial rite of passage of his organization: a young man is castrated while Axon's officers sing a stupefying two-syllable chant that could pass for "Seig Heil." Immediately after this, the young man performs the solemn offering of his own testicles in a sanctuary while a threatening blowing of horns is heard at an almost imperceptible level. In the next sequence, raucous music again: another mind-numbing march gives rhythm to Axon's military gang as they brutally confront a band of protesting civilians. The march is then abruptly replaced by a string quartet, reminiscent in its ornamentation of Corelli or Lully, which roughly reversions the orchestral score we heard during the urban holocaust images in some of the film's first sequences. This smooth quartet music scores a new succession of metaphorical images of massacre: Axon's men spilling buckets of red paint on the protesters, punching their stomachs, and pulling out red bulbs, sawdust, red fruits, leaves, a white dove. Axon's vignette ends with the corps of police reciting a sort of quiet, occult litany.

The seventh toll: architect Lut from Pluto. In a futuristic, avant-garde home, Lut, a grown-up man cladded in a kimono, plays hide-and-seek with a group of children with Micky Mouse ears. This deceivingly innocent tableau, in which Jodorowsky actually hides a sarcastic hint at pederasty, is musicalized by chamber orchestra music reminiscent of Haydn or Mozart. The next sequence has Lut on a walk across a failed multi-family complex he built, followed by a group of rich investors. The group is accompanied by relaxed jazz. The presentation of a new dwelling project, the "City of Freedom" (a compound of – literally – tombs for resting, planned for the popular classes), features a striptease show with greasy burlesque music.[19]

The seven characters' presentation ends and gives way to a new phase in the film: that of their quest for immortality in the holy mountain of Lotus Island. Soft, melancholy contemporary instrumental music is heard in the background. The characters sit attentively inside the Tower, listening to The Alchemist as he elaborates on holy mountains of different spiritual traditions and summons them to form a group, enlighten together, and achieve immortality in Lotus Island, because otherwise no money or power will save them from death. Contrastingly, a light-hearted, peppy tune escorts them to a round table with a hearth in the middle where they surrender their riches, burning wads of cash. The music stops for a minute while they laugh out loud at The Thief, who was discovered stealing some bills. The tune resumes, energetic and vigorous, and becomes trance-like by the mantra-like repetition of a melodic line (the tabla, dilruba, and sarangi are back and in full force) while wax effigies of the seven characters, The Thief and The Written Woman (their self-images, according to The Alchemist) burn at the hearth, becoming disfigured and destroyed.[20]

The journey begins for the newly formed group. Sequences in a rugged landscape full of vegetation (evocative of Machu Picchu), where the Klen and later Lut undergo a healing process by a local sage man, are characterized with two tracks: a zampoña (wind instrument) version of the huayno "Ojos azules," composed in 1947 by Gilberto Rojas Enríquez from Bolivia, and the other a two-guitar Chilean waltz.

A forlorn variation, played by guitar and bassoon, of the neo-Baroque motive of the lambs' sequence is heard at a moment of both generosity and communion in which the group encounters another local sage, a woman who grinds for them a green potion on a molcajete (mortar) out of wild plants. The Alchemist explains that the plants are "humble guardians of the secret" because "they remained as they were at the moment of Creation."

A chirimía (an oboe-like instrument) and drum sound while the pilgrims get naked and run playfully on the fields, and, led by a third sage, undergo a powerful hallucinatory trance on a pre-Hispanic ceremonial site. This tune cross-fades with a distorted, eerie succession of "magnified" sounds (most probably, by the effect of drugs): the group's own panting, the movements of ants, a dog, a beetle, and other bugs, the falling of a stone. A wailing chorus and rattling intensify this nightmare of sound.[21]

Mistakenly believing that one of them drowned in a basin, the group puts the water into a hole in the ground while the third sage and two boys play a funeral march with a cornet and snare drum. More rattling sounds in the background while the chimpanzee and one of the women in the prostitutes' sequences (Ana de Sade) lie in the lotus position.

The transformation continues in a ceremony of metaphorical death. The pilgrims weep, hold each other, agonize, and then recover and embrace happily while strings and wind instruments play the same wistful music of the holy mountains' explanation. As this track unfolds, we recognize variations of tunes present in past initiatory sequences of the film: the ascension of the wax double, the burning of money. The Alchemist pleads that they surrender pleasure, pains, friends, lovers, family, past, all notions of possession. The sequence gives way to a triumphant zoom-out shot of the pilgrims standing at the top of a pyramid.

Before sailing to Lotus Island, The Alchemist shows a vision to The Thief should he, now half-illuminated, intend to work miracles: a thundering electronic buzz ominously scores an image of children greedily fighting with each other for bread after he multiplies bread for the feeding of multitudes. Later, while the pilgrims travel on a ferry the forlorn tune of the wild plant communion sequence is heard again: a nostalgic note, perhaps, as they seemingly approach their goal. During this voyage, The Alchemist summons The Thief to throw overboard The Dwarf, who is nothing but a monster contained in this mind; the former does this with great pain over an anguished variation of the music heard when they shared the joint at the beginning of The Thief's quest.

Immediately after they arrive at the island, the pilgrims are received by an ecstatic Bar Owner (José Antonio Alcaraz) in lederhosen who takes them to his "Pantheon Bar," a chaotic feast among crypts of dancing and eating, merrymakers in costumes from different historical periods, quacks and charlatans, a string quartet, and at least two rock bands. The music heard is a deafening, brassy hard rock that takes up the tune of a previous spectacle in the film, the Conquest of Mexico.

At last the group begins to climb the holy mountain and meets with hard-ships over a sorrowful version of the money-burning theme. Then a gloomy *ostinato* of cellos connects various vignettes of each character traversing their worst nightmare. Additionally, a piano tinkles when Klen dreams of falling golden coins, a maddened trumpet (the same strenuous effect heard in the sequence in which The Thief destroys the wax figures) signifies the maddened dogs of Axon's dream, violin chords are squeaked when Lut is about to be castrated, *glissandos* are heard when Berg is covered by tarantulas, lost drums when Fon encounters a decrepit androgynous hermaphrodite.

The pilgrims spot nine Immortals at a distance. After falsely executing The Alchemist (at the last minute he substitutes his body for a lamb), The Thief parts with the loyal Prostitute who, together with the chimpanzee, had followed him through his travels: another version of the lambs' theme, now reconciling and soft, scores this farewell. No music whatsoever accompanies The Alche-mist's final reckoning to the seven planet-characters, in a kind of underlining of the idea that they (and we) are now facing stark naked reality: "We came in search of the secret of immortality. To be like gods. And here we are . . . mor-tals. More human than ever. If we have not obtained immortality, at least we have obtained reality. We began in a fairy tale and we came to life! But is this life reality? No. It is a film. Zoom back, camera!" Then we see the film's crew. After Jodorowsky resumes his speech and the group slowly disbands, the final credits roll beneath a white screen, and the nostalgic version of the lambs' theme, the same we heard during the sea trip, plays again.

* * *

The Holy Mountain's finale underlines one of the film's pre-eminent readings: its character as an ambitious *satire* against a whole world order, including the commodification of counterculture in which the film and Jodorowsky's work could be inserted. Since the first sequence of the stripping of the Marilyns – a statement concerning mass culture and Hollywood – thinly veiled diatribes are thrown against capitalist consumerism, propaganda, the military industry and cool-blooded interventionism, social control, state repression, and the spuri-ousness of official religion, among other major topics of the twentieth century. The demystification of fake idols and the use of travesty (and transvestism) is systematical, and an acid tone appears time and again in the film.[22] More extensively, *The Holy Mountain* can be read as a reflection on the contemporary status of icons and their suffering of "transferences, inversions, multiplications and vexations."[23]

An important part of the film's music – arguably pertaining to the adroit work of Frangipane – thus cooperates with this satirical spirit through intertextual strategies. There are the numerous examples of pastiches: those of Nazism marches (when brutality and fascism are alluded to, specifically in the Conquest of America reenactment with the frogs and chameleons and in Axon's organization), of sword-and-sandal soundtracks in all their boisterousness (apropos the commercialization of religion), of chamber music (to convey the bourgeois atmosphere of Lut's, or else to contrast Axon's murderous repression), and of rock (when contemporary young pop and rock culture is vilified for its possible concealed reactionary inflection, as with Isla's weapons or in the celebration of phoniness and superficiality in the Pantheon Bar). Moreover, the music selection for some sequences of enlightenment set in archaeological locations is absolutely generic – lending an "Amerindian" sound – as it bears little to no connection to the sites portrayed and their historical tradition. This echoes the film's visual logic of the amalgamation of an array of non-Western imageries and rites in an exercise of exoticization which includes psychoindigenism.[24]

The musical pastiche strategy might also be considered in light of the soundtrack of *The Holy Mountain*'s predecessor, *El Topo*, also credited to Jodorowsky (with arrangements by Nacho Méndez and additional music by John Barnham).[25] Just as *El Topo* uses/parodies the very recognizable narrative conventions and imaginary of Westerns (the wandering horse-riding protagonist, an arid atmosphere, duels, shootings, justice vs. social corruption, etc.), it also dips into the most identifiable music associated with the genre. Composers such as Richard Hageman, Cyril J. Mockridge, Dimitri Tiomkin, and Ennio Morricone (leader of the then-recent current of Spaghetti Western) had consolidated such sound in the precedent decades. Jodorowsky's soundtrack, at least in its main theme (the "fanfare"), evokes those conventions, not to mention the use of guitars and ocarina.

And yet, a closer watch (and listening) of *The Holy Mountain* allows us to elucidate the film's ambiguous and paradoxical character: as much as it mocks the proliferating spiritual practices in the transition between the 1960s and 1970s (exemplified by one of Alexandro's tickets of entry, Ichazo's method), it *may be*, in practical terms, an initiatic experience in its own right, testified to by the intense cult following it has developed since its theatrical releases.[26] The music created by Don Cherry and company for certain sequences, in all its sincerity and earnestness, does not convey a sense of irony but has an immersive, pathos-filled quality that takes us by the hand throughout numerous stages of sacrifice and detachment: consider the opening sequence, the destruction of the Christs, the Ascension with balloons, the entrance to The Alchemist's tower, the burning of money and effigies. Apart from that, it is possible that Jodorowsky very deliberately recruited Cherry for the soundtrack due to the latter's impulse of concentrating different world traditions in his music, in an analogous manner as the director intended in the film's narrative.

Another conspicuous element (and a new layer of complexity) becomes tangible after the music recap: its obedience to at least certain Hollywood silver-screen industry canons. As much as *The Holy Mountain* is an alternative film, it follows the style of the grand-scale symphonic orchestrations that were experiencing a revival in the early 1970s (parallel to a reappraisal of household composers such as Bernard Hermann and Erich W. Korngold) along with, uncoincidentally, a new generation of epic releases.[27] Another frequent recourse, widely extended in mainstream cinema of the 1960s, is present: the strong presence of melodic lines that manifest repeatedly – expressing different moods and situations – throughout the film (a practice, at least partially, born out of the industry requirement of releasing a song with such a melody as a commercial strategy).[28] The overriding theme in *The Holy Mountain* is the one that first identifies the Thief and his Dwarf in their vagabonding across dystopia, perhaps stressing the importance of that archetypical voyage as the backbone of the story to the point that it ultimately sends the audience home while the end credits roll. The neo-Baroque style of this melody, among other tracks described above, may also be inscribed in the Baroque trend that was part of an "early music revival" movement of the twentieth century.[29] In the realm of cinema, trends of symphonic music had become recursive in auteur cinema since the 1950s, in both "genuine" works of classical music or in "à la manière" contemporary compositions.[30]

In addition to the Baroque musical influence, *The Holy Mountain* draws upon at least other two common cinematic resorts. One of them is the use of Mozartiana – which, in the description by Michel Chion,[31] is outstanding in its effectiveness in expressing human frailty – to contrast with images of brutality. This general principle of concert music/sadism (even if not particularly using Mozart) is evoked in the Axon repression sequence and the silent violence of Lut towards the children.[32] Another resort is the representation of demure, bourgeois attitudes, markers of "the Establishment," through easy-listening music (associated with *elevator music*, *beautiful music*, and *Muzak* and other denominations that rose in popularity in American society of the 1950s).[33] An example of this is the depiction of Fon's world.

Last but not least, it is important to unlock the door to a more comprehensive inquiry regarding the role of music in the early Jodorowsky corpus, in which many elements prominent in *The Holy Mountain* are harbingered. Even in his early incursion into cinema, the short *La cravate* (The Transposed Heads/The Severed Heads, 1957, co-realized with Saul Gilbert and Ruth Michelly), a score is omnipresent: the story being told completely through mime, music accompanies every action. Sound features repeatedly in the documentation and the existing records of Jodorowsky's theater production and actions. It appears in the form of rock (the band Los Ángeles Negros is present on stage of 1962's *La ópera del orden*) and in the musical "playing" of Manuel Felguérez's *Mural de Hierro* by drummer Micky Salas, plus a mosaic text that included daily news, poetry, and drug formulas. It appears, too, in the quirky musical instruments invented for the Gran Efímero Pánico de San Carlos (1963),[34] in the presence of Sibelius, Liszt, and percussive free jazz in *Melodrama sacramental* (1965), and as a scripted sound collage in the "auto sacramental pánico" *El túnel que se come por la boca*.[35] Additionally, other listed spectacles where music was key were the projected rock-and-roll version of *Hamlet* in the first half of the 1960s; showcases *H30* (1967) and *Alfa-Gungadin* (1968) (which featured the meeting of different genres: bossa nova, Motown, pop, rock, classic) and the play *Zaratustra*, which featured music and songs by Las Damas Chinas, the improvisation ensemble formed by Jodorowsky and his regular associates Luis Urías and Henry West.[36]

The soundtrack to *Fando y Lis* (credited to Pepe Ávila and Héctor Morelly) and that to *El Topo* also fit in the common ground of these experiences and *The Holy Mountain*. The latter resorts to a number of shocking juxtapositions of sight and sound in sequences in which an almost physical sensation is demanded for the spectator: scratches at a moment when corpses are shown, a ball bouncing with an unearthly echo when Fando's moribund mother appears, squeaking machinery in lieu of the voices of a group of drag queens who entice Fando and Lis, etc. Music from an instrument "from the past," the harpsichord, is used in a violent sequence: the abuse of Lis by a group of adult men. Sometimes energetic jazz music bursts in the strange, desolate world traversed by the two protagonists; more frequently, their music comes from the quaint ragtime of the gramophone they carry with them. But above all, there are musical themes (as mentioned, something common in the decade) that irrigate most of the soundtrack. Two of them are childlike circus marches, with ritornellos: the more innocent "¡A Tar! ¡A Tar!" (Tar being the fictional city to which Fando and Lis are heading) and the more irritant and dissonant "¡Qué bonito es un entierro!" ["What a lovely thing a burial is"]. A third theme, with neo-Baroque traits, expresses the melancholic nature of the co-dependent relationship between the eponymous characters.

Sight and sound collages of "shock value" are also present in *El Topo*: bees and the strange chirpings of birds are heard over the image of a massacred town, an old waltz while young Franciscans are abused, electroacoustic ambiences reign in the desert, jazz sets the scene for a cantina, the roar of a lion is heard while a Black man is beleaguered by the town's rich ladies. A resounding ball (the same idea used in *Fando y Lis*, perhaps) and Eastern invocations barge in at determined points in the story. Furthermore, as stated above, beyond the combination of conventional score and other more experimental resources (a strategy shared with both *Fando y Lis* and *The Holy Mountain*), its score is in great part a pastiche of the recognizable western genre score. This is in line with the crafted way in which Jodorowsky was able to make use of the language and formats, not only of happening and alternative performing arts, but of mass media (proved by diverse experiences such as comic books, TV programs, musical theater, science fiction) in order to convey his ideas and his artistic expression.[37] His capacity for "mimicking" (at an uncertain point between homage and parody) the resorts of film scores seems to be attuned with his interest in reconfiguring and rearticulating the raw material of mainstream and popular culture(s) into his own. The fact that after *El Topo*, a "cowboy film," he had declared an interest in making two more features, a "gangster film" (which would evolve into *The Holy Mountain*, loosing much of the genre but keeping the notion of villainy) and another, unmade, which would have been a "pirates film"[38] points towards this general interest in his work. Moreover, the sentimental character of a great part of passages of the three soundtracks reveals an interest, associated with conventional cinema, in addressing the audience's empathy.

Overall, Jodorowsky's music and sound repertoire reveal that he omnivorously – and very much disregarding "high" and "low" cultural categories – devoured everything and anything needed for the project, and that a collage logic of an intertextual tapestry often prevailed (such was the intended idea of the unmade version of Frank Herbert's *Dune*, which would have required music from different rock groups, Pink Floyd and Magma, for different motifs).[39]

The Holy Mountain remains a remarkable example of this intertextuality, an exercise of the cerebral that coexists with an appeal to emotions and the cathartic in sequences as potent as the waltz between grenadiers and civilians or the massacre scored by tranquil chamber music. Apart from its endless spilling of images, the Jodorowskian machine is designed to entice the ears.

NOTES

1. Cuauhtémoc Medina, "Pánico recuperado/Recovering Panic" in *La era de la discrepancia. Arte y cultura visual en México 1968–1997 (segunda edición) / The age of discrepancies. Art and visual culture in Mexico 1968–1997 (second edition)*, ed. Olivier; Debroise and Cuauhtémoc Medina (México: UNAM / Turner, 2014), 92–105; Alessandra Santos, *The Holy Mountain* (New York and Chichester West Sussex: Columbia University Press, 2017); Cuauhtémoc Medina, "Un rito de antiiniciación: *La montaña sagrada* de Alejandro Jodorowsky" in *XXVIII Coloquio Internacional de Historia Del Arte, La Imagen Sagrada y Sacralizada, Vol. II* (Mexico City: Instituto de Investigaciones Estéticas – Universidad Nacional Autónoma de México, 2011), 693–708; Ben Cobb, *Anarchy and Alchemy: The Films of Alejandro Jodorowsky* (London: Creation Books, 2006); Bilge Ebiri, "Ascending The Holy Mountain," in *Booklet for Fando y Lis/El Topo / The Holy Mountain/ Psychomagic, a Healing Art* (ABKCO, 2020), 39–46.
2. The film version I worked with for this chapter is the restoration recently edited by ABKCO which includes the soundtrack album. It includes a great part of the score

featured in the film. The music tracks are titled: 1. Trance Mutation, 2. Pissed and Passed Out, 3. Violence Of The Lambs, 4. Drink It, 5. Christs 4 Sale, 6. Cast Out and Pissed, 7. Eye of the Beholder, 8. Communion, 9. Rainbow Room, 10. Alchemical Room, 11. Tarot Will Teach You/Burn Your Money, 12. Mattresses, Masks and Pearls, 13. Isla (The Sapphic Sleep), 14. Psychedelic Weapons, 15. Rich Man In a Fishbowl, 16. Miniature Plastic Bomb Shop, 17. Fuck Machine, 18. Baby Snakes, 19. A Walk In The Park, 20. Mice and Massacre, 21. City of Freedom, 22. Starfish, 23. The Climb/Reality (Zoom Back Camera), 23. Pantheon Bar (Bees Make Honey).

3. Medina, "Un rito de antiiniciación," 698–699.

4. The exact nature of Jodorowsky's involvement in the composing/musical improvising process of *The Holy Mountain* remains uncertain to me. On December 3, 2021, I had a telephone conversation with Luis Urías, a multidisciplinary artist and close collaborator of Jodorowsky in the 1960s and 1970s. He told me that Jodorowsky "had a great ear but no formal training." Urías suggests that Jodorowsky and professional musician Henry West might have created the music (as they proceeded in the play *Zaratustra*) in New York, and that Don Cherry would have likely contributed the arrangements. On the other hand, after reading Andy Votel's research, it is evident that Don Cherry and the band had much more agency (with Jodorowsky being close to their process), and that, later on in the production, the academically trained Ronald Frangipane answered Jodorowsky's requests for bits and cues. Andy Votel, "The Holy Mountain (the Original Sountrack) (Liner Notes on LP Sleeve)" (ABKCO/Finders Keepers, 2014).

5. Music and Records ABKCO, "The Holy Mountain: Original Soundtrack (Vinyl)," para. 1, accessed October 11, 2002, https://www.abkco.com/store/holy-mountain-original-soundtrack-lp/

6. Votel, "The Holy Mountain (the Original Sountrack) (Liner Notes on LP Sleeve)" (ABKCO/Finders Keepers, 2014), para. 3.

7. Votel, "The Holy Mountain," para. 3.

8. Qtd. in Votel, "The Holy Mountain," para. 3.

9. The soundtrack album was planned to be released immediately after the film's debut but several events, including Jodorowsky's long-time fallout with Allen Klein, did not allow this to happen until four decades later. Votel, "The Holy Mountain," para. 7.

10. Emilio García Riera, *Historia documental del cine mexicano, vol. 16*, 2nd ed. (Guadal: Universidad de Guadalajara, 1992), 30.

11. Ethnomusicologist Alonso Arjona kindly helped in identifying traditions, instruments, and sound elements of the Eastern and Latin American music in the film. "Other Cherry albums, such as *Organic Music Society* and *Eternal Now*, feature drone-tone ragas similar to those that provide the backdrop for the intense title sequence of the film. Most comparable is the track *Tibet* (from *Eternal Now*) (. . .)." Votel, "The Holy Mountain," para. 3.

12. Musician Patricia Morales Schechinger kindly helped in spotting the early music references in the film and their temporality. Film, television, and stage composer Delerue (1925–1992) is known for his interest and use of Baroque techniques (such as bass continuo) and instruments in soundtracks. Perhaps his most famous work with these characteristics is in *Night for Day* [*La nuit américaine*], François Truffaut, 1973.

13. Luis Alvarado, a Peruvian sound art expert, kindly helped with the identification of the Andean music in the film. He hints that the ensemble which recorded these bits might have been from Cusco (as suggested by the instruments used).

14. The sword-and-sandal or *peplum* film subgenre has its origins in Italian cinema and its heyday was from the late 1950s to the mid-1960s. Some of the most famous films that portrayed the Roman militia in a biblical setting include *Ben-Hur* (William Wyler, 1959), *Barabbas* (Richard Fleischer, 1961), and *The Robe* (Henry Koster, 1953). Miklós Rózsa

(*Ben-Hur*) and Alex North (*Spartacus*, *Cleopatra*) are prominent sword-and-sandal composers. Regarding this particular cue, Andy Votel points out that "(t)he opening orchestral pounds (. . .) follow a similar progression, signature and pace to the title track to the title track *Puzzle* by The Mandrake Memorial." Votel, "The Holy Mountain," para. 6. (Ronald Frangipane had produced the album *Puzzle* in 1970.)

15. Mexican popular music expert Pável Granados confirmed on November 2, 2021 that the version used was recorded in the 1950s by Marimba Orquesta La Poli de Tuxtla, directed by Ricardo Sánchez Solís.

16. This music resembles "Desireless" from the Don Cherry album *Relativity Suite* (1973), as well as appearing as a theme in other Cherry releases. Votel, "The Holy Mountain," para. 3.

17. Medina, "Pánico recuperado/Recovering Panic," 103–105.

18. "(. . .) tracks such as (this) contain the cyclic prog rock guitar parts and orchestral percussion that give empathetic nods to Cherry's traditional flutes and horns found elsewhere in the film." Votel, "The Holy Mountain," para 6.

19. Andy Votel reckons that the "over-saxed lost striptease track in the film also sounds similar to Elephant's Memory saxophonist/vocalist Stan Bronstein's work on Yoko's wacky 'I Felt Like Smashing My Face In A Clear Glass Window.'" Votel, "The Holy Mountain," para. 6.

20. On November 25, 2021 I interviewed the pianist Ana Ruiz, who played with Cherry in the late 1970s with her group Atrás del Cosmos, and artist and composer Naima Karlsson, also archivist of her grandparents Moki and Don Cherry. Naima stated that this track in particular reminds her of a particularity in Don's work – its "singability" – which allowed him to transmit his musical ideas to colleagues. Andy Votel points out that "(t)he track *Trans Love Airways* on the *Relativity Suite* LP (recorded in New York City on Valentine's Day, 1973, virtually parallel to *The Holy Mountain* sessions) united Charlie Haden, Moki Cherry and The Jazz Composer's Orchestra to form the basis for the music in the iconic scene where Jodorowsky's nine principal characters enter a giant yellow eye-shaped room to part company with their earthly treasures." Votel, "The Holy Mountain," para. 3.

21. Sound effects expert Gonzalo Gavira participated in the film and is most probably co-creator of this montage.

22. Santos, *The Holy Mountain*, 75–97; Medina, "Pánico recuperado/recuperado Panic," 102.

23. Medina, "Un rito de antiiniciación," 694.

24. Medina, "Un rito de antiiniciación," 699.

25. The director recently told the story that he wanted to compose the soundtrack but had no music training. The solution was to invent a musical notation system in which he assigned notes to different friends and then invited them to come over to his house. The order in which the guests arrived would construct the melodic line. *Jodorowsky Remembers El Topo* (ABKCO, 2020).

26. Santos, *The Holy Mountain*, 34–58.

27. Michael Chion, *La música en el cine* (Barcelona: Paidós, 1997), 158–60.

28. Chion, *La música en el cine*, 142–145.

29. This interest could be linked with the rise of Baroque Pop (as a genre) and the pedagogical use of that musical style in the Suggestopedia teaching method.

30. Chion, *La música en el cine*, 254–263.

31. Chion, *La música en el cine*, 256–257.

32. Michel Chion highlights the contrasting use of Mozart and the extreme narrative situation as a common cliché and cites as an example *Il portiere di notte* (Liliana Cavani, 1974), in which an encounter between an SS guard and his former victim takes place at the opera. Chion, *La música en el cine*, 256–257. I put forward another interesting example, which is the use of Mozart's String Quartet No. 15 in Pier Paolo Pasolini's *Il fiore delle mille e una*

notte (*Arabian Nights*, 1974), in which the gentleness of the music is contrasted with the impoverishment of the setting.

33. Keir Keightley, "Music for Middlebrows: Defining the Easy Listening Era, 1946–1966," *American Music*, vol. 26, no. 3 (2008), 309–335, https://doi.org/10.2307/40071710

34. Tamar Barzel, "'We Began from Silence': Toward a Genealogy of Free Improvisation in Mexico City: Atrás Del Cosmos at Teatro El Galeón, 1975–1977" in *Experimentalisms in Practice. Music Perspectives from Latin America*, eds. Ana R. Alonso-Minutti, Eduardo Herrera, and Alejandro L. Madrid (New York: Oxford University Press, 2018), 217.

35. Rita Eder, "Dos aspectos de la obra de arte total: experimentación y performatividad/ Two Aspects of the Total Work of Art: Experimentation and Performativity" in *Desafío a la estabilidad. Procesos artísticos en México 1952–1967/Defying Stability. Artistic Processes in Mexico*, ed. Rita Eder (Mexico City: UNAM/Turner, 2014), 64–81; Angélica García, "Manuel Felguérez y Alejandro Jodorowsky/Manuel Felguérez and Alejandro Jodorowsky" in *Desafío a la estabilidad. Procesos artísticos en México 1952–1967/Defying Stability. Artistic Process in Mexico 1952–1967*, ed. Rita Eder (Mexico City: UNAM/ Turner, 2014), 108–111; Angélica García, "Desplazamientos desde la escena teatral" in *Genealogías del arte contemporáneo en México (1952–1967)*, ed. Rita Eder (Instituto de Investigaciones Estéticas – Universidad Nacional Autónoma de México, 2014), http:// www.ebooks.esteticas.unam.mx/items/show/46. Sound artist and researcher Manuel Rocha Iturbide came to notice this interest in sound while reading Jodorowsky's book *Teatro Pánico* (1965), from which he cited (in his own translation): "Sound collage in darkness: door handle – crackling of a small door opening – crackling of a big door – crackling of an enormous door – Roar of King-Kong and chains – the interjection Aj! Said by a German – Gurgles – the voice of a man: five, four, three, two, one, cero." Manuel Rocha Iturbide, "Sound Art in Mexico," n.d., para. 8, https://www.academia. edu/8101338/Sound_art_in_Mexico.

36. Barzel, "'We Began from Silence,'" 218–220; Daniel Escoto, "Interview with Luis Urías (Unpublished)," 2019.

37. Daniel Escoto, "1, 2, 3, 4, 5 a Gogó: Pop, Avant-Garde, and TV in Late-Sixties Mexico," *The Journal of Popular Culture*, vol. 54, no. 1, 27–46; Mauricio Matamoros, "Crononauta" in *Desafío a la estabilidad. Procesos artísticos en México 1952–1967*, ed. Rita Eder (México: UNAM/Turner, 2014), 180–181; Mauricio Matamoros, "Aníbal 5" in *Desafío a la estabilidad. Procesos artísticos en México 1952–1967*, ed. Rita Eder (México: UNAM/ Turner, 2014), 260–263.

38. Jodorowsky quoted in Medina, "Un rito de antiiniciación," 697.

39. Frank Pavich, *Jodorowsky's Dune* (USA and France: Sony Pictures Classic, 2013).

CHAPTER 9

Outlaw Artists and Esoteric Media: International Copyright and Alejandro Jodorowsky's Illicit Media Practice

Andrew Ventimiglia

With the release of his visionary film *El Topo*, Alejandro Jodorowsky is widely credited as the first filmmaker to have created the "ritual" of the midnight movie.[1] In fact, the entirety of his career is notable for the idiosyncratic ways in which his films have been marketed, distributed, and exhibited. Jodorowsky's first feature, *Fando y Lis*, inspired riots at the Acapulco Film Festival and was subsequently banned in Mexico; his entry into the U.S. film scene involved his arrival – "wild-eyed [and] shaven-headed"– in New York City with a print of *El Topo* under one arm; and his first taste of success occurred with a private screening of the film at the Museum of Modern Art during which half the audience walked out.[2] But these idiosyncratic efforts resulted in Jodorowsky successfully booking a run of weekday midnight screenings at the Elgin Theater in 1970.[3] From there, word of mouth publicity and the cultivation of an aura of mystery around him and his films resulted in *El Topo* becoming a staggering success through alternative and explicitly countercultural strategies of outreach. The success of Jodorowsky's early feature films as prototypical cult movies illuminates his unique status as a filmmaker whose fame is linked not simply to the content of his films but also to their unique strategies of distribution.

Further, the success of these distribution strategies depended on Jodorowsky and his distributors' careful attention to copyright law. Whoever owned the rights to his films wielded the control necessary to successfully distribute them in such a way as to maximize their auratic value. The controversial copyright owner for Jodorowsky's first films was the producer Allen Klein whose company ABKCO purchased the rights to *El Topo* and funded (and subsequently owned the rights to) Jodorowsky's follow-up film *The Holy Mountain*. However, despite an initially productive relationship, in

1975 Jodorowsky found himself in a copyright dispute with Klein, resulting in the distributor pulling both *El Topo* and *The Holy Mountain* from circulation. The prints for these films were locked away and supposedly destroyed. Thus, Jodorowsky's films – originally actively marketed as cult experiences existing outside the traditions of normal motion picture art – suddenly literally existed outside the boundaries of the film industry. Any attempted screenings were rendered illegal offenses.

In response, Jodorowsky began to circulate copies of his films to video bootleggers in every country he visited. Eventually Klein tracked down one of these pirates and threatened them with a lawsuit. Jodorowsky assumed responsibility for the piracy and defended his actions as illegal distributor of his films. He thus found himself in the counterintuitive role of pirate of his own work.[4]

This chapter argues that, rather than disrupting Jodorowsky's unique capacity for film promotion, this copyright dispute and its link to an "outlaw" distribution strategy had the effect of heightening his films' illicit qualities, thereby demonstrating the filmmaker's continued savvy at strategic circulation. By exploring this moment in Jodorowsky's career, I demonstrate that his legal maneuvers – particularly as he lost formal control of his films – amplified the esoteric message of his early cult successes. This approach holds particularly true for *The Holy Mountain*, a film that was heavily influenced by Oscar Ichazo's Arica School, an organization that similarly found itself embroiled in copyright disputes around ownership of the esoteric symbol the enneagram. This chapter thus further indicates that Jodorowsky was not alone in his illicit media practice but instead shared a tendency with religious media producers of that era to use copyright law to strategically shape the distribution and control of spiritual media.

THE ESOTERIC PRODUCTION AND DISTRIBUTION OF *THE HOLY MOUNTAIN*

El Topo's run at the Elgin Theater was an unequivocal success. The film was screened at midnights (and 1 a.m. on Fridays and Saturdays) every night from December 1970 to the end of June 1971. The film was barely advertised. Instead, it generated attention because of the aura of mystery that surrounded it. As Ben Cobb writes, the film "would work best if it felt like the closely guarded discovery of a select few scene-makers and hipsters. The power of their influential word-of-mouth-recommendation alone would, [Elgin Theater owner Ben Barenholtz] believed, be the perfect promotional campaign."[5] This unique approach to distribution fit with the content of the film as a unique event designed to generate psychedelic or spiritual effects in the viewer. In this regard, Jodorowsky considered his films – particularly his subsequent feature *The Holy Mountain* – analogous to psychedelics that have the power to transform.[6]

El Topo's run drew the attention and admiration of John Lennon who recommended the film to Allen Klein, a figure famous for his management of major music acts including the Beatles and the Rolling Stones. While Klein was most successful in the music industry, he was already somewhat familiar with the mechanics of film management and promotion. Klein had produced and distributed his first film – *Without Each Other* – in 1962. He modeled his approach on United Artists, which had pioneered a new model wherein a motion picture company could independently finance and produce a film – and retain the rights to the resulting product – rather than relying on the Hollywood studio system.[7] Interested in finding success in the film industry – and pleasing his important client and Jodorowsky fan John Lennon – Klein bought the rights to *El Topo*, pulled it from the Elgin Theater, and began marketing it to a (slightly) broader audience.[8] He also signed Jodorowsky to an exclusive deal with ABKCO and provided funding for his subsequent film *The Holy Mountain*.[9]

From its inception, Jodorowsky's third major filmmaking effort *The Holy Mountain* was an ambitious project whose experimental production was heavily influenced by radical theater techniques developed earlier in his career.[10] While *El Topo* leaned heavily on mythic narratives and elements from Hollywood genres like the western, *The Holy Mountain* was steeped in Gnostic and occult imagery as well as contemporary spiritual belief systems like transpersonal psychology. Jodorowsky mobilized a plethora of global religious symbols and scripts to create an overwhelmingly dense and visually sumptuous filmic experience.

While the import of much of this religious imagery is open to interpretation – and is even considered to be intentionally "desacralizing" to the extent it appears as a critique of traditional forms of religious hierarchy and authority – Jodorowsky constructed the film to resonate with the countercultural spiritual zeitgeist.[11] In short, the film's narrative centers on a troop of religious seekers led by an alchemist (played by Jodorowsky) who pursues the key to immortality by ascending a holy mountain to meet the masters at the summit. The film characterizes individual attachments to national, racial, gender, or class identity as illusionistic and as productive not of unique subjectivities but rather of petty conflict, intergroup violence, and self-delusion. These attachments must be abandoned to obtain transpersonal and universal enlightenment.

The film's narrative, and Jodorowsky's central role as The Alchemist, helped create and reinforce his status as a radical filmmaker and a countercultural spiritual authority figure. In this regard, religious studies scholar Jeremy Guida has analyzed Jodorowsky as a charismatic leader (in the manner originally theorized by Max Weber) whose real-life spiritual influence – evidenced by his role as a practitioner of an invented method of therapy called psychomagic as well as his extensive experience with Tarot reading – has been reinforced both by his filmic self-representation and his ability to craft a liminal space in the screening of his films as midnight movies.[12] Further, and reflecting the core message of *The Holy Mountain*, Jodorowsky has claimed that, as a Chilean-born Jewish son of Russian immigrants currently living in France, he was a stateless citizen of the world. In a 1978 interview he said, "I don't want to have roots . . . I decided to make the sacrifice to not have any roots in order to reach pure spirit. It's very difficult because . . . you are not Jewish, you are not Christian, you are not anything . . . Then you are human . . . Without nationality."[13]

Like *El Topo*, *The Holy Mountain* met with success upon its release, running as the midnight screening at New York's Waverly Theater for sixteen months until April 1975. However, Klein's careful control of distribution may have limited its broader potential when he decided to exclusively contract the film as a double bill with *El Topo*. Nonetheless, this limited distribution strategy continued to feed into Jodorowsky's overall cult mystique as the film's scarcity produced an esoteric value around select midnight film screenings around the United States.[14]

During the film's run, tensions developed between Klein and Jodorowsky regarding the planning of their next project, a filmic adaptation of the best-selling erotic novel *The Story of O*. Hoping to capitalize on the massive international success of pornographic films like *Deep Throat* and *I am Curious (Yellow)*, ABKCO was on the verge of striking a deal worth $200,000 to begin production when Jodorowsky suddenly backed out of the project.[15] Jodorowsky subsequently described the dilemma as one in which he would have given up his artistic honor if he had agreed to make the film. In retaliation, Klein pulled all copies of *El Topo* and *The Holy Mountain* out of international circulation.[16] As sole copyright holder, Klein promised to bury the films and keep them buried, which he did until 2008 when Klein and Jodorowsky finally reconciled.[17]

While Klein had officially repressed *The Holy Mountain*, Jodorowsky – in response to Klein's legal action – traveled around the world as a one-man distributor, putting black market VHS copies into circulation and handing them to international distributors to ensure that pirated copies of his film were available to all who sought it.[18] In the process, Jodorowsky created a shadow market for his films that functioned as an extension of their earlier midnight movie status. According to scholar Alessandra Santos, Jodorowsky "begged fans to pirate copies," which, in turn, "triggered a cult phenomenon of replication that placed VHS copies in video stores, perpetuating the film's mystery and fetishization."[19] This trajectory is reminiscent of the cultures of analog media consumption explored by media studies scholar Lucas Hilderbrand wherein he describes the circulation of degraded or bootlegged copies of films – sometimes even in a gift economy of exchange amongst fans – as a challenge to the mechanics of control provided by modern copyright law.[20] In this context, *The Holy Mountain* became a product around which a countercultural cult following could rally to the conscious exclusion of the mainstream Hollywood market and its legally-conformist mass audience. What Jodorowsky lost in his legal financial stability through a major distributor he gained in cult status as a marginal yet charismatic figure on the fringes of the media industry.

ESOTERIC MEDIA AND THE LAW

What deserves emphasis in the narrative above is that Jodorowsky's success as a cult filmmaker and his subsequent role as illicit media distributor are deeply linked based on his sustained interest in alternative and even non-economically motivated models of distribution and exhibition. While his initial international rise to fame generated profits for producers like Allen Klein, his subsequent role as outlaw did not. In this regard, we might better understand Jodorowsky's films as specific instantiations of esoteric media – a subset of religious media – rather than traditional commercial media, whether made within the Hollywood or emerging independent film system.

Esotericism is a term used to characterize a broad set of religious teachings focused on ascertaining the hidden or occult nature of reality. As defined, esotericism includes both doctrinal and non-doctrinal components, the latter involving the management of these teachings: esoteric doctrine is kept secret in part to distinguish between initiates and non-initiates.[21] *El Topo*'s distribution explicitly played on these tropes of esoteric knowledge given the framing of the film as a cult object and attendance to a screening as a "midnight mass."[22] Given the need for control over esoteric teachings in order to strategically distribute them to select members, copyright law has featured as a novel contemporary legal mechanism to manage esoteric media, particularly in the United States. Conspicuous examples like the Church of Scientology and the Osho movement involved long-standing and sometimes aggressive legal efforts to protect select teachings and practices from public circulation, ensuring they were only made available to (paying) initiates.[23]

Among those esoteric practitioners savvy about legal control over the distribution of their media was Oscar Ichazo, the creator of a school of thought known as the Arica system. Like Jodorowsky, Ichazo described himself as a kind of religious cosmopolitan interested in syncretizing aspects of the world's religious traditions to create a new method of spiritual training. Ichazo considered himself a "student of Zen, Sufism, Yoga, Buddhism, Confucianism, I Ching, and the Kabbalah," and built the Arica system from various components of those religions to generate a comprehensive training designed to achieve transpersonal and transcendental understanding.[24] At its height, the Arica Institute ran over thirty branches worldwide and charged as much as $3,000 per student for its ability to produce a profound mystical experience in its pupils.[25] Ichazo's early success was founded on a series of months-long training sessions he conducted in Arica, Chile that attracted a number of central players in North and South American counterculture including Chilean psychologist-cum-shaman Claudio Naranjo, dolphin interaction researcher and designer of the sensory deprivation tank, John Lilly, and transpersonal psychologist Jack Downing.[26] This core group of followers and colleagues provided the key transnational network through which Ichazo developed his reputation; a reputation that eventually led Alejandro Jodorowsky to hire Arica leaders to be spiritual consultants throughout the filming of *The Holy Mountain*.

Jodorowsky wanted to model his performance as The Alchemist on that of a spiritual Master, and Ichazo was chosen as that figure. Jodorowsky hired Ichazo to enlighten him and then made the film's cast and crew undergo a rigorous two-month training that involved "a strict regimen of sleeping four hours a night, dieting, exercising, meditating, practicing yoga, and studying other mystical traditions."[27] Jodorowsky has described this tutelage under Ichazo as fundamental to the process of making *The Holy Mountain*. In his book *Psychomagic* he reflected on this relationship, writing, "I needed to understand the mind of a sage. I did not have this mentality, and I was aware of my limitations. So I hired a guru, Oscar Ichazo . . . who told me one day, 'You are going to imitate me for some time, because I have given you knowledge that you did not have: I have marked your virgin soul.' The soul imitates for a while what it has awakened to."[28]

In addition, two members of the Arica School acted as consultants during *The Holy Mountain*'s production. Their influence is evident in the symbolism and spiritual ideas expressed in the film. Most conspicuous is the presence of a key figure – the enneagram – which is frequently visible throughout the film. The enneagram is a nine-pointed figure used by Ichazo in his self-development workshops and spiritual retreats. Each point on the figure represents a given "ego fixation" (or personality type) that one must overcome on the path to universal transcendence and enlightenment. While the symbol itself has a longer history directly traceable to Russian mystic G. I. Gurdjieff and presumably further back into early Sufi mystic traditions, Ichazo claimed to have elaborated a whole new system articulating the symbol to the constituent elements of personality and their interrelations: expressions Ichazo then copyrighted as his own unique intellectual property.[29]

Ichazo's interest in carefully controlling the interpretation and use of the enneagram was evident in a 1991 copyright lawsuit that he pursued against

Harper & Row for publication of the book *The Enneagram: Understanding Yourself and the Others in Your Life* by author Helen Palmer.[30] Ichazo believed that this trade book divulged details of his exclusive esoteric system, and he used his legal rights to attempt to punish this perceived infringement. Ichazo lost the case at both district and appellate levels for several reasons, including that he had claimed elements of his copyrighted system as "an unalterable fact of nature," which would render them unentitled to copyright protection and, more importantly, that Palmer never even had access to the secret material since it was only made available to initiates. Only Ichazo's interviews were widely available to the public, and Ichazo's "conceded policy of withholding materials from the public" had the unintentional result of working against his infringement claims.[31]

Ichazo's desire to patrol the circulation of his teachings as part of an esoteric strategy that affirmed his role as protector and mediator of profound spiritual knowledge was likely part of his appeal for Jodorowsky that extended beyond the content of Ichazo's teachings. Further, while Ichazo's subsequent lawsuit foundered on the doctrinal details of copyright – and likely significant skepticism from the presiding judges – his legal strategy uniquely harmonized esoteric distribution methods with the overall logic of international copyright law, which was designed to allow rights holders a high degree of granular control over media while, at the same time, facilitating their movement across transnational economic circuits of exchange. In this respect, Ichazo's strategies differed little from Jodorowsky's early (legally sanctioned) distribution efforts via the emergent midnight movie circuit. And just as Jodorowsky and his distribution agents widely circulated trailers for his cult films selling them as unique transformative experiences, so too did Ichazo create two separate tiers of media in circulation. The first tier included interviews and letters – marketing materials – that served to recruit potential followers; the second, a protected inner realm of hidden wisdom available only to those who agreed to an explicit and exclusive spiritual relationship with the Arica Institute. Thus, Jodorowsky's esoteric Arica training is evidenced simultaneously across the production, distribution, and exhibition of *The Holy Mountain*.

By foregrounding the esoteric dimensions of Jodorowsky's media distribution strategy, it becomes clear that – counterintuitively – the loss of control over his films via copyright disputes with Allen Klein did not diminish his capacity to maintain the films' spiritual allure. If Ichazo marshaled the logic of authorial rights and the legal privilege of regulation to access to maintain control over his esoteric knowledge within a particular network of circulation, Jodorowsky conversely transformed the loss of legal ownership of his films, alchemy-like, into an equivalent increase in their spiritual and aesthetic value. Part of the reason for this difference is because of the unique history of copyright in Hollywood film, a history that demonstrates Hollywood's use of copyright as a tool for industry consolidation often to the detriment of unique visual artists like Jodorowsky.

HOLLYWOOD COPYRIGHT AND THE OUTLAW AUTEUR

Alejandro Jodorowsky has often been considered an explicitly anti-Hollywood and anti-mainstream filmmaker.[32] He began his career in live theater as a performer and stage director as well as a leading figure in the Artaud-inspired Panic Movement before turning to film for his early short *La Cravate* and his controversial first feature *Fando y Lis*.[33] His subsequent creative output has remained similarly eclectic, ranging from films to novels to comic books and on to his extended work as a Tarot reader and psychomagic therapist while living in Paris. As such, he was unlikely to fit into the model of industrial filmmaking dominant in the United States.

The figure of the filmmaker as author/auteur in the sense usually imagined in copyright law – which secures for "authors and inventors the exclusive rights to their writings and discoveries" – is largely disconnected from the actual assignment of copyright in film. Production companies utilize a work-for-hire doctrine in which they hold the copyrights to their employees' creations even if the origin and value of the work is not necessarily attributable to the corporate entity.[34] In his history of copyright in Hollywood, Peter Decherney writes that most film copyrights were held by studios or production companies as corporate authors and, further, that these copyrights were treated as fully transferable commodities, an approach contrary to the myth of the romantic author in copyright and the tradition of moral rights evident in other countries such as France and Germany.[35] However, the period of the late 1960s and early 1970s also witnessed the emergence of the idea of the director as auteur who was uniquely responsible for the creative vision of a film production even when working within the rigid Hollywood system, as was evident by celebrated American filmmakers such as John Ford or Douglas Sirk.[36] Nonetheless, while these directors might have been recognized and esteemed within critical and scholarly circles, their increased clout as artists did not necessarily translate to legal control over their films' copyright. Instead, the increased visibility of director/auteurs operated more as a marketing technique leveraging the celebrity of filmmakers in distribution without necessarily changing the legal arrangements governing the industrial relationships behind the scenes.[37]

Given his rise in celebrity during a period in which the idea of auteurism in film was increasingly recognized, Alejandro Jodorowsky fit within the model of auteur-driven filmmaking even as he expressed little interest in the economic value of his increasing name recognition.[38] But Jodorowsky's status as auteur was consistently one in which he acted as provocateur and even outlaw within the staid worlds of theater and film. In a 1970 interview with *The Drama Review* – in the interim period between the release of *El Topo* and the filming of *The Holy Mountain* – Jodorowsky described industry practices and mainstream tastes as forms of censorship and his own work in the Panic Movement as "criminal theater."[39] In a number of surprisingly prescient comments, Jodorowsky claimed that "art should be for the few, for initiates like a masonic group, who go into a home to become changed," and further that it was better to put one's artistic efforts on film "so that if it is censored, it can be stored in cans. It may sit for twenty years, but one day it is screened."[40] This latter comment was already based on his experience with Mexico banning his first film *Fando y Lis*, but it also anticipated the fate of his subsequent two films.

Jodorowsky also represented himself in both interview and artistic practice as someone who failed to recognize the (legal, cultural, artistic) jurisdiction of national borders.[41] As previously noted, Jodorowsky largely considered himself a stateless citizen of the world for whom conceptions of national identity and culture only limited the range of human expression possible.[42] Further, it was the failure of *Fando y Lis* to give Jodorowsky entry into Mexican filmmaking (where he had been working in theater), particularly the film's subsequent repression, that propelled him to cross the border to New York with a print of *El Topo* under his arm.

Jodorowsky's risk-taking behaviors and provocateur persona indicated the degree to which his success was grounded less in the traditional distribution of successful films than in the very practices of distribution – either through the act of carrying prints and VHS tapes to viewers or through the utilization of non-traditional networks for circulation – that Jodorowsky cultivated even prior to his relationship with Allen Klein. As Jeremy Guida writes, Jodorowsky's charismatic authority, and thus his success as a cult auteur, has consistently relied on repeated instances of "flouting risk."[43] This approach resulted in the very act of viewing Jodorowsky's films – both as a midnight movie and later in pirated form – as an act of cultural and even legal rebellion.

Because of this history of antagonism to systems of legal and economic control, one might look at Jodorowsky's falling out with Allen Klein with a certain degree of skepticism. At a minimum, Jodorowsky was extremely adept at quickly turning his loss of copyright into another instance of hegemonic control against which he had made a career of rebelling. After Klein and Jodorowsky's business partnership fell apart, Jodorowsky used his copious interview opportunities to frame Klein as a villain whose legal control of copyright masked the greater injustice of alienating a filmmaker from his works. Klein made little effort to counteract this framing as he withdrew every print of *El Topo* and *The Holy Mountain* and refused requests from theaters and festivals to screen the films for over twenty years.[44] According to Jodorowsky, Klein claimed that he was "going to lock the negatives of his films in a safe as of now, and until the day he dies, no one will ever see them."[45] The language Jodorowsky used to describe Klein since their dispute demonstrates the animus with which he saw this representative of industry. In his autobiography, he described Klein as a "cultural murderer, an accursed gangster, and a repugnant vulture who hoped for my death so that he could enrich himself with posthumous screenings."[46] Elsewhere, he wrote that Klein was an "artistic killer. A murderer. It is a crime. When a criminal burns a picture or a painting, it is criminal."[47]

Consonant with his role as outlaw auteur, Jodorowsky's response to this dispute was to circulate pirated copies of his own films in defiance of Allen Klein, the formal copyright holder. While his own accounts of his participation in this bootleg market differ slightly across interviews, he undoubtedly supported the creation of a market of illicit film copies. In one interview, Jodorowsky claimed he found a negative of one of his films (it is unclear if he is referring to *El Topo* or *The Holy Mountain*) in Mexico and then gave it to "robbers" to pass along to film pirates.[48] According to Alessandra Santos, Jodorowsky also mentioned that "he was responsible for circulating video copies of his films that spawned pirated versions – a move to guarantee that his films would be seen – and that he begged fans to pirate copies."[49] However Jodorowsky was involved, soon his films generated a second-generation cult audience who first found his films through these pirated versions: versions whose relative lack of accessibility and bootleg status led to the films' esoteric mystery and fetishization.[50] While we might imagine that Alejandro Jodorowsky would have been better served if he maintained control of his films' copyrights and used that control to distribute them as he wished, his conflict with Klein led Jodorowsky to operate in a space surprisingly suitable for his own career trajectory: the international spaces between and beyond traditional legal jurisprudence.

ABKCO V. *JODOROWSKI* AND THE OBSTACLES OF INTERNATIONAL COPYRIGHT

In narrating his role as pirate of his own films, Jodorowsky made special mention of his films circulating across various countries in Europe and North America. In his autobiography he wrote, "I gave them away for free to pirates in every country I visited. Although of poor quality, they managed to sell in Italy, Chile, Japan, Switzerland, Russia, and other countries for about thirty years."[51] This promiscuous circulation notably contrasted with the limited distribution strategy that Klein utilized prior to their conflict, even as the films' pirate status maintained Jodorowsky's esoteric outlaw authority. In this way, Jodorowsky became a figure more aligned with the international underground and avant-garde rather than the "international" – read globally famous – director Klein had hoped Jodorowsky would become.[52] This alternative network was both more closely aligned with Jodorowsky's artistic sensibilities and existed firmly outside the mainstream film industry and its rigorous copyright permission system.[53]

Jodorowsky's films as distributed in bootleg markets are a testament to their informal global distribution patterns. A common VHS copy on the market was a version of *The Holy Mountain* made from a Japanese release that Alessandra Santos describes as having "been censored and edited with blurry dots covering nudity or any sight of pubic hair."[54] This copy was presumably produced from the negative of the film found by Jodorowsky in Mexico. Other bootleg copies included a VHS PAL version of *El Topo* taken from masters that were supplied to the BBC (and used for a transmission of the film on March 21, 1997) that was in Spanish with English subtitles.[55] In this sense, these copies carried the traces of their international circulation paralleling the "aesthetic of access" – signs of degradation, wear, decay, and distortion characteristic of bootleg films – that Lucas Hilderbrand theorizes in his book *Inherent Vice.*[56] These copies also circulated in international spaces that were hard to patrol legally – what Hilderbrand calls a "legal limbo" – even if the bootlegs would formally be considered illegal due to legal reciprocity between countries in international intellectual property agreements.[57]

Eventually these bootlegged copies drew the legal attention of Allen Klein and ABKCO. As Jodorowsky tells it, Klein used the internet to track down one of these international pirates and threatened the individual with a lawsuit. In response, Jodorowsky "decided to assume responsibility for the 'piracy' and defend [himself] legally" thereby resulting in the lawsuit *ABKCO Music & Records Inc.* v. *Jodorowski.*[58] Given the complicated nature of international piracy and the challenge of locating liability within networks of distribution, the lawsuit was administratively complex and centrally involved questions about copyright jurisdiction. Proceedings for the lawsuit were initiated in France where Jodorowsky lived. In the dispute, Jodorowsky "contended that he owned the copyright," thereby evoking, at least rhetorically, the idea that he maintained a certain degree of moral rights in the film regardless of the legal transfer of copyright to Klein. However, the proceedings quickly became muddled as a U.K.-based company – MovieMail – was discovered as also having illegally distributed the film (and which claimed it was given the authority to do so from the filmmaker himself) while a third party initiated proceedings against both ABKCO and Jodorowsky, claiming that it was "entitled to certain video rights in all countries other than the United Kingdom and the Republic of Ireland."[59]

Given that, as a 2002 judgment on the case noted, copyright law is territorial, the international circulation of the film forced different notions of authorship and ownership of the film into conflict. In the U.K., "the producer or financial backer of the film . . . is the owner of the copyright. In French law, the general position . . . is that the persons responsible for the intellectual input into the film . . . generally share the copyright. The position in these two countries is therefore fundamentally different."[60] Because of the contrasting nature of the rights in dispute, the proceedings in the U.K. were temporarily halted until the courts could collectively decide how to ensure harmony between the different jurisdictions' legal conclusions.[61] The case proceedings, complicated as they were by the multijurisdictional nature of video piracy, provided a compelling illustration of the power of Jodorowsky's outlaw distribution strategy. This strategy uniquely affirmed and reinforced Jodorowsky's interest in being a "stateless" figure producing universal art: art which, by its illicit distribution, undermined the legal boundaries of the nations through which that art circulated. In Jodorowsky's engagement with and resistance to copyright law, it became apparent that the meaning and import of his work was instantiated through its conflict with the law, the obstacles it established, and the limitations it created.

Had these lawsuits been allowed to work their way through the legal system, they would inevitably have been resolved in a suitable manner to reaffirm the harmony of the international copyright system; the disjuncture revealed in the law eventually sutured by juridical argument and analogy. Further, had Jodorowsky lost the lawsuit, he might have faced significant financial loss. Instead, Jodorowsky and Klein resolved their personal differences, and the case was settled out of court. Jodorowsky claimed that he called Allen Klein's son Jordi who agreed to settle so that they could mutually profit from a formal DVD release of the film. When they met to decide the conditions of the settlement, Jodorowsky reunited with Allen Klein and they both embraced. The filmmaker claimed, "The hatred fell away from my body like a tattered old overcoat."[62] After this reconciliation, Jodorowsky worked with ABKCO to restore the films, after which a newly remastered copy of *The Holy Mountain* was screened in 2006 and the film was distributed to cinemas again shortly thereafter.[63]

CONCLUSION

To fully account for the success of Alejandro Jodorowsky as a filmmaker and outré celebrity, scholars must look not only to the content of his works but also to the unique ways in which those films were marketed and distributed. In doing so, it becomes evident that Jodorowsky – even when he was not in control of the copyright for his landmark films – was incredibly savvy at managing the affordances and obstacles of media distribution to create an image of himself as an outlaw filmmaker whose overall mystique suggested he shared characteristics with the esoteric masters he ably portrayed in his most spiritual film *The Holy Mountain*. By foregrounding the story of Jodorowsky's copyright battles with Allen Klein over the films *El Topo* and *The Holy Mountain*, I argued that Jodorowsky turned disadvantage into value, particularly when it came to his latter efforts to circulate bootleg copies of his films to international audiences.[64] In the process, his films continued to operate in the way that they were originally designed as cult films: they were experiences in which the ways that the audience encountered the films – as midnight movies, as bootleg DVDs, as illegal festival screenings – enhanced their esoteric and potentially transformative content. Thus, a key part of Jodorowsky's legacy is in the unique ways he made his films (in)accessible by engaging with and challenging the mechanisms of international copyright law.

NOTES

1. J. Hoberman and Jonathan Rosenbaum, *Midnight Movies* (New York: Da Capo Press, 1983), 80.
2. Ben Cobb, *Anarchy and Alchemy: The Films of Alejandro Jodorowsky* (London: Creation Books, 2007), 68–9, 111; Hoberman and Rosenbaum, *Midnight Movies*, 93.
3. Ben Cobb, *Anarchy and Alchemy*, 111.
4. The lawsuits are briefly described in Alejandro Jodorowsky, *The Spiritual Journey of Alejandro Jodorowsky* (Rochester, VT: Park Street Press, 2005), 238–239. Litigation was initiated in both France and the United Kingdom resulting in some confusion about which jurisdictions should take priority. Details on these two cases are described in *ABKCO Music & Records Inc. v. Jodorowski* [2003] E.C.D.R. 3 (2002).
5. Cobb, *Anarchy and Alchemy*, 111–112.
6. Cobb, *Anarchy and Alchemy*, 126. See also, David H. Fleming, "Head Cinema as Body Without Organs: On Jodorowsky's Bitter Pill Films and Their Spinozian Parallels" in *Unbecoming Cinema: Unsettling Encounters with Ethical Event Films* (Bristol: Intellect, 2017), 101–134.
7. Fred Goodman, *Allen Klein: The Man Who Bailed Out the Beatles, Made the Stones, and Transformed Rock & Roll* (Boston, MA: Mariner Books, 2015), 31.
8. Hoberman and Rosenbaum, *Midnight Movies*, 95.
9. Alessandra Santos, *The Holy Mountain* (New York: Wallflower Press, 2017), 23.
10. Santos, *The Holy Mountain*, 28.
11. Alessandra Santos describes *The Holy Mountain* as a "desacralizing cult film" that "questions long-held beliefs, institutions of power and societal dynamics." Santos, *The Holy Mountain*, 7. Adam Breckenridge makes a similar argument in "A Path Less Traveled: Rethinking Spirituality in the Films of Alejandro Jodorowsky," *Journal of Religion & Film*, vol. 19, no. 2, article 2 (Fall 2015). My analysis here does not necessarily disagree with these interpretations except to note that many of the Gnostic and esoteric traditions – or more precisely American countercultural interpretations of those traditions – that Jodorowsky references similarly criticize traditional religious authority in order to assert new forms of spiritual authority based on other alternative or secret practices and modes of transmission. For instance, see Jacob Needleman's definition of esotericism in *The New Religions* (New York: Jeremy P. Tarcher/Penguin, 1970), 213.

12. Jeremy Guida, "Media Review: Producing and Explaining Charisa: A Case Study of the Films of Alejandro Jodorowsky," *Journal of the American Academy of Religion*, vol. 83, no. 2 (June 2015), 537–553. On psychomagic, see Alejandro Jodorowsky, *Psychomagic: The Transformative Power of Shamanic Psychotherapy* (Rochester, VT: Inner Traditions, 2004). On Tarot, see Alejandro Jodorowsky and Marianne Costa, *The Way of Tarot: The Spiritual Teacher in the Cards* (Rochester, VT: Destiny Books, 2004).

13. Quoted in Cobb, *Anarchy and Alchemy*, 21–22.

14. Santos, *The Holy Mountain*, 34. Hoberman and Rosenbaum also claim that Klein only scheduled the film to run on Friday and Saturday nights at midnight to "'protect' Jodorowsky from the critics," and the film was never released in Los Angeles at all. *Midnight Movies*, 107.

15. Jodorowsky claimed that the $200,000 was an advance on his salary as director that would be given immediately upon signing a contract. Jodorowsky, *Spiritual Journey*, 237–238. For the economic success of pornographic films like *Deep Throat* as well as the threat they posed to Hollywood filmmaking, see John Lewis, *Hollywood v. Hard Core: How the Struggle over Censorship Saved the Modern Film Industry* (New York: New York University Press, 2000).

16. In his Allen Klein biography, Fred Goodman claims that Jodorowsky took Klein's money and then claimed he would not make the movie. Goodman, *Allen Klein*, 228.

17. Goodman, *Allen Klein*, 275.

18. Jodorowsky, *Spiritual Journey*, 238.

19. Santos, *The Holy Mountain*, 42–43.

20. Lucas Hilderbrand, *Inherent Vice: Bootleg Histories of Videotape and Copyright* (Durham, NC: Duke University Press, 2009). Mention of bootleg gift economies is on p. 189.

21. Antoine Faivre, "Esotericism" in *Encyclopedia of Religion*, ed. Lindsay Jones, 2nd ed., vol. 4 (Detroit, MI: Macmillan Reference, 2005), 2842.

22. Hoberman and Rosenbaum, *Midnight Movies*, 94.

23. On copyright and esotericism, see Andrew Ventimiglia, *Copyrighting God: Ownership of the Sacred in American Religion* (New York: Cambridge University Press, 2019), 184–189. On Osho, see Hugh Urban, *Zorba the Buddha: Sex, Spirituality, and Capitalism in the Global Osho Movement* (Berkeley: University of California Press, 2016).

24. On the Arica system, see John C. Lilly and Joseph E. Hart, "The Arica Training" in *Transpersonal Psychologies*, ed. Charles T. Tart (New York: Harper & Row, 1975), 329–351. On Ichazo, see Oscar Ichazo, *Interviews with Oscar Ichazo* (New York: Arica Institute Press, 1982). The quote comes from the opinion in the case *Arica Institute, Inc. v. Helen Palmer and Harper & Row Publishers* 970 F.2d 1067 (1992).

25. Cobb, *Anarchy and Alchemy*, 127.

26. Jeffrey Kripal, *Esalen: America and the Religion of No Religion* (Chicago: University of Chicago Press, 2007), 177–178.

27. Santos, *Holy Mountain*, 27–8. Details from Jodorowsky's individual spiritual training with Ichazo are recounted in Cobb, *Anarchy and Alchemy*, 128.

28. Jodorowsky, *Psychomagic*, 182, 199. Jodorowsky's description here of imitating in order to fully embody the role of a spiritual master for *The Holy Mountain* broadly reflects his overall approach to performance in which he induced his actors to, in the words of Alessandra Santos, "experience themselves as the characters or . . . become the character, which is a precept of the theater techniques of Antonin Artaud." Santos, *The Holy Mountain*, 29.

29. On the enneagram, see Lilly and Hart, "Arica Training" and James Moore, "The Enneagram: A Developmental Study" (2004). On the transmission of the enneagram from G. I. Gurdjieff to Ichazo to Jodorowsky, see David Pecotic, "Mountains Analogous?

The Academic Urban Legend of Alejandro Jodorowsky's Cult Film Adaptation of René Daumal's Esoteric Novel," *Journal for the Academic Study of Religion*, vol. 27, no. 3 (2014), 367–387. On Ichazo's rationale for asserting property rights in the enneagram, see Oscar Ichazo, "Letter to the Transpersonal Community" (1991). To clarify, the enneagram alone could not be registered for copyright, but the enneagram plus Ichazo's written explication of its meaning was registered amongst other materials – diagrams, manuals, training regimes – that were central to the Arica system.

30. Helen Palmer, *The Enneagram: Understanding Yourself and Others in Your Life* (New York: Harper & Row, 1991).

31. *Arica Institute, Inc. v. Helen Palmer and Harper & Row Publishers* 970 F.2d 1067 (1992).

32. Santos, *The Holy Mountain*, 29.

33. Hoberman and Rosenbaum, *Midnight Movies*, 88–93.

34. On the work for hire doctrine, see Catherine Fisk, *Writing for Hire: Unions, Hollywood, and Madison Avenue* (Cambridge, MA: Harvard University Press, 2016) and *Working Knowledge: Employee Innovation and the Rise of Corporate Intellectual Property, 1800–1930* (Chapel Hill, NC: University of North Carolina Press, 2009).

35. Peter Decherney, *Hollywood's Copyright Wars: From Edison to the Internet* (New York: Columbia University Press, 2012), 112. On the myth of the author, see Martha Woodmansee, *The Author, Art, and the Market: Rereading the History of Aesthetics* (New York: Columbia University Press, 1996); and *The Construction of Authorship: Textual Appropriation in Law and Literature*, ed. Martha Woodmansee and Peter Jaszi (Durham, NC: Duke University Press, 1994).

36. Decherney, *Hollywood's Copyright Wars*, 123.

37. Of course, literary celebrity has also historically been used as a marketing technique in a similar way. This celebrity function is closely linked to the "author function" famously theorized by Michel Foucault. On literary celebrity, see Loren Glass, *Authors Inc.: Literary Celebrity in the Modern United States 1880–1980* (New York: New York University Press, 2004).

38. In a 2018 interview for *The Paris Review*, Jodorowsky claimed, "I have freedom as a director because I make *cine de autor*. But now there are very few filmmakers of that kind because you don't make any money." Elianna Kan, "Buy High, Sell Cheap: An Interview with Alejandro Jodorowsky," *The Paris Review* (March 8, 2018). Available at https://www.theparisreview.org/blog/2018/03/08/buy-high-sell-cheap-an-interview-with-alejandro-jodorowsky/ (last accessed December 29, 2021).

39. Sergio Guzik, "A Mass Changes Me More: An Interview with Alexandro Jodorowsky," *The Drama Review: TDR*, vol. 14, no. 2 (Winter 1970), 70, 73.

40. Guzik, "A Mass Changes Me More," 75, 72.

41. George Melnyk calls Jodorowsky a "transcontinental" artist. "The Transcontinental Cinema of Alejandro Jodorowsky," *Film International*, vol. 6, no. 4 (2018), 59–69.

42. "What the Mexican has is that he is a human being, as the Russian is a human being, as the Chinese is a human being, as the North Americans are human beings. We should make a theatre of human beings." Guzik, "A Mass Changes Me More," 75. However, we might note that Jodorowsky can be considered in relation to various national and regional filmic traditions rather than simply appropriated by the Western cult canon. This point is made in Dolores Tierney, "Mapping Cult Cinema in Latin American Film Cultures," *Cinema Journal*, vol. 54, no. 1 (Fall 2014), 131.

43. Guida, "Media Review: Producing and Explaining Charisma," 545.

44. Ben Cobb, "Midnight Rambler," *Sight and Sound*, vol. 17, no. 5 (May 2007), 92.

45. Jodorowsky, *The Spiritual Journey*, 238. While this story is plausible given that there are many indications in Klein's life that he let personal grudges get in the way of

business decisions (and that the films had a healthy life in bootleg copies, as explored further below), Hoberman and Rosenbaum suggest that the lack of formal distribution for these films might have also been because they quickly became a dated product of the counterculture and thus were not economically valuable. The authors quote Ben Barenholtz who described *El Topo* as "strictly a product of the '60s. It wouldn't make a dime today." They also mention that Klein was "toying with the idea of rereleasing [*El Topo*] in a dubbed English version . . . raising the spectre of midnight nostalgia." *Midnight Movies*, 108–109. On Klein's approach to business, see Goodman, *Allen Klein*.

46. Jodorowsky, *The Spiritual Journey*, 238.

47. "Interview with Alejandro Jodorowsky," CFRB AM, Toronto (September 4, 2000). In perhaps the most florid language used to describe the dispute, Jodorowsky claimed that Klein hated him because Jodorowsky "saw [Klein] eating a huge sandwich full of rotten pork right in front of the orphanage he was expelled from for stinking too much." The quote comes from an unattributed online article called "El Topo and the Conceit of Alejandro Jodorowsky." Available at https://web.archive.org/web/20020106154606/ http://www.spiderstratagem.co.uk/eltopo.htm (last accessed, December 30, 2021).

48. Ed Halter and Michael Galinsky, "The Universal Language: An Interview with Alejandro Jodorowsky," *Cinemadmag* (Summer 2000).

49. Santos, *The Holy Mountain*, 42. See also, Jodorowsky, *Spiritual Journey*, 238; Cobb, *Anarchy and Alchemy*, 173.

50. Santos, *The Holy Mountain*, 43.

51. Jodorowsky, *Spiritual Journey*, 238.

52. Hoberman and Rosenbaum quote Klein as having said "My whole idea was to build him up as an international director." *Midnight Movies*, 95.

53. On copyright and the artistic avant-garde filmmaking scene, see Decherney, *Hollywood's Copyright Wars*, 185–191. David Fleming also compares Jodorowsky to work in the avant-garde like Kenneth Anger and Maya Deren. His description of Jodorowsky as "plurifilmic" and intertextual in a manner that parallels his syncretic use of spiritual traditions in his films suggests another way that his films resist traditional copyright as grounded in the idea of originality in favor of "combinatorial creativity." David Fleming, "Head Cinema as Body without Organs," 109. On "combinatorial creativity," see Maria Popova, "Combinatorial Creativity and the Myth of Originality," *Smithsonian Magazine* (June 6, 2012). Available at https://www.smithsonianmag.com/innovation/combinatorial-creativity-and-the-myth-of-originality-114843098/ (last accessed January 2, 2022). Finally, Alessandra Santos notes that *The Holy Mountain* had a rich "afterlife" through fan art, showing that these newly created works based on the film continued "to violate the copyright laws that Jodorowsky's film fans helped break while copying and distributing hundreds of bootleg tapes for decades." Santos, *The Holy Mountain*, 50.

54. Santos, *The Holy Mountain*, 42–43.

55. Information comes from "The Symbol Grows: Alejandro Jodorowsky" website, which collected news articles and information about Jodorowsky and his films. Information about the BBC version is available at https://web.archive.org/web/20110725102851/http:// www.hotweird.com/jodorowsky/ukvhs.html (last accessed January 2, 2022).

56. Hilderbrand, *Inherent Vice*, 15.

57. Hilderbrand, *Inherent Vice*, 32.

58. Jodorowsky, *The Spiritual Journey*, 238.

59. *ABKCO Music & Records Inc. v. Jodorowski* [2003] E.C.D.R. 3 (2002).

60. *ABKCO Music & Records Inc. v. Jodorowski* [2003] E.C.D.R. 3 (2002).

61. This procedure followed Article 21 and 22 of the Brussels Convention, which regulates legal disputes between different members of the European Union. Given Brexit, these

cases would have been resolved differently today. Ultimately, the judge in the U.K. case decided that legal proceedings should not have been halted (as previously decided) while the French case proceeded, because the cases involved different parties and thus were only distantly related.

62. Jodorowsky, *The Spiritual Journey*, 239–240; Cobb also describes this reconciliation in "Midnight Rambler" and Goodman similarly describes it in *Allen Klein*, 275–276.

63. Santos, *The Holy Mountain*, 44–45.

64. We might even include here reference to Jodorowsky's ill-fated *Dune* project, whose mystique was enhanced by the fact that it was never made and thus rendered forever inaccessible.

CHAPTER 10

Resistance in Alejandro Jodorowsky's *Santa Sangre*

Alessandra Santos

An undressed man is perched on top of a tall, bare tree stump. He is inside a large room, bathed in light coming through a high window. The window is disproportionally small, and the man, who thinks he is a bird, wants to escape his confinement and find liberation. He rejects the prepared human food doctors offer him, and screaming like an eagle, he devours raw fish instead. These are the opening shots in Alejandro Jodorowsky's *Santa Sangre* (1989). This bird-man is the protagonist Fenix (Axel Jodorowsky), who longs to escape not only physically, as we will learn later, but mentally he also needs to escape the oppression of traumas and his violent impulses.

Santa Sangre represents the complexity of Jodorowsky's cinema in multiple aspects. His films offer intricate visuality and sound, provocative and poetic scripts, challenging productions and contentious receptions, and, ultimately, controversial and often violent topics. In addition, the political dimensions of Jodorowsky's films cannot be understated. In my previously published work about his cinema, I claimed that considering the dissident historical contexts of his films, and the industry Jodorowsky provokes (Hollywood), the assumption that his films have a bombastic impact may be not considered outrageous.[1] For an attentive viewer, his controversial films are often imbued in political connotations, or overt political statements and postures. Jodorowsky's cinema offers multiple interpretations and numerous possibilities for analysis, especially considering the director's equally inspiring and controversial signature aesthetics. The anarchical rebelliousness early critics attributed to Jodorowsky still holds up to his most recent autobiographical cinema productions, attesting to Jodorowsky as a controversial counterculture iconoclast,[2] visionary and rebellious.[3]

The main goal of this chapter is to argue that Jodorowsky's films may be read as cinema of resistance through filmic denunciations and proposed

Figures 10.1‒ 2 Adult Fenix as the birdman, perched in the asylum

liberations, or through complications of actual notions of resistance and conformity.[4] Specifically, I will examine the role of anti-authoritarianism in *Santa
Sangre*. From a particular lens, Jodorowsky's cinema dismantles hierarchies
through filmic strategies, and negotiates poetic resistance in a refusal of normativity, overtly against structures of oppression. Paradoxically, Jodorowsky's
films may also be placed within contexts of oppressive patriarchal systems,
particularly in alignment with shock value, exploitation topics, violence against
women, problematic queer representation, and portrayals of disability ‒ also in
alignment with cult cinema in its complexities. I investigate how *Santa Sangre* operates in an orchestrated chaos of rebelliousness and occasional outrage,
and in organized critiques of injustices. I argue that resistance in Jodorowsky's
films follows a supposed "tradition of rupture" aligned with avant-garde and
art cinema tendencies, also juxtaposed to cult cinema's scandalous spectacle,
and to Jodorowsky's loyalty to theater as creative strategy. Given the film's
complexity, and the limited scope of this chapter, I focus on manifestations of
resistance within specific aspects, without engaging in *Santa Sangre*'s history
of production and reception.

RESISTANCE

Resistance has been defined in many different forms. While critic Barbara Harlow's book *Resistance Literature* (1987) linked literary works to organized national liberation struggles, certainly there are multiple forms of resistance expressed in artistic works. While speaking of a cinema of resistance, the most obvious case is in reference to films that directly comment on resistance to oppressive political regimes.[5] In a 2013 Lincoln Center Cinema of Resistance film festival in New York City,[6] curators Dennis Lim and John Gianvito quoted French director Jean-Luc Godard declaring that "it was no longer enough to make political films. One must make films politically." In European film history, Godard has manifested a level of political engagement in filmmaking that revolutionized the notion of what comprises political cinema. To the curators, films of resistance are "radical in both content and form, ever mindful of the relationship between politics and aesthetics. Ranging from the Vietnam War to Occupy Wall Street, addressing conflicts in Algeria, Ireland, and Afghanistan, these films offer an essential view of cinema's historical and continuing role in revolutionary culture." In explicit terms, there are films which are overtly concerned with organized resistance to varying degrees. For example, the Argentine Octavio Getino and Fernando Solanas's *The Hour of the Furnaces* (1968), presents an anti-colonial message of liberation from neo-colonialism in Latin America, aligned with the movement Third Cinema.[7] Note also Godard's films that engage in opposition to the Vietnam War and to capitalism, particularly *Tout Va Bien* (1972). Even though Jodorowsky was not a member of an organized cinema movement, his film *The Holy Mountain* (1973) also participates in the anti-war movement, offering a strong critique of unethical capitalism and consumerism, and of colonialism in Latin America.

To turn to a more systematic study of resistance, according to Jocelyn Hollander and Rachel Einwohner, who developed a typology for studying resistance, "scholars have used the term resistance to describe a wide variety of actions and behaviours," and that given the level of variation, there is little consensus as to what resistance means.[8] However, there are common traits such as opposition to oppression and refusal, particularly when acting in autonomy, rendering agency as one fundamental characteristic of resistance. As these critics examined, there are multiple modes of resistance, including social movements and protests, but also behaviors, appearances, or breaking silence, for instance. There are also variations in scale of resistance and different targets. Resistance, therefore, does not only entail armed struggles or direct action, but it can certainly manifest through artistic expressions in diverse forms.

Resistance in a discussion of Jodorowsky's cinema is directly defined as resistance to power and authoritarianism, but also to conformism and violence. Michel Foucault, who carefully theorized disciplinary society, acknowledged the relational complexity of resistance, claiming: "where there is power, there is resistance, and yet, or rather consequently, this resistance is never in a position of exteriority in relation to power."[9] Foucault attributed a point of contact between what is resisted (power) and the act of resistance in itself. To resist is to engage in complex relational power networks, and "their existence depends on a multiplicity of points of resistance: these play the role of adversary, target, support, or handle in power relations."[10] In that sense, my reading of Jodorowsky's cinema of resistance takes into consideration the various interactions within networks of power, such as the state and the family.

In the context of their critical study of Latin American exploitation film, critics Victoria Ruétalo and Dolores Tierney have observed:

> how Latin American exploitation cinemas [. . .] *may* represent a form of contestation and resistance not just to dominant (i.e., Hollywood-derived classicism's) stylistic aesthetic and narrative norms, for example, Alejandro Jodorowsky's 'cinema of cruelty' approach in *El Topo* (1970) [. . .] but also to the bourgeois art cinema models that many of the New Latin American Cinemas (despite their rhetoric) ultimately aspired to.[11]

From this perspective, Jodorowsky's cinema functions in multivalent resistances, aesthetically and politically, and in relation to cinematic approaches and genres. To study Jodorowsky's cinema within the exploitation cinema lens is directly aligned with cult cinema studies, without precluding resistance, but complicating it, as I will explore below. In a way, cult cinema may also be considered as resistance because it is ultimately concerned with breaking norms and conventions.

Jodorowsky's cinema of resistance may be considered artistic political action through filmmaking. While some critics may see Jodorowsky's cinema as too controversial or too idiosyncratic to consist of artistic acts of resistance, I see numerous possibilities given the political content and contexts which his cinema engages. It is important to note that, as critics have discussed, Jodorowsky's cinema is intrinsically related to Antonin Artaud's Theater of Cruelty. From the director's early artistic pursues in theater, to his adaptations of theatrical techniques to cinema, Artaud remains one of Jodorowsky's main inspirations. In *The Theatre and its Double*, Artaud proposes theater as "an essential disintegration of the real by poetry," and as a "hymn to anarchy and wholehearted revolt."[12] To follow these analogies, Jodorowsky's cinema attempts to disintegrate previously held assumptions through poetic revolt and resistance. If we accept that rebellious and renegade concepts instigate and organize Jodorowsky's cinema,[13] those traits may be directly connected to the notion of resistance as an operating principle. As cinema of resistance, Jodorowsky's films seek to unsettle norms, artistic and societal, creating constellations of filmic images and concepts that invite viewers to disrupt their understanding of reality.

It is important to point out the differences between resistance and transgression. To Foucault, transgression entails a process of desacralization, and ultimately it is "an action which involves the limit," and crossing lines in complex trajectories that often include excess.[14] In that sense, resistance may entail transgressions, but they are not equivalent. It is important to point out this distinction in relation to a discussion of Jodorowsky's cinema because, as part of cult cinema, his films also employ filmic transgressions. To cult cinema critics Ernest Mathjis and Jamie Sexton, "cult cinema's modes of reception are informed by debates around how they break boundaries of morality and challenge prohibitions in culture, how they dispute commonsense conceptions of what is normal and acceptable, and how in doing so they confront taboos."[15] These actions may allude to modes of resistance, and in some cases cinematic transgression may be an act of resistance to social mores and dictates. In elucidating these nuances, the goal is to establish how a cinema of resistance may use multiple strategies, including transgressions. In cult film theory, the concept of freakery is a form of cinematic transgression "in particular because of its singular focus on deviant human bodies as sites of transgression,"[16] and because the performance of difference also complicates the relationship between actor and character and character and audience. Filmic transgression offers a contrast and often a confrontation between the characters' deviances and the audiences' normativity. Cult films also engage with distinctions of taste and excess, which may invoke a kind of freedom in audiences.[17]

SANTA SANGRE

After making the cult midnight films, *El Topo* (1970) and *The Holy Mountain* (1973),[18] and after failing to complete the well-documented *Dune*, Jodorowsky took a hiatus as a filmmaker in the 1980s, with the exception of *Tusk* (1980), a film the director disowned by saying "Don't see *Tusk*. I bury that film."[19] Almost a decade later, he made *Santa Sangre* (1989) co-written by the director himself, Claudio Argento and Roberto Leoni. Because of the film's association with Argento[20] and because of the film's gory themes, *Santa Sangre* is known as a horror film. More specifically surreal-horror due to the director's artistic tendency to explore surreal imagery and outlandish artistic direction. Undoubtedly, *Santa Sangre* falls under the horror category considering the protagonist's trajectory as a serial killer of women. As such, this film would deserve an analysis according to genre, particularly as a body-horror film and to gender politics as represented in horror cinema.[21] Nevertheless, scholarship on *Santa Sangre* is scarce, apart from film reviews published upon release in the early 1990s. More recently, contemporary critics have offered important cultural and psychoanalytic interpretations.[22] An international co-production (Italy and Mexico), the film was shot in Mexico and it presents an exuberant and whimsical visuality in production design, as is typical of Jodorowsky's cinema.

Roger Ebert claimed that "to call *Santa Sangre* a horror film would be unjust to a film that exists outside all categories. But in addition to its deeper qualities, it is a horror film, one of the greatest."[23] In innovative and original text, images, and sounds, *Santa Sangre* re-signifies the horror genre to present resistance to authoritarianism, conformism, and violence. The film tells the story of Fenix (played by Jodorowsky's sons Axel Jodorowsky as an adult, and Adán Jodorowsky as a child). In the beginning, the protagonist is committed to a psychiatric hospital in a hallucinatory state in which he believes to be a bird of prey, an eagle. At this point in the film, Fenix was presented as dehumanized, eating raw fish voraciously, with hospital staff hoping he would "eat like a human." The eagle functions as an allusion not only to Fenix's state of mind, but also to his past. In a series of flashbacks, we learn that Fenix grew up in a Mexican circus as an aspiring child magician with an American circus owner father, Orgo (Guy Stockwell), and a Mexican mother, Concha (Blanca Guerra) who was a trapeze artist and the leader of a religious cult.

The late 1980s brought the end of the Cold War, and in Mexico, as in the rest of Latin America, this period saw an end to most U.S.A.-supported authoritarian regimes, the start of re-democratization processes, and the beginning of programmatic insertions of neo-liberal policies in the continent. In Mexico, specifically, this was the end of a period known as the Dirty War,[24] which was characterized by authoritarianism and brutal state violence backed by the United States. In Jodorowsky's films set in Mexico and later in Chile, there is a consistent explicit political commentary outlining a posture to resist totalitarian abuses of power in those countries.

In many senses, Jodorowsky's cinema functions as a post-colonial critique of power relations established through the colonial legacy in Latin America, and also a critique of capitalism and United States corporation neo-liberalism and neo-colonialism.[25] Critics Josetxo Cerdán and Miguel Fernández Labayen discuss how the "problematic relationship of Jodorowsky with Mexican culture and its national symbols is again a point of discussion" with critics of *Santa Sangre*, and that many popular cultural elements in the film "function as intertextual commentaries on Mexican traditional culture and national identity."[26] *Santa Sangre* presents indigenous peoples and traditional rituals such as the Day of the Dead, which plays a prominent role in one particular sequence. From the early days of *El Topo*, Jodorowsky had already explored various elements of folk spirituality, combined with outrageous violence and surreality in a western genre that directly references U.S. culture. In *The Holy*

Mountain, the exposure of American tourists and industry in Mexico, and of state authoritarianism, creates a post-colonial critique of economic and historical imperialism. In the case of *Santa Sangre*, there is a juxtaposition of local and folk elements with the American presence and influence, as represented in the father figure in this transnational film with a target international audience. The contextual neo-colonialism in Latin America plays a central role in Jodorowsky's persistent filmic exposés of authoritarian impositions.

In *Santa Sangre*, Fenix's American father, Orgo, the blonde circus's ringleader and knife thrower, is a screaming metaphor of American imperialism in Mexico. The circus is called "Circo del Gringo," and the big tent is star-spangled and has the American flag colors, as does the father's topcoat. The father also has the symbol of mighty imperialism, an eagle, tattooed on his chest. In an early sequence, we see the circus parade through town waving U.S. flags proudly, as young Fenix rides an elephant with Aladin (Jesús Juárez), who later becomes his companion in crime.

Figure 10.3 Young Fenix rides an elephant with Aladin

Orgo is authoritarian, domineering, and violent. The father cheats on his wife with the circus Tattooed Woman (Thelma Tixou), and plays knife games to spice up his sexual pursuits as well as mind games to dominate Concha to the point of hypnotizing her into submission. The effect of the dominant father borders on caricature, and yet it is eerily representative of a realistic boisterous machismo, engaging with critiques of domination, reinforcing the film as resistance to patriarchal imperialism. Young Fenix is devastated at seeing violence against his mother, and the first resistance identified in *Santa Sangre* targets the father's authoritarianism, which also doubles as a resistance to U.S. imperialism in the not-so-subtle patriotic elements of the American father. In a defining filmic moment, young Fenix succumbs to the father's authority and undergoes a macabre initiation rite, when the father gives Fenix a tattoo at

Figures 10.4–5 Orgo tattoos the young Fenix

knife point, replicating the father's own tattoo of an eagle on his chest. After completing the tattoo on his young son, Orgo proclaims "Now you are a man, just like me." Ironically, Fenix replicates his father's legacy of violence when he later becomes a serial killer of women using a knife, just like his father. The oppressed becomes the oppressor, in an embodied manifestation of the tyrant. As a metaphor for the country, Mexico's new generation embodies the historical violence of its colonizer.

From the film's opening credits, we see a background of deep red. The film's title refers to Concha's religious cult called Santa Sangre or Holy Blood. Concha started her church to worship a girl saint and martyr called Lirio, who had her arms cut off by rapists, explaining the church's symbol of intertwined arms. The girl tried to fight the rapists off with all her strength, but they raped her and let her die in a pool of blood.

Concha claims they built the church in the exact location of the crime, where a miraculous pool of blood still exists. Adepts of the church submerge themselves in the pool in a macabre initiation. In the sequence in which we

Figures 10.6– 8 Murals representing the history of the martyred saint Lirio

learn the Santa Sangre church's history, there are crucial elements to advance the film's critique of authoritarianism. The first scene presents a confrontation between Concha and her followers with the police, because the landowner developer wants to destroy the church with bulldozers. In a typical Jodorowskian visual strategy, armed soldiers face the audience with their guns (much like in *The Holy Mountain*), offering the threat to Concha as a threat to the

Figures 10.9– 10 Military police confront the congregation of Santa Sangre

public. Concha defiantly claims that they are not afraid of this encounter with the wealthy landowner's authority, and the police state's authority. In a striking scene, her church members sing a song claiming "the end of the world is near, all hope ends here"[27] as a limousine approaches with an eminent member of the Catholic Church, Monsignor (Sergio Bustamante), to appease the conflict. After learning about the church's history, Monsignor endorses the destruction of the cult's "abomination." Monsignor operates as yet another patriarchal force behind oppression, and Concha resists the authoritarian forces of state, Church, and money.

In a gendering of the father's authority, Concha finds Orgo betraying her with The Tattooed Woman, and she throws acid on his genitals, castrating him. This is the revenge moment for the violence he inflicted on her, ultimately portraying Concha as a submissive, abused, and betrayed woman, who worshipped a victim of rape but who also found her agency to castrate her husband. The film, however, does not leave this revenge without vindication because, immediately after, Orgo cuts off Concha's arms before committing suicide, preferring to die after castration. Young Fenix witnesses these events, suffering considerable trauma and eventually confinement in an institution. The exaggerated and gruesome sequence between Orgo and Concha foreshadows the ultimate violence drama in the film when Fenix, later in life, becomes his mother's arms and starts killing women. As a complication to Concha's resistance to Orgo's authority, Fenix embodies his mother to commit his own acts of violence against women.

After escaping the psychiatric hospital, Fenix is free but continues to live a life of delusions and submission, which are revealed at the end of the film. Some of the most fantastic and visually striking elements are the moments when Fenix performs with Concha in cabaret shows and pantomimes as his mother's arms. In perfectly synchronized acting, mother and son become one entity, and Fenix's life is reduced to serving his mother, which is later revealed to be a ghost and an illusion. Fenix, the magician, conjured up his mother through his imagination. He dresses Concha, applies her makeup, feeds her, plays the piano for her, and performs pantomime stories, operating as his mother's puppet. The theatrical techniques that characterize Jodorowsky's cinema are in full display during Concha and Fenix's act called "Concha and her Magical Hands." The first time they appear on screen, they recreate the mime "The Creation of the World" (1972) by Marcel Marceau, Jodorowsky's mime teacher. The effects contribute to an artistic cinema that employs multiple theatrical tactics.

Figure 10.11 Concha and her Magical Hands

And yet, the film pays homage to Hollywood horror as well. Fenix is obsessed with James Whale's film *The Invisible Man* (1933), recreating scenes from it repeatedly, in a reflection of his own invisibility under the towering presence of his father and mother. His insanity and violence are symptomatic of his loneliness and isolation. Concha tells him that without her he is nothing, and it is this nothingness without a will that creates the monstrosity he becomes.

Fenix seduces women in order to kill them and bury them in his garden after performing a ritual of painting them white. Allegedly, Jodorowsky developed the story after a chance encounter with a Mexican man, Goyo Cardenas, a lawyer and journalist who murdered many women under "the evil presence of his mother."[28] Jodorowsky was influenced by the fact that after imprisonment, Cardenas supposedly did not remember committing the crimes, as though possessed by his mother. Ultimately, Fenix's crimes could be a replication of the father's violence against women, or they could be read as an internalization of the mother's self-hatred. The new Concha, the one who controls Fenix in the second half of the film, is also domineering and forces Fenix to commit crimes. In a sense, the film portrays Fenix as a disturbed character who needs to resist parental domination and violence, not only in his "liberation from maternal domination."[29] To follow the initial metaphor of Fenix as the son of an American imperialist man and a superstitious Mexican woman, Fenix needs to break from his own oppression.

One of the main characters who serves as a catalyst for Fenix's transformations is his childhood friend and love from the circus, Alma[30] (Sabrina Dennison as an adult and Faviola Elenka Tapia as a child). Alma is a Deaf orphan who is a tightrope walker and Fenix's magician assistant. She goes away with The Tattooed Woman after Orgo's death, is forced into prostitution by her adopted mother, and also has to face male brutality when The Tattooed Woman brings soldiers to rape her for money. In a terrifying scene, The Tattooed Woman tells the soldiers they can do anything they want with Alma because no one can hear. The girl defends herself and escapes, which leads to her finding Fenix again. Alma, another innocent victim of violence against women and of precarious social conditions, is the character who ultimately liberates Fenix. It is through her act of love that Fenix resists violence and frees his hands from the hallucinatory authority inflicted by his traumatic history.

From the beginning, *Santa Sangre* stipulates a series of parameters to indicate resistance to violence against women through the character of Concha and her church, while at the same time portraying Fenix's crimes against women. This paradox engages with Foucault's claim about relational networks of powered resistance. To resist something is to highlight it, and to engage with the axis of power. Visually speaking, this film confronts violent acts in order to dismantle their power, without excuses or apologies for the brutality of those actions. It is Alma's strength, her courage to walk on a tightrope on fire, and her ultimate love for Fenix that awakes his humanity. His final transformation from monstrous bird of prey to human brings back the magician who dreams of creating flowers out of thin air. His "alma," or soul, returns to him.[31]

At the end of the film, it is Alma who awakens Fenix back to his agency, when he reclaims his hands to himself. He resists killing Alma according to Concha's wishes, and he kills his mother's ghost instead. Another flashback

Figures 10.12–13 Alma's love liberates the phoenix from the ashes

reveals to the audience a repetition of multiple scenes showing Fenix acting as his mother's hands, and Concha appears now not as a human without arms, but as a ventriloquist wood puppet. Alma reveals to Fenix the ghosts of his past and of his delusions. Concha's puppet is properly disposed of with the help of circus clowns and his companion Aladin, all also ghosts from the past, all burned in a bonfire of Concha's artifacts. The revelations of the ending culminate when the police arrive and ask him to raise his hands. Fenix raises them in complete autonomy and agency claiming "my hands, mine." Alma's love liberates the phoenix from the ashes.

In terms of paradoxical elements, *Santa Sangre* engages with cult cinema conventions – albeit transgressive conventions of rupture – that may be considered to be conforming to exploitation cinema. For example, one of the most controversial sequences of the film takes place in a seedy part of town with marginalized characters including drug dealers, street walkers, and pimps, and, most importantly, employs actors with Down syndrome who in a night out from the institution end up partying with Fenix, consuming cocaine, and having sex with prostitutes. The ethics of representation are questioned, and yet this transgression may be read as resistance to normativity and inclusion.

There is an elephant funeral with a somber circus parade, including mourning clowns wearing black and a black American flag, and the elephant is thrown in a shantytown ditch. Poor children rush to harvest the elephant's meat, possibly in a commentary that the American Orgo only gives scraps to the locals. The element of extreme poverty and squalid famished characters composes Jodorowsky's "social realist" repertoire amidst the usual Surrealist imagery, in yet another metaphor for Mexico/U.S.A. relations. There is a bodybuilder character in drag, "Mexican wrestling idol El Santo (who is transexually transfigured into la Santa),"[32] complicating gender norms when Fenix asks to fight "the strongest woman in Mexico." As is often the case with Jodorowsky's cinema, these images produce an ambivalent effect. The underworld represented in his films may serve as a sign of extreme inclusion, or it may serve as a spectacle that objectifies vulnerability, disability, difference, marginalization, and violence. As Dolores Tierney writes, "Latsploitation also carries with it negative associations. As with blaxploitation, there is an implied degradation of the subject matter: a belittling of Latin American locales through the perpetuation of continental and national stereotypes of the weird, the violent and the savage," not associated to a more cosmetic version of "postcolonial artistic autonomy."[33] Nevertheless, films like *Santa Sangre* actually offer an inclusive cast of characters who don't always represent a sanitized Latin America.

In addition, the portrayal of violence against women may paradoxically serve as a vehicle to advocate against violence.[34] Nevertheless, this filmic convention is still applying the horror film commodification of violence through gory gendered spectacles where women are the target. Brenda Austin-Smith argues that

> as Ernest Mathijs and Jamie Sexton observe, the associations of cult cinema with a male viewer of a certain age, has meant that sexual content has often taken a conventional form, intensifying rather than questioning the norms of cinematic depictions of gender. For these reasons, many associate cult cinema with a philosophy of transgression that sees the elimination of restraint (on depictions of sexualized violence against women, for example) as a sign of political and aesthetic progressiveness.[35]

Not that these multiple themes and representations of difference fall under the same category, however, transgressive elements may seem to escape the logic of resistance from one perspective precisely because of the intended shock value that escapes resistance to authoritarianism. Nonetheless, there may be a claim of autonomy even in the most transgressive scenes in this film, representing the double edge of highlighting transgressions from normativity as resistance. Within Fenix's altered mental state, there is trauma; within the violence against women portrayed in the film, there is advocacy against violence.

RECENT RESISTANCE

The autobiographical film *Endless Poetry* (2016) is the sequel to *Dance of Reality* (2013),[36] both written and directed by Jodorowsky, loosely based on his autobiographical book of the same title. In the first film, we follow the character Alejandro's childhood, upbringing in the small Chilean town of Tocopilla, and coming of age as an adolescent confronting his own social class in relation to poverty and inequalities. His father, an authoritarian figure himself, becomes a fighter against fascism, and endures punishment and torture for his rebelliousness, portraying the consequences to resistance. In *Dance of Reality*, the allegory for a country under a violent authoritarian regime is evident, evoking General Pinochet's ultra-nationalism and the horrors Chile endured during a long dictatorship.[37] In *Endless Poetry*, the family's journey continues in Santiago, focusing on Alejandro becoming an independent young man, and his ultimate transformation as an artist. If *Dance of Reality* portrays a Chile under authoritarian attack and resistance to oppression, *Endless Poetry* continues its journey of resistance to authoritarianism and totalitarianism, also conflating paternal authority with national repression. This film is an exhilarating visual journey, in a complex film and ode to resistance and poetry.

Endless Poetry is very different to *Santa Sangre*, but conceptual points of contact are evident. The film blends genres in a coming-of-age story and sensorial carnival, where the mother, Sara (Pamela Flores), operatically sings all of her lines. *Endless Poetry* offers exuberant imagery and sound, exploring Jodorowsky's theatrical perspectives and the ever-present circus. Once again, the initial confrontation and resistance in this film comes when Alejandro goes against his father's impositions. In the beginning, the father Jaime (Jodorowsky's son Brontis Jodorowsky) wants Alejandro (played by his son Adán Jodorowsky as an adult and by Jeremias Herskovits as an adolescent) to become a medical doctor, but Alejandro is determined to be an artist. Jaime is overly concerned with money and prohibits his son from pursuing poetry because it is only for "homosexuals," and because poetry does not make money. Even though I will not analyze *Endless Poetry* in detail here, it is important to highlight the continuity of Jodorowsky's cinema of resistance. In his return to cinema, the director explored a setting close to his personal trajectory, and yet new to his filmic experience, Chile. Almost thirty years after making *Santa Sangre*, there is a continuous anti-authoritarian stance which conflates the father's authority with brutal state authority. Ultimately, *Endless Poetry* also presents an underworld of art and renegade characters who are intensely humanized.

Jodorowsky's cinema of resistance exposes the legacy of colonialism, and how collective and personal traumas persist in internalized structures of domination, power relations, and hierarchical structures. Forces of patriarchy, such as misogyny, racism, and violence, which are essential for processes of colonization and to authoritarian regimes, are embedded in former colonies like Mexico and Chile. It is only after the colonial patriarchal model of authoritarianism is challenged that we may escape violence in the Americas. While excavating deeper into Jodorowsky's cinema, we may see how his tales of horror and resistance offer poetic possibilities for transformation. In the end sequence to *Endless Poetry*, guided by the older Jodorowsky himself, the young Alejandro has a final confrontation with his father and a fist fight. He tells the father: "not giving me anything, you gave me everything. Not loving me, you have taught me the absolute necessity of love."

NOTES

1. Alessandra Santos, *The Holy Mountain* (New York: Columbia University Press, 2017), 1.
2. Ben Cobb, *Anarchy and Alchemy: The Films of Alejandro Jodorowsky* (London: Creation, 2007), 5.
3. Ernest Mathijs and Jamie Sexton, *Cult Cinema: An Introduction* (Oxford: Wiley-Blackwell, 2011), 70.
4. Most if not all of Jodorowsky's films may be interpreted as cinema of resistance, including *Fando y Lis* (1968), *El Topo* (1970), *The Holy Mountain* (1973), *The Dance of Reality* (2013), and *Endless Poetry* (2016). This chapter will focus on *Santa Sangre* (1989); however, a similar approach may be applied to his other films and writing.
5. For example, an online search indicates that the Harvard Film Archives organized a Cinema of Resistance festival in 2020, including films "animated by the spirit of protest and designed to call out oppression and demand justice," https://harvardfilmarchive. org/programs/cinema-of-resistance-9. Another film series, curated by Nora Philippe in 2017 in New York City, presented French films that offer "particular resistance to political regimes," including the Italian director Gillo Pontecorvo's *The Battle of Algiers* (1966), https://frenchculture.org/events/6092-cinema-resistance-nora-philippe
6. https://www.filmlinc.org/series/cinema-of-resistance/
7. Third Cinema was an organized film movement in Latin America in the 1960s and 1970s which promoted a resistance to Hollywood and a commitment to political cinema of liberation. This wave of filmmaking also included the Brazilian Cinema Novo movement under the same political parameters. Both movements were inspired by Italian neorealism cinema. Solanas and Getino wrote a manifesto in the 1960s advocating Third Cinema, and Brazilian filmmaker Glauber Rocha wrote a manifesto "Aesthetics of Hunger" in 1965. Please see Robert Stam, Richard Porton, and Leo Goldsmith, *Keywords in Subversive Film/Media Aesthetics* (Hoboken, NJ: Wiley Blackwell, 2015), 148–149.
8. Jocelyn Hollander and Rachel Einwohner, "Conceptualizing Resistance," *Sociological Forum*, vol. 19, no. 4 (2004), 534.
9. Michel Foucault, *The History of Sexuality*, vol. 1 (New York: Pantheon Books, 1978), 95.
10. Foucault, *The History of Sexuality*, vol. 1, 95.
11. Victoria Ruétalo and Dolores Tierney, eds., *Latsploitation, Exploitation Cinemas, and Latin America*. (New York: Routledge, 2009), 5.
12. Stam, Porton, and Goldsmith, *Keywords*, 113–114.
13. Several critics have discussed the notion of rebellion in Jodorowsky's cinema, including Mathijs and Sexton (*Cult Cinema*, 70), and Ben Cobb who called him a renegade filmmaker (Cobb, *Anarchy and Alchemy*, 13).

14. Michel Foucault, "A Preface to Transgression" in *Language, Counter-Memory, Practice: Selected Essays and Interviews*, ed. and trans. by Donald F. Bouchard (Ithaca, NY: Cornell University Press, 1977), 32–33.

15. Mathijs and Sexton, *Cult Cinema*, 97.

16. Mathijs and Sexton, *Cult Cinema*, 102.

17. Mark Jancovich, "Cult Fictions: Cult Movies, Subcultural Capital and The Production of Cultural Distinctions," *Cultural Studies*, vol. 16, no. 2 (2002), 306–322.

18. For detailed history, criticism, and analysis of *The Holy Mountain*, and for more about Jodorowsky's trajectory as a cult filmmaker, please refer to my own Cultographies series book dedicated to this film. See Alessandra Santos, *The Holy Mountain*.

19. From an interview with J. LaBine as quoted in Cobb, *Anarchy and Alchemy*, 190.

20. Claudio Argento (b. 1943) a producer and screenwriter mostly involved with horror films, most notably producing George Romero's *Dawn of the Dead* (1978). Claudio Argento is also the brother of Dario Argento, an internationally renowned horror film director.

21. For the intricacies of gender in horror films, please see Daniel Humphrey's "Gender and Sexuality Haunts the Horror Film" in Harry Benshoff, ed., *A Companion to the Horror Film* (New York: John Wiley and Sons, 2014).

22. Please see Josetxo Cerdán and Miguel Fernández Labayen, "Arty Exploitation, Cool Cult, and the Cinema of Alejandro Jodorowsky" in Victoria Ruétalo and Dolores Tierney, eds., *Latsploitation, Exploitation Cinemas, and Latin America* (New York: Routledge, 2009).

23. Roger Ebert, *Santa Sangre* review (1990), https://www.rogerebert.com/reviews/santa-sangre-1990

24. The Mexican Dirty War was a period between the 1960s and the 1980s which was part of the historical seventy years uninterrupted rule of the Partido Revolucionario Institucional party, characterized by state power, corruption, and violence. For more historical details see Santos, *The Holy Mountain*.

25. Refer to Justin Edwards and Rune Graulund's chapter on the "Postcolonial Grotesque" (2013), which approaches Jodorowsky's films as post-colonial cinema. In my study on *The Holy Mountain* I discuss in detail how the film may be considered a post-colonial critique (87).

26. For a detailed discussion on Mexican popular culture elements in *Santa Sangre*, refer to critics Cerdán and Fernández Labayen's article "Arty Exploitation, Cool Cult, and the Cinema of Alejandro Jodorowsky," including Christopher Kelly Ortiz and *The Representation of Sexuality in Contemporary Mexican Cinema: 1970–1990*, dissertation, 1995.

27. The film's excellent original sound score and soundtrack are by film composer Simon Boswell.

28. Cobb, *Anarchy and Alchemy*, 213–214.

29. Cerdán and Fernández Labayen, "Arty Exploitation, Cool Cult, and the Cinema of Alejandro Jodorowsky," 110.

30. Alma is played by Deaf actress and playwright Sabrina Dennison, ASL consultant and Director of Artistic Sign Language for the Huntington Theatre in the U.S.A.

31. Critic George Melnyk argues that *Santa Sangre* is a film about Jodorowsky's healing art of psychomagic (65). George Melnyk, "The Transcontinental Cinema of Alejandro Jodorowsky," *Film International*, vol. 16, no. 4 (2018), 65.

32. Cerdán and Fernández Labayen, "Arty Exploitation, Cool Cult, and the Cinema of Alejandro Jodorowsky," 108.

33. Dolores Tierney, "Latsploitation" in Ernest Mathijs and Jamie Sexton, eds., *The Routledge Companion to Cult Cinema* (New York: Routledge, 2019), 90.

34. Violence against women and LGBTQ communities is at an alarming rate in Latin America. Violence against women and transwomen is most predominant in Central America, Brazil, and Mexico. According to the United Nations, 38 percent of women in Latin America have experienced domestic violence, and the rate of femicide is rising, https://www.un.org/en/observances/ending-violence-against-women-day

35. Brenda Austin-Smith, "Cult Cinema and Gender" in Mathijs and Sexton, *The Routledge Companion to Cult Cinema*, 143.

36. Both films were funded with help from fans through crowdfunding methods, https://www.artnews.com/art-news/news/alejandro-jodorowsky-is-crowdfunding-his-latest-feature-film-4742/

37. Dictator Augusto Pinochet ruled during the brutal military regime in Chile from 1973 to 1990, when many thousands of people were persecuted, disappeared, tortured, killed, and exiled.

CHAPTER 11

Inherit and Repair: Self-erasure and Allegoric Montage in Jodorowsky's *The Caste of the Metabarons*

Francisco Javier Fresneda-Casado

INTRODUCTION

Within the scope of Latin American science fiction, the presence of Alejandro Jodorowsky can be understood within a consolidation period encompassing the years 1940 to 1960. In addition to translations coming from the U.S., France, the U.K., and the U.S.S.R., we find authors such as Rafael Bernal, Guillermo Zárraga (under the pseudonym Diego Cañedo), and contributions made by Juan José Arreola and Carlos Fuentes. In 1964 Jodorowsky, alongside Colombian author René Rebetez, published two issues of *Crononaut* science fiction magazine in which they combined surrealist and psychedelic elements under the rubric of "panic science fiction" ("ciencia ficción pánica").[1] Let us remember that Jodorowsky, with Fernando Arrabal and Roland Topor, was one of the creators of the "panic" genre aimed at the radicalization of European Surrealism's expressive and thematic repertoire so as to "to mock the boredom of surrealism (. . .) to incorporate elements despised by surrealism."[2]

Given that, the artistic production of the Chilean in the ambit of comics is genealogically bound to the dissemination of Latin American science fiction. Jodorowsky's involvement in graphic novels stems from a long-term artistic career encompassing puppeteering, theater, and filmmaking, and it can be understood as a medium coalescing all these activities. More specifically, we will tackle his graphic novel production as a reciprocal extension of his activity as a filmmaker, or even as a sort of surrogate medium that responds to the material impossibility of making a film. "To me, my latest comics are movies. If I can't turn them into movies, I make them comics (. . .) If they don't let me in the film industry, I have the individual power to make comics."[3] Here we have two crucial traits: on the one hand, a notion of interchangeability between the graphic novel and cinema implicitly posited by Jodorowsky, and the way in which this fluidity of mediums affects the narrative structure of his scripts, where concepts of "origin" or "identity" are expanded and vulnerated. In particular, I am interested in using these notions as guidelines pertaining to *The Caste of the Metabarons* saga, published in eight volumes by French editorial house Les Humanoïdes Associés between 1992 and 2003 with illustrations by Argentinian Juan Giménez.[4]

In its conception, *The Caste . . .* combines narrative formulas taken from space opera, science fiction, Japanese martial culture, and Greco Latin tragedy, waiving a plot that encompasses a non-specified number of centuries, as a variety of characters come and go along the genealogical tree of the Metabarons. The visual structure proposed by Giménez aims to arrange these fluid temporalities by means of vignettes that work cinematically, or, following Deleuze, that "make cinema," less due to the related content than by its organization made out of "blocks of movement/duration."[5] Time here is created first as an operational structure, as a skeleton composed by durational images that sustain the gaze and the span of reading thanks to the twofold articulation of the vignettes, thus distinguishing the "plasma" or background page and the inline created by the images contained in the vignettes "framing and distinguishing one portion of space-time from another."[6]

I

The graphic novel builds its narrative temporality upon a syntax that is also cinematic, and where the vignettes mimic cinematic framing. In *The Caste* we find ample interstellar landscapes, death combats described through counter-planes and close-ups with dramatic facial expressions, or massive explosions occupying the entire surface of the page. But in order to better understand the links between the cinematic image and the saga made by Jodorowsky and Giménez, it is worthwhile to examine some of the aspects present in films such as *Fando y Lis* (1968), *El Topo* (1970), and *The Holy Mountain* (1973), attending to the correspondences that can be established in regards to the visual repertoire of "head cinema," "Hollywood LSD," or "western" film genres. Going beyond the pragmatic consumption of head films "intended to be seen or retrospectively associated with drug use as a reception practice,"[7] the LSD films that proliferated in the 1960s and 1970s attempted to recreate the subjective effect of hallucinogens consumed through the use of "avant-garde stylistics"[8] such as editing based on the use of overlays, fades, color or contrast saturation, increased sound, or slow-motion sequences.

This approach towards filmic matter and its modification in some of its fundamental features has been described by Benshoff as a "suture, one based on the convergence of neurochemistry (in the spectator's sensorium) with the visual and aural effects of the cinematic apparatus."[9] In this sense, images from the film and the mind intertwine and amalgamate under the canopy of a hallucinatory "lingua franca," generating a particular relationship of co-dependency – perhaps of perceptual nostalgia – since the access to hallucinatory perception is deferred or shared towards the filmic image. It is no longer enough to hallucinate reality through the use of drugs, since hallucination is here oriented towards a field of images that have already been mimetically foreshadowed. The film images pretend to be filmed hallucinations, and in doing so they promise to reconstruct the experience of the one who seeks to feel under the influence of drugs, verifying this state through the contemplation of images.

However, the visual field displayed by Jodorowsky in films such as *El Topo* (1970) and *The Holy Mountain* (1973) seems to pursue less the expressionist recreation of an LSD hallucination than its overcoming, placing it within a different perceptual magnitude. Thus: "If a young boy takes acid and experiences a change, the least a film can do is give him more than acid gives him; you must give him the pill."[10] This ambition to shift film reception into a mystical transformative experience is materialized in peculiarities such as the profuse use of the continuous shot – allowing it to induce transitions of a cognitive order throughout the duration of the sequence, and close-ups that posit the viewer as the object's observed subject.[11] One can imagine if Jodorowsky's intentions were to turn the film image into an immediate catalyst for altered states of consciousness, or rather use it as a representational or symbolic field whose apparent lack of meaning could be more understandable – or at least more significant, thanks to altered states of consciousness produced by the ingestion of substances such as LSD or marijuana. We must remember that already at the end of the 1950s we see the arrival of the *Vortex Concerts* by Jordan Belson and Henry Jacobs, where, despite presenting concerns analogous to those of Jodorowsky – Oriental philosophy, experimentation with hallucinogens, or Jungian psychology – the audiovisual output is located at a great distance in terms of visual and narrative abstraction from the Chilean's film production. Here, I would think that one of Jodorowsky's priorities is to suspend and ideologically problematize the viewer's point of view through the use of a filmic syntax that is partly divergent from commercial cinema, in addition to a repertoire of bodies, symbols, and narratives that are sympathetic with the cultures associated with the consumption of hallucinogens during the 1960s and 1970s.

Notably, *El Topo* deeply connects with main tropes of the so-called Spaghetti Western – a genre already indebted to the style of comic strip graphics, comic book and graphic novels – which shares the iconoclastic character that is distinctive of Jodorowsky's films in opposition to the conservative and mythological tone of the western as a great North American film genre; one that, among other things, reduces the American territory to the United States;

empty, free, and available to the colonists; one that describes the continent's inhabitants as "primitive" and inscrutable enemies. Given that, the Spaghetti Western introduces variations and anomalies:

> These films reappropriated key icons, plots, and situations from the genre, draining them of their moral and mythic significance. However, through the foregrounding of parody, violence and sadism, which were meticulously detailed through intricate cinematic framing, an often-saturated and overloaded soundtrack and a motley crew of bizarre characters, the Spaghetti Westerns proved a distinct version of the genre.[12]

Following Grady, it is possible to find stylistic similarities between this genre, inaugurated by director Sergio Leone with *The Dollars Trilogy* (1964–1966) and that of comic books such as *Blueberry*, drawn by Jean "Mœbius" Giraud – who also drew the series *The Incal* and collaborated with Jodorowsky in the unproduced adaptation of *Dune*. These shared similarities can be seen in the relationships between the "cutting effects" and the "framing" of the scenes, where the entire vast landscape appears in focus, and the alternate sequencing of counter-shots and close-ups typical of comic scenes.[13] *The Caste*'s narrative time also stretches towards scales that can only be emulated in cinema; as in the sixth volume of the saga, custodian robots Tonto and Lothar manage to escape the destruction of the "metabunker" caused by the Baron by taking refuge in a remote sub-planet where they will proceed with the reconstruction of the facilities encompassing "less than two centuries."[14] At an equally significant level, in these comics we can find hyperbolic speech balloons – where the container shape adapts or frames the content of the text – as well as a profusion of onomatopoeic resources that can be comparable to the use of sound effects in the films of Jodorowsky and that eventually allow him to make audiovisual montage by means of correspondences. Through the use of voiceover, studio post-production, and film loop or montage effects, the soundscapes of *Fando y Lis*, *El Topo* or *The Holy Mountain* are superimposed upon the visual, sometimes exceeding it in importance, as happens in the vignettes of *the Incal*, *Blueberry* or *The Caste of the Metabarons*.

II

Despite its only apparently traditional outlook, the Western as a trope – now shared in printed matter and the screens – turned the West into "a site of surreal and anarchic possibilities."[15] In that, we must give all the credit to this narrative environment, for it is fictional, yet uneasy and unfamiliar. One of *The Caste*'s salient features is the combination of temporal and narrative discontinuities that make a story without a traceable epistemological origin, since it introduces one of its fundamental characters in another saga – in *The Incal*, even before *The Caste* begins – and employs constant leaps and temporal recurrences that allow for the characters' lived time to be either indeterminate or discontinuous. But before expanding on time's functioning here, it is convenient to recognize the narrative arc of the saga made by Jodorowsky and Giménez as tracing the genealogical tree of this dynasty of warriors. In what follows, my intention is to underline some characteristics that I consider essential to *The Caste*, which will allow us to relate the characters' identities with the temporalities created by Jodorowsky.

Initially, the lineage of the Metabarons seems to exist halfway between the pirate community and the medieval noble heritage, being an extended family united under the clan structure and an unswerving work ethic. According to the order of publication of the eight volumes comprising the saga, the Metabarons' bloodline is composed by Othon the great-great-grandfather, Honorata the great-great-grandmother, Aghnar the great-grandfather, Oda the great-grandmother, Steelhead the grandfather, Doña Vicenta Gabriela de Rokha the grandmother, Aghora the father-mother, and No Name, the last of the Metabarons.

Through the Bushitaka – a strict code of conduct that the authors seem to have adapted from notions of Japanese Bushido – the Castaka family regulates itself under prevailing tropes. In every generation, the male son on his seventh birthday endures a ritual mutilation by the father in which the severed part will be replaced by a cybernetic prosthesis; then, at the age of sixteen, a ritual combat ensues in which the son must annihilate the father.[16] Mutilation is understood as a necessary process in which the male descendant demonstrates his ability to survive. This emphatically masculine ritual reproduces the idea of the male as an individual entity, a condition that is obtained by eliminating his immediate peer. Thus, man is truthful only when he kills his "double." For Jodorowsky, the patriarchal ritual is also justified from a natural perspective, where human and non-human species – such as the Magon monkeys of the planet Perdita where Aghnar resides – are organized through combats where the victor assumes the rank of "patriarch."[17]

Jodorowsky has raised the saga's narrative structure by overlapping timelines. On the one hand, the reader's immediate narrative access is mediated by Tonto and Lothar, the robotic servants of No Name who chronologically reconstruct the Metabarons' bloodline from the great-great-grandfather to the current moment. Tonto thus guides the description of such a bloodline whilst waiting on the rather messianic return of its master. From the first page, the reader will be confronted with two seemingly antagonistic temporal vectors; one that traces back the origins of the dynasty, another that suspends the present in preparation for the Metabaron's advent. But this twofold temporal structure becomes more convoluted; unbeknownst to Lothar is the fact that its robotic armor hauls the body of Steelhead, the fifth Metabaron defeated in singular combat by its daughter Aghora. So the witness of Lothar's account throughout the entire narration is in reality the missing piece of the tale – a Metabaron deprived of memory whose body is concealed within its very robotic servant. This masterful plot twist offers further insight into Jodorowsky's conceptualization of the Metabarons with regards to the configuration of their identities, always in the midst of an improbable axis between fluidity and rigidity.

Pivotal here is the conceptualization of the "cyborg," which for Jodorowsky has particular connotations, for he enhances the classical significance of the term – based on the mere incorporation of exogenous or artificial components within a living organism[18] while paying heed to the social, chimeric traits pointed out by Donna Haraway in her *Cyborg Manifesto* (1986). However, Jodorowsky does not comply in full with some of the fundamental statements presented in the manifesto; for one, the rendition of a "post-gender world."[19] As we will see, Jodorowsky seems reluctant or oblivious to this possibility, although genuinely interested in exploring the relationships between corporeality and identity as it clearly appears in much of his filmography and activity as a comic book writer. As early as his first foray into film *La Cravate* or *The Severed Heads* (1957) – where two rival suitors repeatedly replace their heads in order to attract their disputed beloved – the body is posited as something that can be modified, and in doing so it either affords substantial changes in an individual, or allows for an identity assumed to be incomplete, which has to continue in another being. I think of Jodorowsky carrying his son Brontis in *El Topo*; of the comic series *Alef-Thau* (Jodorowsky and Arno, 1983–1998) where the protagonist is born without arms or legs and is carried by different creatures while recovering its limbs; of Fando transporting Lis in the homonymous film; and in the frequent representations of disabled people that proliferate in *El Topo* (1970), *The Holy Mountain* (1973), or *Santa Sangre* (1989).

However, the relationship established between Jodorowsky and these bodies is ambivalent to say the least. At first glance, showing new realities and sensorialities, the presence of people with disabilities, cross-dressers, or the homeless might seem equalized as non-divergent from the "panic" world they inhabit.[20] But the author seeks just the opposite; to shock the audiences.[21] Moreover, Jodorowsky directly links some of these identities with his attraction to the "monstrous." In Jodorowsky's words:

(. . .) the picture who (sic) impressed me for all my life was "le Bossu de Notre Dame" (The Hunchback of Notre Dame) (. . .) with Charles Laughton. I saw that and I became in love of the monster, I imitate the monster all the day . . . later, another picture came . . . it was the first Frankestein, like . . . Boris Karloff. Also, I loved! I loved the monster!

I think from this moment I started to love monsters . . . all my life. I make all kind of art thinking that one day I will need that for the movies (. . .) When I became very very very famous in Mexico in the theater (sic) . . . that's the history of Fando and Lis . . . I read that play, I put that play in the theater . . . for one year I was playing that . . . Fando and Lis. I like monster! One day . . . Jewish Mongolian boy with the big mouth and . . . some kind of retarded mental man come to see me . . . I was so . . . so . . . I wouldn't say 'in love' because . . . myself . . . I'm not gay . . . in love in the aesthetical way . . . the monster . . . I said "you will be my assistant director" and my chauffeur, my driver (. . .) in a way, I was always in danger . . . when I was directing an actor (he) was between me and the actors . . . we need to push him away . . . but I loved the guy! (. . .) When I finish to shoot that, he committed suicide (. . .) This is why Fando and Lis begin with dedicate (sic) to the memory of Samuel Rosemberg . . . (he) was the monster.[22]

This problematic conflation of neurodivergence with the monstrous unequivocally marks with derogatory and condescending notes Jodorowsky's fascination upon subjects that, irrespective of the artist's intentions, are still considered to have a spicy, exotic otherness.[23] In the name of the ideological examination to which either the audience or the readers are subjected – that is, one's alleged tolerance to "challenging" narrative content, these subjects selected by Jodorowsky are still reduced to a mere aesthetic supplement that allows for a work of art to be presented as provocative. Jodorowsky's attempt to make the audience responsible for judging the subjects presented before them ultimately turns the artist into the disingenuous one, for these subjects have been profiled, picked, and epistemologically defaced even before the artwork is made.[24] Through a very particular mode of association, certain antagonistic traits such as "the monstrous" and "love" can configure a subject insofar as these characteristics remain impervious to each other, so the subject stands out of the tensions produced by these polarized descriptors which are individually identifiable. This point clarifies the way each of the Metabarons' identity is constructed; less a transgression of boundaries that would cancel identification itself, and more a process of amalgamation that begins from a very particular understanding of the monstrous – that is; the author's questionable fascination by difference – which transits towards the heroic. The saga is constructed upon irresolvable dichotomies that configure every character as if a "patchwork (. . .) measured not only by the quality of the patterns that compose it but above all by their heterogeneity, each pattern remaining well identifiable and differentiated from the others."[25]

Following Mellier's study on the Metabarons, the saga is articulated dialectically "between monster and lack" in which the external traits of the monstrous – in most of the cases, a mutilated limb – act as the anteroom of an ulterior process of augmentation which "does not restore, but increases" the functions of all these missing parts.[26] To repair oneself, one must surpass the previous state, and not only at the physical level. Although contested,[27] I argue that within the Metabarons' narrative universe the sensorial and bodily modifications go hand in hand with cognitive and emotional shifts that cast the characters' identity. I am thinking here in how Othon's emotional impact left by his castration makes him cruel and solitary,[28] or the final passage of saga in which No Name has the senses of his tongue activated by tasting honey, then realizing the feeling of love and defining his commitment to "cleansing evil from the universe."[29] By integrating "protonic" upgrades into oneself, each Metabaron incarnates a new sort of individual that equalizes mutilation and augmentation: "This presupposes a redefinition of the relationship between identity and otherness, the organic and the mechanical, the human and the material, the body and the body's consciousness."[30] In the context of *The Caste*, bodily modifications occur due to several main causes: the ritual mutilation process in the initiation of each Castaka, the militarization of the body through the introduction of bombs inside of it, or as a result of warlike confrontations. Losing the integrity of the body makes it possible to undermine any given identity, and at the same time extends it towards an infrastructural environment, where the new cybernetic dimension of the body is accompanied by a new scale for presenting the individual and his personality. In this way, each mutilation allows not only for the expansion of the individual towards machinic environments, but also the general progression of the saga as such.

We have Othon Von Salza in the first volume turning his accidental emasculation into a "multi-protonic pelvis"[31] that allows him to connect to his aircraft; Aghnar in the second volume losing his feet during the initiation ritual – thereby regaining the lost body weight due to his intoxication with the epiphytic antigravity spice and later on, an arm in combat; Steelhead in the fourth volume literally losing his head in the midst of the rarefied domestic dispute starring his father Aghnar and his grandmother-mother Honorata disguised as his wife Oda – who is going to lose ten fingers at the hands of Steelhead and ultimately commit suicide alongside Aghnar; once again Steelhead in the fifth volume being assembled with the head of Zran Krleza, the last living poet, thereby becoming an entity known as Melmoth; in the sixth volume Doña Vicenta Gabriela de Rokha removing her eyes in order to restore the memory of her newly cloned father; in the same volume Melmoth blows his head off and becomes Steelhead again, then sacrifices one of the Siamese twins born by Vicenta in order to engineer Aghora, the one that partially possess a woman's body and a man's brain (sic), and who will synthesize sperm from her own male brain tissue in order to inseminate themselves and give birth to the last heir, No Name, who ironically only suffers a minor cut in his right eyebrow during the ultimate combat against his grandfather Steelhead. The Caste highlights how the identity of its members is simultaneously fluid and restricted. Fluid because in its development the dynasty exchanges family roles.[32] Restricted because we find exchange of gender identities although these generally operate under binomials where the males assume the tasks of warfare and hybridization with machines and systems, and the females assume the reproductive activities and upbringing. Throughout the saga we can see how this rigid family structure finds limits and paradoxes in maintaining its own existence through an obsessive commitment to its own durability by means of procreation. Cascarino is clear in pointing out the delimitation of roles present in the dynasty:

> only men can perpetuate the Caste and become Meta-Barons (. . .) Aghora is therefore masculine: he is The Father-Mother and not The Mother-Father, and to prove it, he also modifies his body by cauterizing his chest. Despite all the bodily transformations that the Meta-Barons undergo over the course of these eight albums, one constant remains: they are all men. Women, on the other hand, are objects of men's desire. Necessarily beautiful, their value is linked to their fleshly body and to its exaggerated sexualization by the trait of Giménez. If the mutilation of the male body can be followed by the addition of mechanical prostheses and then increase the power and value of this body, the mutilation of the female body necessarily devalues it by diminishing its beauty and then leads, in the short term, to its destruction.[33]

And so these characters incorporate diverse technologies – the cybernetic implants already mentioned, and military infrastructures such as the dynasty's Metabunker – a hybrid between a fortress and a space vessel – without allowing such amalgamation to blur distinctive gender and family categorizations. And I would like to think that ultimately there is no contradiction in terms here, for the Metabarons are the favorite executioners of the empire, and, as such, their features will be coalesced forming polarized yet cohesive entities. Informed by Frank Herbert's six-book *Dune* saga, the Metabarons' reality is composed of a conglomerate of universes in dispute between cosmic creatures and a multitude of factions under the aegis of an imperial structure ruled by the Emperoress – a twofold, Siamese creature that incarnates power from its dichotomous male-female presence. The social realm in which the Metabarons are professionally involved – either as wealthy nobiliary members and mercenaries[34] – resembles an intergalactic Habsburg-like dynasty in permanent interaction and conflict with other archetypes of power that renders the saga's political imaginary as composed by medieval and early modern agents: the Technopope, the Ekonomat, the Techno-techno guild, the Troglosocialik colonists, the Paleo-prophet, the Magnate or the Shabda-Oud are some of the principal interlocutors and rivals with whom the Metabarons interact.

III

The Caste also complies with the formal requisite of imperial power; one that is transmitted upon the death of the immediate predecessor. What confirms imperial belonging is not only a matter of bloodline and biological causality, but a "speech effect" that turns the family candidate "appointed" as the heir.[35] Following Hardt and Negri, we could see how the incarnation of the empire carried out by the Metabarons is in addition to the despotic, biopolitical, expressed towards and from the physical integrity of the body,[36] which for a Metabaron is essentially incomplete or failed until his ritual amputation, the moment that designates his clan membership and the status of his heir. Throughout the pages of *The Caste* we can perceive how the noble heritage of the protagonists simultaneously requires a reconstruction – of bodies, architectures, nobiliary titles – and the production of a loss that sustains the durability of the lineage itself. By losing the integrity of the body, the heir will be Metabaron; by embodying cybernetic limbs, the Metabaron revives the identity of the clan. It is striking how the vast majority of the protagonists are physically very similar to each other; as if Jodorowsky were underlining not so much consanguinity but the obligation that, fundamentally, the empire continues and extends in the same individual, generation after generation. Let us not forget that similarly, Jodorowsky has conceived cinema as a generative act where, literally, the director begets his actors.[37] The characters that we see in this space opera are also different manifestations of a unique emblem of power. In *the Origin of the German Tragic Drama* (1928), Walter Benjamin reflects on Saavedra Fajardo's *Idea of a Christian Political Prince* (1642) a book of emblems that echoes Machiavelli's *the Prince* (1532) or Bruck's *Emblemata Política* (1618) by making a visual, allegorical compendium of imperial traits. Tellingly, the *Symbolum* number sixteen in Saavedra Fajardo's book – displaying a table with two identical rolled pieces of clothing facing each other – is entitled as "*purpura juxta purpura dijudicanda*" ["purple ought to be judged with purple"].[38] The quintessential color of the empire is an endless scroll that preserves the continuity of the imperial lineage, one that is noticeable only under a particular set of conditions. Not by chance, the Spanish diplomat recommends not to compare his purple clothing "in plain light," for one has to "put it next to the purple mantles of your glorious fathers and grandfathers, and notice if it contradicts the purple of your virtues by looking on them."[39]

Similarly, I would like to think of *The Caste*'s pages as a cinematic reel in which its characters exist by extending its lineage, one in which the designated subjects are replaceable, made out of interchangeable parts although ultimately the same subject. Jodorowsky's script presents these warriors as a sheer operational existence that is the same for all of them – conflict, conquest, annihilation, and reproduction. The inner self only emerges when its martial code collides with individual traces of personhood that never last, for the empire always imposes. This mode of existence, based on inheritance and repetition, also includes self-erasure as a necessary condition. As we have seen, Jodorowsky insistently draws examples throughout the entire saga: bodies that are shared, replaced, or reused; or family members who reappear with different family functions, to name but a few. The last heir – the one who ultimately refuses to continue the lineage – has to be nominally erased from the dynasty, thus becoming No Name. As his direct ancestor forebodes: "since his role is greater than even his identity, he will have no name."[40] And yet, deviation from the imperial sequence does nothing but reaffirm it at the temporal level, for it "effectively suspends history and thereby fixes the existing state of affairs for eternity";[41] something that in the comic saga might find two notable indicators. One is the constant change of what I would like to name "narrative scales" within the Metabaron's storytelling, which describe the extreme shifts from human-scale scenes – such as conversations and intercourses – to non-human scale scenes – notably the leaps into parallel universes or into planetary-scale alien creatures. The latter is a concrete manifestation of the former that somehow synthesizes both scales, turning every Metabaron into a multi-modal agent able to navigate every conceivable mode of reality. And, crucially, this ability illustrates the way in which empire exists; by means of intermittencies between historic foreground and background, the empire's agents can transgress the border that separates human-scale narrations from cosmic-scale storytelling.

Already in the second volume of the saga, the metabunker is attacked by the police[42] and the custodial robots Tonto and Lothar decide to activate a "bio-electrogram"[43] of the Metabaron, an ephemeral materialization of their master – or more precisely, of his stored information, which nevertheless is capable of existing for five minutes. This demi-character appears recurrently in different issues of the saga, seemingly not marking a great difference with the Metabaron, since both have the same excellence in combat[44] and receive equal treatment by Tonto and Lothar as the "real" Metabaron. Here I see how the Metabaron exists spectrally; he disappears but survives as a translucent albeit transcendent hologram that blends ghostly into the background of the vignettes, indicating once again how his identity continues beyond the physical margins of the individual. This apparent resolution of opposites as presence and absence, multiplicity and identity exists insofar as Jodorowsky postulates the narrative reality of *The Caste* in such a way that the opposites become similar, even connective realms. This necessary mediation between notions of identity and change – or between the aforementioned scales that each Metabaron navigates – can be better understood if we take into account the notion of "constellation" that Benjamin posits in the *Trauerspiel*:

"the representation of the context within which the unique and extreme stand alongside its counterpart."[45] Then we have a comic strip where the individual and its very lack of individuality are systematically put at stake within the very core of a narrative structure in which family and dynastic identity count the most, but have been subsumed within another structure in which identity overrides individuality: empire. Benjamin again: "The Trauerspiel has no heroes, only constellation of heroes (. . .) are not tragic characters, but suited to the mournful play."[46] This "play" – which is the path to classical natural history in Benjamin – actualizes the notion of "fate" as the prevalent temporality in antiquity and relocates it within a transtemporal scope in which nature always loses the battle against time. Any continuity has been lost, and what remains are fragments, outlines, and kindlings without a necessary origin, which unfold and sprout as "dialectical images" that adumbrate a modality of time that

> visit living beings externally, bringing together, breaking up, destroy-ing, and so forth. Time in this moment can be phrased variously – as theological preordination, as character variation within the limits of tax-onomy, as that which enables monsters or fossils – all of which estab-lishes the premise of continuity through which things either survive or disappear.[47]

In this saga there is no longer a divine language, nor are the gods heard – on the contrary, they are exterminated, as it happens to Jejoh the Pure in the fourth volume.[48] And if the language here is still indicative of the relationship between humans and gods, it has already been outpaced by the stories that robots tell each other, inventing neologism after neologism where being a "mecahysteric" or a "roboidiot" approximates them to human emotions even more than the Metabarons. All that remains is lament; that is, the substitution of naming what a primordial god named to incessantly describing things.[49] Here, reality is explained from an origin that exists as a loss; the present is only the distance to such failure, one that is measured in explanations, in laments. And so, the last character in the saga, No Name, tries to break up with the circularity of this imperial myth. For want of an offspring, he opens up the possibility of a new *Ursprung*, a new "primal leap"[50] that turns his existence into a new sign able to be named rather than explained. And his name folds the saga's temporality into a narrative outcome that plays out with the arrow of time, making the last character of The Metabarons saga (1992–2004) into the first in *the Incal* saga made by Jodorowsky and Mœbius more than decade earlier (1981–1988).[51] By being similar to no one, by erasing himself, No Name opens up the possibility of an origin without fate.

CONCLUSIONS

Alejandro Jodorowsky's creative universe dwells in diverse mediums which have been conceived by him as compatible and complementary, whence antagonistic ideas are presented as correlative in terms of importance. His conceptualization of both films and graphic novels intertwines formal and narrative structures, and eventually lays out his activity in comics as a form of response against the financial drawbacks and creative hindrances found in cinema production. Informed either by filmic manifestations such as the "head cinema" or the "LSD films" of the 1960s and 1970s and their emphasis on hallucinatory sensorialities, or the reconfiguration of major genres produced by the Spaghetti Western, Jodorowsky's cinematic approach is profuse in dislocating the sequence, rhythm, and cohesion between images and sounds, aiming for a divergent framing of time that is allegorical in either its fragmentary composition and in the non-teleological temporal modality that it creates. These traits can be found also in his comic production, confirming both mediums as co-extensive.

In this chapter, I have unpacked some temporal manifestations stemming from notions of "origin" and "identity" throughout diverse examples selected from Jodorowsky's body of work, with an emphasis on the first eight volumes of *The Caste of the Metabarons* that he co-authored with Juan Giménez. The importance of this saga outpaces the intertextual role it complies with in the chronology of his comic releases – notably *the Incal* – and stands out as a major creative investment that serves as a catalysis after the 1975 fiasco of his *Dune* adaptation to film and the necessity for "a change of path."[52] A failed film which exists as twenty copies of a comprehensive storyboard and a script whose imagery may well have percolated into a substantive amount of major sci-fi films, notably *Star Wars* (dir. George Lucas, 1977–), *Alien*, and *Blade Runner* (dir. Ridley Scott, 1979 and 1982) to name just a few.[53] Given the fact that Jodorowsky's *Dune* encapsulates fundamental tropes that exist in other major sci-fi films, *The Caste* comic series can be understood as an obstinate reiteration of the same narrative repertoire, but drawn back to the author's agency:

> The Metabaron, all of that, is kind of Dune's paraphrase all the time. I do it my way, I don't care. I am inspired by Dune. If I can't make the movie I want, I do it in a comic. And I have readers, and I express myself, that is, nobody prevents me from expressing myself.[54]

As it happens in his films, Jodorowsky has conceived the formal montage of *The Caste* according to a meta structure in which each one of the eight volumes diffract and encompass themes, characters, and archetypes borrowed from other places taken from his own production, turning this recursive and allegoric production into a multifaceted, somewhat obsessive, recursion into a number of his main preoccupations as creator: the sense of belonging, the construction of the individual, the search for identity, the plurality of beings, in addition to a variety of cases where the body enters in conflict with the mind and the spirit. In *The Caste of the Metabarons* we find all these interests partaking of a number of temporal manifestations, for time is the co-extensive medium that articulates and dislocates all the paradoxes outlined by the author. Therefore we have a retroactive, genealogical narration conducted by Tonto and Lothar that unfolds the Castaka bloodline from its genesis, while the narrative time is located in that of the disappeared last heir, the one that is still unknown to the reader.

Genealogic and messianic time alternate throughout the entire saga, setting up a discontinuous reality that impregnates the way each Metabaron configures his identity. By means of embodying antagonistic elements such as cybernetic implants, third-party body parts, and getting rid of one's own parts, what is given and what is new are equalized within a process of augmentation that does not lead to confusion. Beyond restoration, the self's reparation implies a qualitative leap that increases the possibilities of the individual and consequently of the saga as such. And yet, all these modifications do not cancel the implicit gender and family hierarchies. This point is systematically reiterated by Jodorowsky in order to stress how the Metabarons' agency is arrested by their own status as imperial agents, either as nobiliary members or mercenaries. The gender bias, the loss of body integrity and its reconfiguration do nothing but highlight how the empire itself functions; by means of suspending disambiguation amongst its subjects, every Metabaron becomes entwined with his designated infrastructures and a bodily appearance that is isomorphic yet disposable. The self disappears just enough to maintain the essential operative existence of the character at the expense of the inner self, the feelings – or lack thereof – that punctuate the saga's development with plot twists sustained by unexpected sprouts of love, hate, and solitude.

With every fracture of the norm, the empire reinforces its temporal dimension by means of deferral; either because there is always an heir to be born or a messiah to return. Jodorowsky is precise at rendering every Metabaron as the cardinal expression of the empire; an individual without selfhood nor boundaries, with the capacity to leap from human to non-human modes of reality, or to disappear from the scene leaving behind a hologram with the same prerogatives as oneself. The medium in which all these operations occur is an allegorical time that conflates polarized entities under the rubric of a pre-existent fate whose weight is so pervasive that any secession from the rule still leaves room for a messianic return. In this sense, the last Metabaron, No Name, acts as the emblem of Jodorowsky's allegory by reuniting antagonistic realities that are necessary for the empire to exist. The one that erases himself from its lineage, the one that remembers the feeling of love and disappears into deep space, the one that recalls his humanity by means of love, is yet to be the promise of a new story to be told.

NOTES

1. Y. Molina-Gavilan, A. Bell, M. A. Fernandez-Delgado, M. E. Ginway, L. Pestarini, and J. C. Toledano, "Chronology of Latin American Science Fiction, 1775–2005," *Science Fiction Studies*, vol. 34, no. 3, On Latin American SF (November 2007), 373.

2. R. Neustadt, "Alejandro Jodorowsky: Reiterating Chaos, Rattling the Cage of Representation," *Chasqui*, vol. 26, no. 1 (May 1997), 204. My translation. "(. . .) burlar el aburrimiento del surrealismo (. . .) de incorporar elementos despreciados por el surrealismo."

3. R. Neustadt, "Las prerrogativas de la imaginación: Una conversación con Alejandro Jodorowsky," *Confluencia*, vol. 11, no. 2 (Spring 1996), 209. My translation. "Para mi, mis últimos comics son películas. Si no los puedo hacer en cine, los hago en comics. Yo soy como una rebelión, ¿entiendes? Si en cine no me dejan, yo tengo el poder individual de hacer comics."

4. For the purposes of this argument, I will focus on the first eight volumes of the series, to the detriment of later published series: Charest and Janjetov 2008, Pastoras and Giménez 2015, Frissen, Secher, and Henrichon 2015.

5. G. Deleuze, "Having an Idea in Cinema" in *Deleuze and Guattari: New Mappings in Politics, Philosophy and Culture*, eds. Eleanor Kaufman and Kevin Jon Heller (Minneapolis: University of Minnesota Press, 1998), 15.

6. T. García, *Dr Strange: A Hero of the Mind*, trans. Robin Mackay (Urbanomic/Documents, 2016), https://www.urbanomic.com/document/doctor-strange/

7. D. Church, "The Doors of Reception: Notes Toward a Psychedelic Film Investigation," *Senses of Cinema*, no. 87 (June 2018), https://www.sensesofcinema.com/2018/feature-articles/the-doors-of-reception-notes-toward-a-psychedelic-film-investigation/

8. H. Benshoff, "The Short-Lived Life of the Hollywood LSD Film," *The Velvet Light Trap*, no. 47 (Spring 2001), 31.

9. Benshoff, "The Short-Lived Life of the Hollywood LSD Film," 37.

10. A. Jodorowsky, *El Topo: A Book of the Film by Alexandro Jodorowsky*, ed. Ross Firestone (New York: Douglas/Links, 1971), 97.

11. D. Fleming, "Head Cinema as Body without Organs: On Jodorowsky's Bitter Pill Films and Their Spinozian Parallels" in *Unbecoming Cinema: Unsettling Encounters with Ethical Event Films* (Bristol: Intellect, 2017), 126.

12. W. Grady, "For a Few Comic Strips More: Reinterpreting the Spaghetti Western through the Comic Book" in *Spaghetti Westerns at the Crossroads: Studies in Relocation, Transition and Appropriation*, ed. William Fischer (Edinburgh: Edinburgh University Press, 2016), 215.

13. Grady, "For a Few Comic Strips More," 216.

14. Jodorowsky and Giménez, *The Metabarons*, vol. 6. Doña Vicenta Gabriela de Rokha (Los Angeles, CA: Humanoids, 2011), 20.

15. Grady, "For a Few Comic Strips More," 216.

16. Jodorowsky and Giménez, *The Metabarons*, vol. 7. Aghora (Los Angeles, CA: Humanoids, 2011), 19.

17. Jodorowsky and Giménez, *The Metabarons*, vol. 3, Aghnar (Los Angeles, CA: Humanoids, 2011), 49.

18. A. Cascarino, "Les Méta-Barons, des cyborgs subversifs?" *ReS Futurae*, no. 14 (2019), https://doi.org/10.4000/resf.3776
19. D. Haraway, *A Cyborg Manifesto. Science, Technology and Socialist-Feminism in the Late Twentieth Century* (Minneapolis: University of Minnesota Press, 2016), 8.
20. "Jodorowsky both asserts and deconstructs the notions of difference and individuality (. . .) he narrates a heterogeneous world in which the notion of 'normality' does not exist." (Neustadt, "Alejandro Jodorowsky: Reiterating Chaos, Rattling the Cage of Representation," 73). If so, one might only wonder why there are recursive characters – such as Jodorowsky himself and his offspring – as protagonists in most of his films. It is worthy inquiring also about the pervasive physical similitude of *The Caste*'s protagonists. In this regard, "majority" predates "normality," and Jodorowsky does not elude the former.
21. "I consider the theatre in Mexico definitively dead. The only way to revive it would be for theatre people to let themselves be jailed, to provoke scandals, as I did six years ago." S. Guzik, "A Mass Changes Me More. An Interview with Alexandro Jodorowsky," *The Drama Review*: TDR, vol. 14, no. 2, Latin American Theater (Winter 1970), 71.
22. J. Moctezuma, R. Viskin, M. Rosemberg, S. Rosemberg, and A. Jodorowsky, Audio Commentary by Alejandro Jodorowsky. *Fando y Lis* [Blu-ray] (Available from ABKCO Music & Records, New York City, 2020). 0'0"–5'0". Transcription is mine.
23. See Huberman for a converse standpoint: "Beyond Exotic: Jewish Mysticism and the Supernatural in the Works of Alejandro Jodorowsky" in *Latin American Jewish Cultural Production*, ed. David W. Foster (Nashville, TN: Vanderbilt University Press, 2019), 55. "To some, Jodorowsky's fascination with Hasidim, Kabbalah, dibbuks, circus attractions, and armless saints may resemble the Orientalist gaze of empire and its selfish love of the freak-show. But that first impression will fade upon recognition of Jodorowsky's deep, perhaps radical investment in difference as a means to break through the quagmires of Western reason and its discontents." I contend that, although Huberman's argument might be valid within the analysis of Jodorowsky's relationship to Jewish mysticism and representations of the sacred, it does not suffice to clarify his selection criteria regarding characters.
24. This example is one of many in which Jodorowsky extrapolates private fantasies – such as his love for monsters – into generalizing statements. The pattern can be found elsewhere: "For example, I have never been raped. I have been told that a political prisoner was raped in jail; I thought that perhaps it would do him good (. . .) Sometimes I think it would be good if they raped me, if four or five queers fucked me so that I would lose this personality" (Guzik, "A Mass Changes Me More. An Interview with Alexandro Jodorowsky," 74). My aim here is less to analyze Jodorowsky's public statements regarding other people than how such ideas shape his characters' conceptual design.
25. Cascarino, "Les Méta-Barons, des cyborgs subversifs?" My translation. "(. . .) se mesure donc non seulement à la qualité des motifs qui le composent mais surtout à leur hétérogénéité, chaque motif restant par ailleurs bien identifiable et différencié des autres."
26. D. Mellier, "Corps, technologies et appareils chez Alejandro Jodorowsky: les cycles de la Caste de Meta-barons et des technopères," *Captures, figures, théories et pratiques de l'imaginaire* (2009), http://revuecaptures.org/article-dune-publication/corps-technologies-et-appareils-chez-alejandro-jodorowsky
27. "If the body can be modified using cybernetic implants, these modifications seem to have little impact on the identity of the individual, which would be located entirely within his brain (the brain of Steelhead having been moved in his torso) (. . .) Thus, the hybridity of the Meta-Barons' bodies does not seem to significantly alter their identity, and Steelhead changes bodies several times without altering his personality. The hybridity of bodies staged in 'La Caste des Méta-Barons' does not therefore call into question the dualisms but is satisfied with their concatenation." (Cascarino, "Les Méta-Barons, des

cyborgs subversifs?"). My translation. "si le corps peut être modifié à l'aide d'implants cybernétiques, ces modifications semblent n'avoir que peu d'impact sur l'identité de l'individu, qui se situerait entièrement au sein de son cerveau (le cerveau de Tête d'Acier ayant été déplacé dans son torse) (. . .) Ainsi, l'hybridité des corps des Méta-Barons ne semble pas modifier profondément leur identité, et Tête d'Acier change d'ailleurs plusieurs fois de corps sans que sa personnalité en soit altérée pour autant. L'hybridité des corps mise en scène dans 'La Caste des Méta-Barons' n'entraîne donc pas de remise en cause des dualismes mais se contente de leur concaténation." Although the case pointed out by Cascarino seems unequivocal – yet we pay heed to the memoryless Steelhead shifting its mood after exchanging cerebral waves with No Name – I believe it does not apply to all the members of the dynasty.

28. Jodorowsky and Giménez, *The Metabarons*, vol. 1, Othon (Los Angeles, CA: Humanoids, 2011), 15.

29. Jodorowsky and Giménez, *The Metabarons*, vol. 8, No Name (Los Angeles, CA: Humanoids, 2011), 66.

30. My translation. "Celle-ci suppose une redéfinition des rapports de l'identité et de l'altérité, du bio et du mécanique, de l'humain et du matériel, du corps et de la conscience du corps." (Mellier, "Corps, technologies et appareils chez Alejandro Jodorowsky: les cycles de la Caste de Meta-barons et des technopères," 2019).

31. Jodorowsky and Giménez, *The Metabarons*, vol. 1, 57.

32. For example, Honorata instructing combat techniques to his son Aghnar – which is the prerogative of men (Jodorowsky and Giménez, *The Metabarons*, vol. 2, Honorata [Los Angeles, CA: Humanoids, 2011]), or the aforementioned duo Oda-Honorata in the fourth volume.

33. My translation. "(. . .) seuls les hommes peuvent perpétuer la Caste et devenir Méta-Barons (. . .) Aghora est donc masculin: il est Le Père-Mère et non La Mère-Père, et pour le prouver, il modifie d'ailleurs son corps en se cautérisant la poitrine. Malgré toutes les transformations corporelles que subissent les Méta-Barons au fil de ces huit albums, une constante demeure: ce sont tous des hommes. Les femmes de leur côté sont objets de désir des hommes. Nécessairement belles, leur valeur est liée à leur corps de chair et à sa sexualisation exagérée par le trait de Gimenez. Si la mutilation du corps masculin peut être suivie de l'ajout de prothèses mécaniques et augmenter alors la puissance et la valeur de ce corps, la mutilation du corps féminin le dévalorise nécessairement en diminuant sa beauté et entraîne alors, à courte échéance, la destruction de ce corps." (Cascarino, "Les Méta-Barons, des cyborgs subversifs?")

34. The secret of the Metabarons' former wealth and the origin of their misfortunes resides in the interior of their native planet Mármola in the form of epiphyte, a kind of stone resin that causes antigravity by contact. After conducting negotiations with the imperial representatives of the galaxy, an agreement is made by which the Castaka will obtain immense commercial benefits from the exploitation of this miraculous substance, giving rise to a fortune that will increase as the story progresses thanks to the inimitable profile that the Castaka possesses as interplanetary soldiers of fortune.

35. "More generally, it can be noted that all Meta-Barons inherit their name only through a speech effect. It is not their biological and genetic lineage that makes them Meta-Barons, but their appointment." Cascarino, "Les Méta-Barons, des cyborgs subversifs?" my translation. "Plus généralement, on peut noter que tous les Méta-Barons n'héritent de leur nom que par un effet de discours. Ce n'est pas leur filiation biologique et génétique qui fait d'eux des Méta-Barons mais leur nomination."

36. M. Hardt and T. Negri, *Empire* (Cambridge, MA and London: Harvard University Press, 2000), 27. The body of the last Metabaron, composed largely of robotic elements, has a life timespan of 30,000 years. (Jodorowsky and Giménez, *The Metabarons*, vol. 8, 50.)

37. "[Jodorowsky] not only writes, produces and directs films, but has also been responsible for composing the music, acting and even fathering some of their main actors, their children." Neustadt, "Las prerrogativas de la imaginación: Una conversación con Alejandro Jodorowsky," 203, my translation. "[Jodorowsky] no solo escribe, produce y dirige películas, sino que también ha sido responsable de componer la música, actuar e incluso engendrar a algunos de sus actores principales, sus hijos."

38. D. Saavedra Fajardo, "Idea de un principe politico christiano: rapresentada en cien empresas" (Milan, 1642), 103.

39. Saavedra Fajardo, "Idea de un principe politico christiano: rapresentada en cien empresas," 104.

40. Jodorowsky and Giménez, *The Metabarons*, vol. 7, 67.

41. Hardt and Negri, *Empire*, xiv.

42. A hint that would expose Hardt and Negri's thesis of the imperial mode of expression as police expression: "The juridical power to rule over the exception and the capacity to deploy police force are thus two initial coordinates that define the imperial model of authority" (17).

43. Jodorowsky and Giménez, *The Metabarons*, vol. 2, 9.

44. Jodorowsky and Giménez, *The Metabarons*, vol. 6, 9–11.

45. W. Benjamin, *The Origin of German Tragic Drama* (London and New York: Verso, 2003), 35.

46. Benjamin, *The Origin of German Tragic Drama*, 132.

47. J. Bourg, "Nature and the Irruptive Violence of History," *History and Theory*, vol. 55, no. 4, Words, Things, and Beyond: Foucault's *Les mots et les choses* at 50 (December 2016), 103.

48. Jodorowsky and Giménez, *The Metabarons*, vol. 4, Oda (Los Angeles, CA: Humanoids, 2011), 12.

49. Bourg, "Nature and the Irruptive Violence of History," 97.

50. Bourg, "Nature and the Irruptive Violence of History," 97.

51. Mellier, "Corps, technologies et appareils chez Alejandro Jodorowsky: les cycles de la Caste de Meta-barons et des technopères."

52. Jodorowsky, *The Spiritual Journey of Alejandro Jodorowsky. The Creator of El Topo*, trans. by Joseph Rowe (Rochester, VT: Park Street Press, 2005), 154.

53. See B. Bishop, "Inside the Greatest Sci-Fi Films Never Made: Before 'Star Wars' and 'Alien,' there was Alejandro Jodorowsky's 'Dune,'" *The Verge*, March 27, 2014, 3.10 p.m. EDT. https://www.theverge.com/2014/3/27/5554126/jodorowskys-dune-interview-greatest-sci-fi-film-never-made. Also M. Gemesi, "Famous Sci-fi Movies Influenced by Jodorowsky's Dune," *Taste of Cinema*, posted on August 14, 2015, http://www.tasteofcinema.com/2015/7-famous-sci-fi-movies-influenced-by-jodorowskys-dune/2/. More to the point: "According to Jodorowsky and Mœbius, specific images from the Dune story board (and the Incal) were appropriated in subsequent films. Roger Sabin notes that Ridley Scott's Blade Runner and The Empire Strikes Back, for example, employed the Dune storyboard in an 'unofficial capacity' (. . .) Sabin informs that Humanoides Associés (the Incal's publisher) refers to the influence in these films as 'homages' (. . .) It is worth noting that members of the team Jodorowsky had assembled for Dune (Mœbius, Dan O'Bannon, Chris Foss and H. R. Giger) later worked together on Ridley Scott's film version of Alien as well as Blade Runner and Star Wars." (Neustadt, "Alejandro Jodorowsky: Reiterating Chaos, Rattling the Cage of Representation," 60).

54. Neustadt, "Las prerrogativas de la imaginación: Una conversación con Alejandro Jodorowsky," 209–210.

CHAPTER 12

Alejandro Jodorowsky, the Unmade, and *The Sons of El Topo*

Matthew Melia

INTRODUCTION: JODOROWSKY AND THE UNMADE

Elsewhere, in a previous text, I explored the ways in which Alejandro Jodorowsky's infamous cult western *El Topo* (1971) and its use of landscape may be critically understood through the lens of the post-war European avant-garde and the "Theatre of the Absurd" as much as through the countercultural milieu of the late 1960s and early 1970s.[1] This chapter serves as a "sequel" of sorts to that chapter by focusing on Jodorowsky's own unmade (as a film) follow up, *The Sons of El Topo*, which was published in comic book/graphic novel form by BOOM! Studios in 2018. This chapter aims to form part of a wider critical engagement with the phenomenon of the unmade and abandoned project, which has been spearheaded by James Fenwick, Kieron Foster, and David Eldridge in their edited collection *Shadow Cinema: The Historical and Production Contexts of Unmade Films* (Bloomsbury, 2020). In the introduction to their book, Foster and Fenwick reference Dan North's *Sights Unseen: Unfinished British Films* as a pioneering text in the study of the unmade and "an attempt to understand the underlying contexts as to why so many film projects fail rather than succeed."[2] They clarify their own approach:

> Our criteria for evaluating what actually constitutes unmade cinema consciously remains as loose as that described by North, in ranging across unfinished screenplays, unmade screenplays, aborted films or fleeting ideas "discarded at the back of an envelope stage."[3]

Jodorowsky is part of a small group of auteurist directors (others include both Stanley Kubrick and Ken Russell) whose career is defined almost as much by the films they didn't make as by those they did. Jodorowsky is, of course, responsible for one of the "Holy Grails" of unmade cinema – his adaptation of Frank Herbert's epic 1965 science fiction novel *Dune*. With the recent release of Denis Villeneuve's 2021 adaptation of Herbert's novel, cultural and critical attention has turned not only to recuperating David Lynch's much maligned (and disowned by the director) 1984 adaptation of the film, but also to Jodorowsky's unmade film, what it and its production *would have been like*. If Fenwick and Foster's book is interested in how lost projects are reclaimed in other ways and re-emerge in other forms (in my own chapter in that book I note, for instance, how Ken Russell's lost projects were never really lost but repurposed in other ways across his career, becoming the raw materials for later projects),[4] then Jodorowsky's own unmade projects are also exemplary of this trend. *Dune* for instance finds a new form not in another film version but in the 2013 documentary *Jodorowsky's Dune* (dir. Frank Pavich) in which the key concept, design ideas, and conceptualizations are distilled within the documentary format. This perhaps is as close as Jodorowsky's *Dune* will come to fruition. Through interviews with the director, access to the design books etc., the documentary allows us to interpret and imagine the final look and design of a film which does not exist. In the documentary, Jodorowsky ruminates gleefully on the potential casting of Orson Welles as the grotesque and corpulent Baron Harkonnen – an actor so large he "ate his movies." Jodorowsky comments on Welles's own habit of abandoning projects and leaving a trail of unmade films, conferring a layer of meta-textuality upon this particular abandoned masterpiece.

This fits in with the methodology of exploring "the unmade" – which to a large extent depends on an interpretation hypothesis constructed from raw archival material and some degree of speculation, hypothesis, and *what ifs?* Investigating and piecing together "the unmade" is to ponder an alternate universe or history of film. While archival approaches are crucial in uncovering and visualizing such projects, conjecture and speculation are also, at least, a part of the same process.

Jodorowsky's ambitious project would have used Pink Floyd for the soundtrack, and would have starred not only Orson Welles but also Salvador Dalí, as well as employing H. R. Giger for its set design. In an online article for *Inverse*, Ryan Britt proposes that it was in fact a "good thing" the film never got made, not only for avoiding fanboy concerns and tantrums over potential changes made to Herbert's story, but for the knock-on effect that it might have had on later science fiction films (would Giger have gone on to design the Xenomorph for *Alien*, for instance?).[5] This is an opinion backed up in the press and in reviews of the *Dune* documentary. Screen International, for instance, notes that:

> Danish director Nicolas Winding Refn (who made *Drive*) recalls being at Jodorowsky's house and being asked if he wanted to see *Dune*.

He showed him the legendary "Dune book," which compiles the script and drawings, and talked him through the story. "If he had have made it, then Dune would have been the first epic film of that nature and not Star Wars," said Refn. "I believe deep down that the people in America didn't make the film because they were afraid of him. Afraid of his mind and what he was going to do with them. People were scared."[6]

Certainly, in the pantheon of the unmade, *Dune* is on a par with Kubrick's equally ambitious and abandoned *Napoleon* project. Like Jodorowsky's film, Kubrick's unmade labor of love exists outside of its original format in the vast amount of pre-production material housed at University of the Arts, London, London College of Communication, the Stanley Kubrick Archive, and at Kubrick's estate in Hertfordshire, UK. Much of this material has been condensed into an expansive published collection published by Taschen (while a mooted HBO television adaptation from the material waits in the wings seemingly indefinitely).[7] Such projects may not exist as a tangible product but they are mythologized as part of cinema folklore and retain a cultural presence despite their absence and non-existence – much of this myth of their myth residing in the folkloric identity and personas of their tempestuous auteurist creators. Both *Dune* and *Napoleon* are epic monuments of unmade Western cinema and of glorious failure (Western cinema's great unmade "White Whales"). They are embedded within its folklore and mythology – the product of two of its most enigmatic auteurs. The same, perhaps, cannot be said for *The Sons of El Topo*. This chapter aims to offer a critical analysis of the "un-production" history of Jodorowsky's unmade sequel, and to consider the reasons for its failure as a project. It will present a close reading of the comic book text(s) and consider the thematic and aesthetic legacy of *El Topo* as it is translated into a different media form, one which Jodorowsky started working with in the 1960s and has increasingly become associated with since the 1990s.

ALEJANDRO JODOROWSKY, COMICS, *ABELCAIN*, AND *THE SONS OF EL TOPO*

The cultural interest surrounding *Dune* has, to some extent, tended to obscure or divert interest away Jodorowsky's other "lost" project, *The Sons of El Topo*. Its (un)production history is fragmentary and disparate and only Ben Cobb in his book *Anarchy and Alchemy: The Films of Alejandro Jodorowsky*[8] has offered any real insight (in print) into the background of this project, although Jodorowsky himself has discussed it in interviews. That *The Sons of El Topo* was a sequel to a cult hit from the early 1970s whose fame (and notoriety) is primarily relegated to the Cult/Jodorowsky cognoscenti is of course one potential reason for its relative obscurity. Interest around *Dune* is augmented by other fandoms and interested parties – science fiction fans for instance for whom Frank Herbert's novels form a sacred and foundational text; and those with an interest in the work of H. R. Giger as well. *Dune*'s appeal lies not only in Jodorowsky but in its status as a multi-authored text and its canonical status within the science fiction genre. *The Sons of El Topo* has no such foundations. Secondly, *El Topo*'s problematic and notorious sexual politics are extended into *The Sons of El Topo* (as I will explore in greater detail below) and may be also accountable for its lack of cultural visibility, especially in the #MeToo age where there is (rightly) a greater awareness surrounding such issues and in which the cultural thermometer is much more sensitive to issues of sexual violence and exploitation post-Harvey Weinstein. Jodorowsky has, as well, infamously put himself in the way of such scrutiny with statements made around his actions during the filming of *El Topo*. In *El Topo: Book of the Film*, he claimed in order to achieve authenticity during the scene in which El Topo rapes his companion (Mara Lorenzio) that "After she had hit me long enough and hard enough to tire her, I said, 'Now it's my turn. Roll the cameras.' And I really . . . I really . . . I really raped her. And she screamed. Then she told me that she had been raped before [. . .] You see, for me the character is frigid until El Topo rapes her, and she has an orgasm."[9]

He later claimed he had fabricated this statement, and, provocatively, to be a feminist. Still, it is interesting to note (and perhaps also an indicator of changes in the industry) how given that these statements were made in 1972, a year after the film was released, it took until 2017 when the Museo del Barrio in New York cancelled an exhibition of his work (coinciding with the emergence of the #MeToo movement), for this statement to be taken seriously.

Furthermore, at one point in the extended development of the project both actor Johnny Depp and goth rocker Marilyn Manson (a close personal friend of Jodorowsky) were attached to star, both of whom have had and are currently undergoing their own #MeToo moments. Incidents involving these celebrities come after the unmade film's genesis, but as part of the historical matrix of its production would no doubt perpetuate its relative obscurity in the annals of the unmade.

If *Sons of El Topo* has been somewhat hidden under the weight of both his earlier great unmade masterpiece *Dune* and potentially also by the weight of Jodorowsky's problematic statements and the surrounding perception of his sexual politics in the era of #MeToo, it has also been buried under the cultural weight of its parent film, which originated (so it has been claimed by cult critics like Jonathan Rosenbaum) the tradition of the midnight movie at the Elgin Theater in New York in 1971. It is the "prototypical cult film," and as Roger Greenspun has noted "During its months of midnight screenings at

the Elgin, Alejandro Jodorowsky's *El Topo* became a secret rite of some importance in New York City."[10] The film (as I have argued previously) engaged
a range of "countercultural" ideologies, including both that of the European
post-war avant-garde and that of the American counterculture of the 1970s. It
famously struck a chord with John Lennon and Yoko Ono, for instance, who
instructed manager Allen Klein to give Jodorowsky a million dollars for whatever he wanted to do next. This turned out to be *The Holy Mountain* (1973) – a
business arrangement which came to a head after Jodorowsky refused to direct
The Story of O for Klein who, in retaliation, took both *El Topo* and *The Holy
Mountain* out of circulation. As Xan Brooks noted in his article for *The Guardian*, "I'm the Last Crazy Artist,"

> Matters reached a head when the director bailed out of Klein's next
> project, The Story of O. "I did not want to make a sexual film, because
> I am a feminist. So Klein says, 'OK, if you don't want to make this pic-
> ture I will take your other pictures and no one will ever see them again'.
> And that's what he did. He took all the copies and he retired them."
> For three decades, the films existed only as poor-quality bootlegs, which
> Jodorowsky would collect and circulate among his nearest and dearest.[11]

Jodorowsky's cult identity as a director and that of his films as cult products
were exacerbated by Klein's withholding of their distribution and circulation.
While much has been written (for better or worse) about Jodorowsky's seminal
film, there has been considerably less attention paid to his unmade sequel, *The
Sons of El Topo*, a project which during the course of its "development" (such
as it was) underwent numerous variations in form and style. It is part of a ros-
ter of unmade films other than *Dune* which have contributed to its director's
auteur status which itself was defined in part by his penchant for collaboration.

The Sons of El Topo finally emerged in 2020 in graphic novel format. Stuck
in development limbo since its inception, the project was forced to adapt into
another form. Comparisons may be made here with the British director and
provocateur Ken Russell. Throughout the last decade of Russell's life financing was increasingly difficult to come by for many of his film projects. During
the last ten years of his life Russell instead turned to making films himself, at
home and in his garden: knowing and self-aware DIY projects released online
and filmed on digital video as a way of circumnavigating the barriers presented to him by the British film industry. In his introduction to the first
volume of *Sons of El Topo*, Jodorowsky writes that in the wake of the cult
success of *El Topo*,

> I wrote a screenplay for *Sons of El Topo* and tried to get it made. Every
> studio in Hollywood looked at me like I was an Alien from outerspace,

and turned me down. A few producers, aficionados, tried their best to help me out, but since film is the most expensive of the arts, none of them managed to scrape together the necessary funds. Years went by, but my dream stubbornly refused to go away. One day, I said to myself, "if I can't shoot my screenplay, maybe I can make a comic out of it." I waited another few years, never losing faith until in 2016 I'm at José Ladrönn the ideal artist to make not so much the usual graphic novel as a "comic book film," every page of which is divided into three widescreen panels so reader-viewers feel like they're watching a movie [. . .] there is no such thing as failure – only new paths opening up.[12]

As with Russell, necessity seems to have been the mother of invention and a factor in adapting *The Sons of El Topo* within the format of the graphic novel. Here we may return to the phenomenon of the unmade film which frequently (and certainly in Russell's case) emerges in a different form elsewhere. Jodorowsky had, in fact, been working within the comic book format since the 1960s when he was living in Mexico City. His first venture into the format was in 1966 with the science fiction *Anibal 5* (illustrated my Manuel Moro), and as Lambiek Comiclopedia reminds us "He in turn drew his own comics, such as the weekly 'Fabulas Panicas' featured in the Mexican magazine *El Heraldo de Mexico*, between 1967 and 1973."[13] As Daniel Kalder indicates in his article "Alejandro Jodorowsky's Dance on the Edge of Meaning," Jodorowsky turned again to the format after the collapse of *Dune* due to a lack of funding. He states "Jodorowsky got into comics following the collapse of his *Dune* film adaptation, which was to feature the talents of French comics artist Jean 'Mœbius' Giraud, *Alien* designer HR Giger, Pink Floyd, Salvador Dali and many others."[14] Writing in 2011, as the Marvel Cinematic Universe was gathering steam, Kalder notes the growing relationship between comic book and film (now ubiquitous) and refers to Jodorowsky as "the greatest traveler between these two realms," and that despite working within the medium for over thirty years, his contribution to comic book culture has gone uncommented on. In another example of the unmade finding a new form elsewhere, Jodorowsky retooled the production designs and research which had gone into *Dune* into his dystopian science fiction graphic novel series *The Incal*. He writes:

[The series] begins as a profane collision of hardboiled SF noir and Fritz Lang's Metropolis, before mutating into a cosmic quest/spiritual voyage as the reluctant hero John DiFool ventures across the universe copulating with aliens, doing battle with "technopopes," persuading the entire universe to take a nice nap, and finally meeting a godlike being called ORH. Toss in a berserk overload of sex and violence, dissolving bodies, symbols, archetypes, metaphysics and a heavy influence from the tarot and you may have a vague inkling of what goes on in The Incal. You won't be surprised to hear that the narrative spirals completely out of control at the end before crash landing in a swamp of impenetrable, New Age blather.[15]

Working predominantly within a science fiction mode, Jodorowsky's so-called "Jodoverse" which began The Incal series in 1981 (and which finished in 2014), with interconnected comic series The Metabarons (1992–2019) and The Technopriests (1998–2006), was way of extending and reframing his cinematic concerns with spirituality, the Tarot, symbology, and transgressive imagery. The Sons of El Topo sits outside of this mythology not only generically but it is also unique in that, rather than being a self-contained comic book mythology, it is one which extends across media from his cinematic work, beginning immediately from the exact point at which El Topo ends.

Just as the graphic novel begins so Sons of El Topo has its origins almost immediately in the wake of the release of the original film when the idea was formed. As Ben Cobb has noted,

> After the release of El Topo in 1970, Jodorowsky remarked [on a potential sequel] "In a few years, I should make a new film . . . Sons of El Topo or The Return of El Topo. Yes about what happens to his son and the little dwarf and the baby." Over the years, this idea developed into a project based around El Topo's sons. Abel and Cain [. . .] The film went through various incarnations with, at different stages, Johnny Depp and Marilyn Manson both attached to star. A press release was even issued in 1997 announcing a spring start date for production. It never happened.[16]

These titles are worth noting as they locate the film referentially within the overlapping spheres of both the European and American western, borrowing from the idioms and calling to mind such titles as The Sons of Katie Elder (dir. Henry Hathaway, 1965), Son of the Renegade (dir. Reg Browne, 1953), or Return of Django (Osvaldo Civirani, 1967). As I have previously argued, El Topo "displaces" the western, interrogating and self referentially subverting its genre conventions especially in the later sequence in which "we find a parody of a wild west town peopled by what Foster Hirsch calls 'Grotesque parodies of acquisitive, rapacious, hypocritical capitalists.'"[17] The Sons of El Topo again self referentially locates itself within the western genre and occupies the same arid, bleak, and (this time) post-apocalyptic landscape as its cinematic forebear. Returning briefly to Jodorowsky's earlier introductory statement regarding the cinematic nature of the graphic novel, although it must be clarified that while each page does not necessarily follow such a pattern (frequently these "widescreen" panels are subdivided into triptychs or rearranged across the page), the intentionality remains to present the story in the expansive style of both the European, Mexican, and American studio western – a style that renders the story in a sort of comic book Panavision or Cinerama.

Here I would like here to clarify the timeline of the project's gestation according to the sources available. The project was first mooted in the aftermath of the release of *El Topo* by Jodorowsky himself who stated his plans for a follow up: "In a few years I should make a new film . . . *Son of El Topo* or *The Return of El Topo*. Yes. About what happens to his son and the little dwarf and the Baby."[18] According to Ben Cobb (the only person to have written at any great length on the production history of Jodorowsky's unmade film), Jodorowsky was forced to "change the title of the film to *Abelcain* and the central characters name to *El Topo*"[19] after the fallout with Klein over copywrite issues. The script itself was not fully developed until some years later. An article in *Cinefantastique* from "El Topo Returns" suggests that Jodorowsky had been working on the (now extensive) script since the 1970s and had by the end of the 1980s completed writing the long awaited follow-up. The article notes that by now the project's title changed from *Abelcain* to *Sons of El Topo*. It adds:

> Involved in producing the film is Charles Lippincot, whose Creative Movie Marketing recently completed NIGHT LIFE, a horror/comedy [. . .] Lippincot called Jodorowsky's script a "classic Cain and Able story with lots of religious symbolism attached to it." Set in the same idiom as surreal desert as EL TOPO, Jodorowsky will again appear as the title character, now evolved into a god-like being. Plans call for casting two of the directors six sons as the offspring of the title.[20]

The resurgence of interest in the potential project in the late 1980s (especially from Jodorowsky) had come off the back of the success of *Santa Sangre* (1989), Jodorowsky's carnivalesque amputee serial killer film, at the Cannes Film Festival where it had been nominated for the Un Certain Regard award (the film had had a run of nominations at various festivals across Europe and the U.S.). Jodorowsky's stock was riding high during the period which had led to increased work on the script and which, as reported in *Cinefantastique*, was (according to Lippincot) "Way too long" and in need of "paring down."[21] However, if Jodorowsky's oeuvre to date had appealed to a set of film cultures more attuned to the transgressive, its appeal was largely lost on Hollywood, causing Lippincot to look elsewhere for funding for *Sons of El Topo*. According to *Cinefantastique*, Lippincot was "looking to Europe and Japan for production funds because – despite the smash success of SANTA SANGRE at the Cannes film festival – Hollywood just doesn't understand Jodorowsky."[22]

The project re-emerged again in the 1990s where according to early publicity for the film, shooting was finally scheduled to begin in the spring of 1997, a full twenty-six years after the project was first mooted. In the intervening years, the project had at various points found its way onto the slate but had never come as close to production. The film was to be produced by Alfonso Arau (who had appeared as one of the trinity of gunslingers in *El Topo*), casting both Johnny Depp and Marilyn Manson as the two central brothers. Manson, a friend of Jodorowsky's, was also, according to Ben Cobb, lined up to star in another potential project, *King Shot*. According to Cobb:

> In 2003 Jodorowsky began work on a different film, to be his last. The story of *King Shot* is based around a "casino in the middle of the desert where gangsters play in a contest with fake shots. There comes one who Is not honest. That is one part of the story, not all. There also comes a young gangster who is on the run [having] stolen diamonds. Back in the desert, scientists have found an enormous prehistoric bone. Then they discover bones everywhere in the desert. A Big enormous hand. It is like *King Kong*.[23]

In Jodorowsky's description of *King Shot* (as recounted by Cobb), he claims the story would be from the perspective of a beetle and that Marilyn Manson would star as a "beautiful woman." Again (and perhaps unsurprisingly given the disparate nature of the story) funding for the project did not happen.

The publicity materials for *The Sons of El Topo*, which included a mock-up poster for the film, pitched the project as "*The Sons of El Topo* recalls *Mad Max* and *the Road Warrior*. Outrageous adventure, explosive imaginary, sensual brutality and tremendous heart . . . *The Sons of El Topo* is destined to become the classic from Jodorowsky." The film climate and culture of the late 1980s to the mid-to-late 1990s perhaps provided the opportunity for the project to become a reality with the emergence of a new independent American film spirit and milieu – a (largely male) collection of young, independent American film directors working outside of the prevailing Hollywood system (albeit financed largely by Miramax and the Weinstein company) and who looked to earlier pioneering independent film auteurs as guiding figures. Not only did the cultural climate of independent filmmaking provide fertile ground for auteurist and transgressive cinematic visions (e.g. Larry Clark or Harmony Korine), in many ways this was a new countercultural cinematic movement that crossed over to the mainstream in figures like Quentin Tarantino. While mainstream Hollywood cinema was recuperating the studio western in the shape of films like *Dances With Wolves* (dir. Kevin Costner, 1990), *Legends of the Fall* (dir. Edward Zwick, 1995) or *Wyatt Earp* (dir. Lawrence Kasdan, 1994), a range of independent approaches to the western (or western-inflected film) appeared, such as *El Mariachi* (dir. Robert Rodriguez, 1992), *Wild Bill* (dir. Walter Hill, 1994), or *Dead Man* (dir. Jim Jarmusch, 1995). These were not just "revisionist westerns," they were revising the revisionist, acid or anti-westerns which had proliferated throughout 1970s independent cinema, and of which, of course, Jodorowsky and *El Topo* had contributed to the evolution. Johnny Depp had previously starred in *Dead Man*, the foremost of the resurgent "Acid Westerns" (a genre Jodorowsky helped invent), a role which no doubt influenced the decision to cast him in *The Sons of El Topo*. Jodorowsky's reputation as the consummate independent and transgressive auteur positions him as the spiritual figurehead of the milieu. Ben Cobb has noted:

> Jodorowsky has been hip Hollywood's inspiration for decades. Dennis Hopper, while struggling in the cutting room with his troubled *Easy Rider* follow-up *The Last Movie*, called Jodorowsky in to re-edit. Jack Nicholson and Peter Fonda got high to *El Topo*. John Lennon crusaded for him. Tim Burton loves him and Johnny Depp signed up to star in his abandoned *El Topo* sequel. He even officiated at the wedding of close friend Marilyn Manson and Dita Von Teese dressed as the Alchemist from *The Holy Mountain*.[24]

But he adds:

> In an industry where "independent" has become a meaningless brand, Jodorowsky was out there by himself. He is a true maverick: working, talking and thinking outside the system. Forget the '90s crop of Sundance Kids (Kevin Smith, Quentin Tarantino, Steven Soderbergh et al.); their forerunners, Hollywood bad-boys Hopper, Nicholson and Fonda; and even "indie" giants Coppola or Scorsese. They label themselves independent. Jodorowsky lives it. The sheer exuberance of his work makes today's cinema feel processed, bland and over-packaged.[25]

THE SONS OF EL TOPO — RETCONNING *EL TOPO*

In the existing critical literature surrounding the comic/film adaptative relationship, emphasis has tended to privilege the comic to film adaptation with much less, if any, attention paid to the transition from films to comics – or comics as an extension of an existing film universe. *The Sons of El Topo* was finally realized in comic book form in 2018, written by Jodorowsky and illustrated by Mexican comic artist José Ladrönn. Published in two parts, the second book, Volume 2, was published in 2019 – its ending setting up and anticipating a third, as yet unpublished, conclusion. Jodorowsky and Ladrönn present an expanding picaresque narrative – a journey taken by two brothers, Cain and Abel (the sons of El Topo) across a violent western-style post-apocalyptic landscape of violence and horror carrying the sainted and incorruptible body of Abel's mother to the grave of their father. One of the first things to note about the transition to this form of graphic storytelling is how it seems not only to have allowed Jodorowsky to extend the narrative of his 1970 film but also to revise it. *The Sons of El Topo* opens with an old man recounting the events of the story to a group of followers as they wend their way through an arid canyon.

Also on their way across the arid desert are a horde of costumed idolaters composed of many religions, unified by a love and desire not for "the saint" but for gold. The crowds are on their way to El Topo's grave – an island of several golden pillars which have emerged from the earth and which are surrounded by a moat of acid. It is the day of the anniversary of El Topo's "sainthood." If earlier publicity for the film had drawn comparisons with George Miller's *Mad Max* franchise, the images provided in the comic are redolent of the post-apocalyptic crowd scenes in Miller's *Mad Max: Fury Road* (2015) released three years prior to the comic. Miller's post-apocalyptic cinematic vision is particularly apparent in the depiction of costume and mask, particularly in the devil-skull masked antagonists in Volume 2.

Only the pure may cross to the island, and Jodorowsky and Ladrönn depict the dissolving in acid of one such impure follower who tries to bluff his way across. This device and opening gambit allows Jodorowsky to "retcon" the end of his 1970 film, in which after freeing the cripples and outcasts from their cave, El Topo (now a monk) immolates himself. The son he previously abandoned as a child and who has since become a monk now dons his father's signature costume from the first half of the film – the black leathers of the gunfighter – and rides off with his father's lover and her newborn son, his half-brother. As I have previously noted,

> At the film's finale, the now grown-up son of El Topo has rejected the spiritual vestments of the monk and has adopted the earlier dark costume of his father – the fetishistic black leather of the gunfighter. This provides a contrast to El Topo himself, who in the final movement has rejected such a costume in favor of the garb of a Buddhist monk.[26]

If the film ends in such an open way – with this new nuclear family riding off into the wastelands, then the comic rewrites this history turning El Topo, before his self-immolation, into "The Saint" a vengeful and transcendent spiritual entity who "was an outlaw who in throwing the doors to his heart open became a saint able to work the greatest of miracles"[27] and who "to punish those swine [the cultists from the film] The Saint set off a cataclysm that covered the land in an arid crust."[28] El Topo is, shortly thereafter, in a scene which would not seem amiss in a Marvel comic, depicted as a levitating god-like being who "to keep Cain from murdering his half-brother forbade one and all from speaking to him or looking on him under pain of death."[29] The foisting of a Cain and Abel narrative onto the end of the film's story forms part of this retconning, and Hijo, El Topo's son in the film (played by Jodorowsky's own son Brontis as a child, and by Robert John as a man) becomes Cain in the comic.

PROBLEMATIC SEXUAL POLITICS

Like its parent film, *The Sons of El Topo* balances both the sacred and transcendental and the profane and carnivalesque. Later, in book two, the picaresque narrative leads the two brothers Cain and Abel (both of whom are representative of the two halves of their father's persona: while Cain is depicted in the gunfighter's black leathers, Abel is depicted as the shaven headed, frocked monk his father becomes in the second half of the film), who are transferring the sanctified body of Abel's mother to the Holy Island, to become involved in the conflict between a Mexican army (whose General believes himself to be a dog) and a convent of men dressed as nuns. The graphic novel format also provides a wider palette and a canvas for Jodorowsky (whose own cinematic vision is filtered through the art of Ladrönn) to take his depictions of violence and especially sexual violence to new extremes. On two occasions, across books 1 and 2, Jodorowsky depicts the problematic images of its central anti-hero, Cain, tying up a female victim by her hair and graphically assaulting her, a woman who, in adhering to the instructions of The Saint (El Topo), refuses to acknowledge him. In another sequence he abandons a female follower to a gang rape. However, her virginity proves "too much" for her attackers (a religious community who subject her to "holy rape") who cannot penetrate her hymen (to the cost of their own genitals). In yet another sequence, Cain satiates his lust with a grotesquely obese woman. As has been noted by reviewers of the graphic novel,

> In one of the movie's more controversial scenes, the protagonist violently rapes a woman who falls in love with him as a result. (In a subsequent interview, Jodorowsky claimed this graphic onscreen attack was not simulated.) The apple doesn't fall far from the tree here, as in the graphic novel, Cain strings a total stranger up by her hair and takes her by force just to reinforce his own existence. In the era of #MeToo, audiences are understandably unwilling to root for a main character who's an unrepentant rapist.[30]

Given the more recent criticisms of both film and director, one might suggest that Jodorowsky's adoption of the comic format in realizing *The Sons of*

El Topo might be influenced by the post-Weinstein cultural climate as much as by the problems in securing funding (the two are probably also interconnected). Others have noted of the text, and have argued, supporting Jodorowsky's self-claims to "being a feminist," that its transgressive and outwardly problematic sexual politics are in fact intended as a critique of toxic masculinity:

> Ironically, the long-awaited sequel to *El Topo*, *The Sons of El Topo*, explores the corollary themes of the mistreatment of women within the second volume. The first pages display Cain allowing for the rape of a character to occur; however, men are unable to defile her. This appears to be a consistent thematic approach for El Topo. It's the idea of men believing themselves to be owed something for their acts of kindness [. . .] This narrative shows the obvious, yet subtle, ways men have problematic ills towards women. One brother, Cain, is outright misogynistic, calling women whores and ignoring their rape. The other brother, Abel, is portrayed to be some sort of saviour for women; however, he himself does this kindness out of a desire for them to reciprocate his feelings. In many ways, the hope is that this artist is passing along a better message to people, illustrating the dangers of toxic masculinity.[31]

DUALITY

The theme of duality and dualism underscores the two graphic novels indicated by the cover art: Volume 1, featuring a close-up image of Cain, and Volume 2, of Abel. Both are two halves of the original El Topo character, with the young Abel appearing as the more diminutive version of El Topo the monk. The comic book format allows both of these two sides to exist simultaneously, and for Jodorowsky to blur the boundaries between good and evil, morality and immorality, violence and pacifism, indicated by the evocative and western gothic image of Cain on the cover of book one and the meditative Zen-like image of Abel on book two. Within the scheme of the narrative Jodorowsky offers further biblical allusions, for example in the character of Lilith, the seductive lover of The General, stolen by Cain and presented as the antagonist in the second half of book two, and at one stage presenting Abel as David forced into combat by Lilith with a giant in order to reclaim his mother's body from the horde. When we first meet Abel he and his mother are working a children's puppet show in which death is pitted against love, underscoring the thematic concerns of Jodorowsky's narrative in a self-reflexive play-within-a-play device. Incorruptibility and purity in the face of death, violence, and evil are central themes of the comics and, in the final panels, Cain divests himself of the gunfighter's death-like black leather costume and refuses the gold in favor of his father's blessing, to the young girl – the victim of gang assault whom he had previously abandoned to her fate.

CONCLUSION

Book 2 ends on a "cliffhanger" with The General reverting to his blood-drenched cannibalistic dog persona and swearing revenge on Cain for stealing his lover, and with the two brothers going on separate quests. At the time of writing there appear to be no plans for a concluding Volume 3, which further emboldens and complicates *The Sons of El Topo*'s status as an unmade/abandoned project. Jodorowsky is currently writing a script for a film adaptation of his graphic novel *The Incal* rumored to be made by the director Taika Waititi.[32] To conclude this discussion, *The Sons of El Topo* is a useful text through which to view and further understand the phenomenon of the unmade project. It is a project which has found form and new life (albeit not in the form that it was originally intended) despite more than thirty years of setbacks and industry pushback. As Peter Kunze notes,

> Rather than focusing on what went wrong so as to prevent future failure, unproduction studies may uncover creative and industrial tensions that, in fact, reveal themselves to be alternative models of success, as in when a writer refuses to compromise her artistic vision or a production team actively works to revise narrative conventions only to be stymied by corporate intervention.[33]

He continues:

> If cultural studies or media industry studies truly hopes to stand in opposition – rather than in service – to the industry, it must resist giving sole attention to the "winners", the heard and the visible. In that way, we can engage in a truly radical critical praxis that seeks to understand and to unsettle, to examine and to expose, to analyse and to mobilize. In failure, we can find an alternative (to) success – one that resists convention and control, empowers the disenfranchised, inspires innovative approaches for media history.[34]

This assessment (albeit in relation to Kunze's study of an unmade film version of Andrew Lloyd Webber's musical *Cats*) is applicable to Jodorowsky's project which has been unbowed by industrial and cultural pressures and which has found a way to emerge in a new idiom and form. It is ironic and self-referential that Volume 3 is as yet unannounced, with the story's future left uncertain, conferring yet another level of incompletion and abandonment on the project.

NOTES

1. Matthew Melia, "Landscape, Imagery and Symbolism in Alejandro Jodorowsky's *El Topo*" in *Reframing Cult Westerns: From The Magnificent Seven to The Hateful Eight*, ed. Lee Broughton (New York: Bloomsbury Academic, 2020), 93–111.
2. James Fenwick, Kieran Foster, and David Eldridge, eds., *Shadow Cinema: The Historical and Production Contexts of Unmade Films* (New York: Bloomsbury Academic, 2021), 4.
3. Fenwick, Foster, and Eldridge, *Shadow Cinema*, 5.
4. Matthew Melia, "Ken Russell's Unfinished Projects and Unmade Films, 1956–68: The BBC Years" in Fenwick, Foster, and Eldridge, *Shadow Cinema*, 91–109.
5. Ryan Britt, "Why *Dune* Fans Should be Thankful Jodorowsky's Film was Never Made," *Inverse* (March 10, 2021) [Online], https://www.inverse.com/entertainment/dune-jodorowsky-villeneuve (March 31, 2022).
6. Mark Adams, "Jodorowsky's Dune," *ScreenDaily* (May 10, 2013) [Online], https://www.screendaily.com/jodorowskys-dune/5056357.article (accessed March 31, 2022).
7. Alison Castle, ed., *Stanley Kubrick's Napoleon: The Greatest Film Never Made* (London: Taschen UK, 2017).
8. Ben Cobb, *Anarchy and Alchemy: The Films of Alejandro Jodorowsky* (London: Black Gas Publishing, Persistence of Vision Series, vol. 7, 2007).
9. Nancy Kenney, "Museo del Barrio Cancels Exhibition Over an Artist's Remarks about Rape," *The Art Newspaper* (January 28, 2019) [Online], https://www.theartnewspaper.com/2019/01/28/museo-del-barrio-cancels-exhibition-over-an-artists-remarks-about-rape (accessed March 11, 2022).
10. Roger Greenspun, "El Topo Emerges: Jodorowsky's Feature Begins Regular Run," *New York Times* (November 5, 1971) [Online], https://www.nytimes.com/1971/11/05/archives/el-topo-emergesjodorowskys-feature-begins-regular-run.html (accessed December 17, 2018).
11. Xan Brooks, "I'm The Last Crazy Artist," *The Guardian* (April 5, 2007) [Online], https://www.theguardian.com/film/2007/apr/05/1 (accessed February 18, 2022).
12. Alejandro Jodorowsky, "Introduction," *The Sons of El Topo* (Los Angeles: Archaia, 2018).
13. *Lambiek Comiclopedia*, "Alejandro Jodorowsky" [Online], https://www.lambiek.net/artists/j/jodorowsky.htm (accessed March 11, 2022).
14. Daniel Kalder, "Alejandro Jodorowsky's Dance on the Edge of Meaning," *The Guardian* [Online], https://www.theguardian.com/books/booksblog/2011/jan/25/alejandro-jodorowsky (accessed March 31, 2022).
15. Kalder, "Alejandro Jodorowsky's Dance on the Edge of Meaning."
16. Cobb, *Anarchy and Alchemy*.
17. Matt Melia, "Landscape, Imagery and Symbolism in Alejandro Jodorowsky's *El Topo*" in *Reframing Cult Westerns: From The Magnificent Seven to the Hateful Eight*, ed. Lee Broughton (London: Bloomsbury, 2020), 100.
18. Conversation with Jodorowsky part two (YouTube) in Cobb, *Anarchy and Alchemy*.
19. Cobb, *Anarchy and Alchemy*.
20. "El Topo Returns," *Cinefantastique*, vol. 20, no. 1/2 (November 1989), 37.

21. Ibid.
22. Ibid.
23. Cobb, *Anarchy and Alchemy*.
24. Ben Cobb, "Mondo Jodo: Anarachy and Alecjemy: The Films of Alejandro Jodorowsky" in *Vertigo* [Online], https://www.closeupfilmcentre.com/vertigo_magazine/volume-3-issue-8-winter-2008/mondo-jodo-anarchy-and-alchemy-the-films-of-alejandro-jodorowsky/ (accessed March 31, 2022).
25. Cobb, "Mondo Jodo."
26. Melia, "Landscape, Imagery and Symbolism in Alejandro Jodorowsky's *El Topo*," 100.
27. Alejandro Jodorowsky and José Ladrönn, *The Sons of El Topo. Volume 1: Cain* (Boom!Studios, 2018), 1.
28. Jodorowsky and Ladrönn, *The Sons of El Topo. Volume 1: Cain*, 9.
29. Jodorowsky and Ladrönn, *The Sons of El Topo. Volume 1: Cain*, 10.
30. Dan Grote, "Sons of El Topo: A Perplexing, Sexually Violent Sequel to 1970 film," *WMQ Comics* (December 12, 2018) [Online], http://wmqcomics.com/reviews/review-sons-of-el-topo-ogn-a-perplexing-sexually-violent-sequel-to-1970-film/ (accessed March 31, 2022).
31. Arbaz Mohammed Khan, "The Sons of El Topo: Abel Vol. 2," *Fanbase Press* [Online], https://fanbasepress.com/index.php/press/reviews/item/10513-the-sons-of-el-topo-abel-vol-2-hardcover-review (accessed March 31, 2022).
32. Matt Grobar, "Taika Waititi to Adapt Alejandro Jodorowsky's Graphic Novel 'The Incal' as film," *Deadline* (November 4, 2021) [Online], https://deadline.com/2021/11/taika-waititi-to-adapt-alejandro-jodorowsky-graphic-novel-the-incal-as-film-1234867589/. (accessed March 31, 2022).
33. Peter Kunze, "Herding *Cats* or the Possibilities of Unproduction Studies," in Fenwick, Foster, and Eldridge, *Shadow Cinema*, 147.
34. Kunze, "Herding *Cats* or the Possibilities of Unproduction Studies," in Fenwick, Foster, and Eldridge, *Shadow Cinema*, 147.

CHAPTER 13

Jodorowsky, Psychomagic, and Subjective Destitution

William Egginton

Alejandro Jodorowsky wears many hats. Trained as a mime and a puppeteer, he imbibed the radical theater aesthetics along with the philosophy of Gaston Bachelard while living in France, where, under the influence of André Breton, he founded the panic group with Fernando Arrabal in the 1970s. There he also earned renown as the creator of graphic novels in a country that reveres the genre. Turning to motion pictures, he revolutionized cinema with only his second film, the ultraviolent Surrealist western *El Topo*, which ignited the midnight movie series at the famed Elgin Theater in Chelsea in the 1960s. Not content to rest on such laurels, the nonagenarian has developed into a full-fledged media guru, with some two million followers on Twitter and a distinctly New-Agey brand of Tarot-themed therapy to his name: psychomagic.[1]

At first glance such diversity might seem the sign of a restless mind, not to say a mind unhinged; but a method permeates Jodorowsky's flirtation with madness. While not a disciple of any school of psychoanalysis, Jodorowsky's time in France, his absorption of the basic tenets and aesthetic impulses of Surrealism, and his reading of French philosophy conspired to cultivate a view of the human psyche that has its clearest correlate in the teachings of the French analyst whose profile emerged in proximity with the Surrealist movement: Jacques Lacan. In what follows I exposit a few examples from Jodorowsky's work that correspond to key elements of this model of the psyche. In particular, I focus on the body's fragmentation by meaning and the emergence of partial objects as lodestones of desire; the figure of the guru as a quasi-analyst figure who functions according to the logic of the Lacanian *sujet supposé savoir*; and the therapeutic process of subjective destitution, in which the suffering subject shatters the ego's complacent attachments to liberate itself from normative structures of power and submission.

Jodorowsky's films, like the artwork of the Surrealist milieu that nurtured him, teem with fragmented bodies. Indeed, in some sense the proliferation of severed arms, castrated testicles, and deformed bodies are only the most visceral manifestation of a vast landscape of visual incoherence and audial dissonance. In Jodorowsky's first film, *Fando y Lis*, the male protagonist's quest as he pushes his disabled lover's body up a hill in a makeshift cart passes through the rubble of a reality in ruins. A musician plays a piano that blazes amid a junkyard of detritus. The soundtrack shimmers with a detached droning akin to swarms of angry hornets – an audible signature so recurrent in his work we might venture to call it Jodorowsky buzzing. In his breakthrough psychedelic western *El Topo*, the gunslinger must fight four antagonists, each of whom has a power to alter lived reality in some fundamental way. In *The Holy Mountain*, a phantasmagoria of visual incoherence, a military leader builds an army of young recruits who willingly sacrifice their testicles to him. After severing them in an initiation ritual he proudly adds them as trophies to a display on his wall. In *Santa Sangre*, Jodorowsky's psychedelic tribute to Alfred Hitchcock's *Psycho*, the protagonist watches as his knife-throwing father severs the arms from his religious fanatic mother – revenge for throwing acid in his face, in turn revenge for his infidelities with their circus's tattooed lady – before slitting his own throat. The list could go on indefinitely; this is but a brief selection of examples from a few films. And yet, far from a random splatter of violent images, Jodorowsky's recurrent rehearsal of fragmentation is motivated by a singular and highly coherent philosophical vision.

This vision begins to emerge from the first lines of *Fando y Lis*. Based on the 1958 play by Spanish playwright and co-founder of the panic group Fernando Arrabal, and written together with him, *Fando y Lis* portrays the quest of the eponymous protagonists to find the mythic city of Tar. After opening with an image of Lis lying on her side and slowly eating a flower, a voiceover during the credit sequence recounts the legend of Tar, the sole city left from a mythical time before "the final war" had broken out. The voiceover speaks in second person, telling the listener that when "you" arrive in Tar, all differentiation will cease, "you will know eternity . . . you will be cat, and phoenix, and swan, and elephant, and child, and old man, and you will be alone and accompanied, and you will love and be loved, and you will be here and there. . . ." At the end of this list the voice concludes, "you will feel ecstasy possess you and it will never abandon you."

The desire of the protagonists to reach Tar is a manifestation of what we could call a drive to transcend particularity, the limitations of location in space and time, the borders of a given identity. Such a desire found its most compelling expression in the work of the great Neoplatonist and Christian theologian, Saint Augustine, when he wrote of his life that it is a "distension in several directions," and declared himself "scattered in times whose order" he could not understand. Faced with such scattering between here and there, now and then, and "storms of incoherent events" that tear the at entrails of his soul, Augustine yearned for "that day when, purified and molten by the fire of [God's] love, I flow together to merge into you."² While Augustine's version was religious and explicitly Christian, the problem of the One and its fragmentation into the many finds its origin in pre-Socratic thought, specifically Parmenides, and was ultimately codified by Plato, perhaps most famously in his dialogue *The Symposium*. There we are introduced in almost comic form to the myth of a prior plenitude to which humans strive by one of Socrates's interlocutors, Aristophanes, who tells the story of primordial spherical beings whose pride and power led them to threaten the gods. In response Zeus split them in half, and since that moment each broken half desperately seeks to reunite with its lost partner. This, Plato writes, is love, "born into every human being; it calls back the halves of our original nature together; it tries to make one out of two and heal the wound of human nature."³

The ancient myth of the human being's dissection and loss of a prior plenitude became the philosophical matrix for Jacques Lacan's understanding of how humans are alienated by language and meaning. From his earliest teachings and writings, Lacan associated the human loss of and desire for the recuperation of plenitude with our linguistic being. In one of his most famous and influential early articles, "The Mirror Stage as Formative of the I as Revealed in Psychoanalysis," he discusses how, in the period during which children start to acquire language, the assumption of a sense of self produces an alienation of one's embodied experience, an externalization through a mirror image of the self that is always at some level a misrecognition. At the most fundamental level and from the earliest moments, the acquisition of selfhood is always simultaneously a loss of original wholeness, and is experienced as a fragmentation, a mortification and dismembering of one's body. The self-image one later composes out of this original wreckage will always retain unconscious traces of that fragmentation, fixations, fetishes, partial objects that will continue to organize the subject's desire later in life. But behind or beyond such local fragmentation remains the myth of redemption, of a wholeness, an ecstatic union that will heal one's original wounds. Such an ecstatic melding with the infinite is strictly impossible, a contradiction with the very temporal and spatial conditions of human knowledge; and thus the place of that full enjoyment is held from early on in the form of a signifier, the name of some ultimate other who has access to what we cannot.

The problem then becomes how the human subject's drive towards an original, illusory wholeness manifests itself or is interpreted within the context of social relations, and how the signifier of its own displacement from such full enjoyment is situated. At the individual level as well as the societal level, the repeated failures to achieve a lasting, eternal peace, to permanently heal the wound of dislocation for the individual, or the antagonisms that are constitutive of social bodies, may be interpreted as temporary setbacks or, worse, intentional blockages, the work of some foreign agent or adversarial other whose presence serves to deprive one of the hoped-for satisfaction. Blocked from achieving satisfaction, the subjects deposit the key to their fulfillment in a hidden object, Lacan's *objet petit a*, that one missing thing that will certainly solve all my problems. Social groups may deposit the key to achieving an elusive coherence and success as a nation, for instance, in the exclusion, suppression, or even eradication of supposed agents of harm. Severe maladaptation can assume the structure of psychosis, paranoid delusions, and hallucinations in an individual, or the kind of enrapturement to totalitarian control I've elsewhere called the psychosis of power.[4] Successful adaptation, the goal of therapeutic interventions or *Ideologiekritik*, requires integrating the impossibility of a final redemption into the psychic structure, accepting the openness of the anchoring signifiers, and ultimately "passing through" the social fantasy holding up an image of attainable fruition and identifying with the pathological symptoms we have created to protect ourselves from the terror of radical contingency.

Lacan came to his own as a theorist and clinician under the influence of structural linguistics, on the one hand, and the Surrealist movement, on the other. While linguistics influenced his idea of how the unconscious is structured – specifically as a complex of elements relating to one another through the operations of metonymy and metaphor, with meaning being sought along a sliding chain of signification anchored by special signifiers that stand in for or hold the place of an absent, ineffable whole – the Surrealists provided a model for an underlying, wild, incoherent imaginary landscape that always threatens to erupt, disrupting the temporary illusions of stability provided by a symbolic détente. For Lacan, the Surrealist proliferation of dreamscapes and liberation of the play of signifiers was a stark reminder in the cultural world of the sea of psychosis on which sail our fragile crafts of reason. If Goya had famously warned that the sleep of reason engenders monsters, Lacan's much-touted return to Freud emphasized how reason's over-confidence had its own monstrous side.

In Lacan's system, then, signifiers giveth and signifiers taketh away. By staying minimally the same in the flux of impressions creating our lived reality, words provide the very pivot on which the perception of self in time can turn, the very basis for what Kant called the sensible manifold to coalesce into something like coherent experience. The very same words, however, mortify us by partitioning lived experience: union with the mother's body is replaced first by a cry, then a word, then a prohibition – a series progressively installing a phantom object calling to us from behind the receding image of a nourishing breast. Gradually a name is assumed, an identity normatively including a gender, and almost immediately implying one that one isn't. Such "gendering" through language is the theme of Lacan's famous invocation of a scene on a train recounted from the diverging perspectives two children, a brother and a sister. As the train pulls up to the station, the boy looks out and says "look, we're at Ladies!" to which his sister replies, "Imbecile! Don't you see we're at Gentlemen."

The point of his vignette is to undermine the classical structuralist model of signification whereby a signifier is related to an image; here, the signifiers Ladies and Gentlemen relate to otherwise identical bathroom doors, and the users' identification with the signifier relies on a certain change assignation, where she or he sits at a moment of assignment, of what Althusser will later call interpellation, and from which moment those terms "will henceforth be two homelands toward which each of their souls will take flight on divergent wings, and regarding which it will be all the more impossible for them to reach an agreement."[5] Impossible because, that is, to bring those wings to earth, to land them on some firm and immobile ground, would be to ground meaning and identity on something it ultimately cannot be: self-contained, self-present being, referring to no other thing than itself.

In the absence of such a landing place, the sliding of one signifier to the other, driven by the capacity language gives us to "use it to signify *something altogether different* from what it says," comes to intermittent and often arbitrary stopping points that momentarily anchor the flow and retroactively produce meaning. Here Lacan credits precisely Surrealism, and its recognition that "any conjunction of two signifiers could just as easily constitute a metaphor" – as noted by its prophet André Breton who cited as an utmost example of poetic beauty Lautréamont's invocation of "the random encounter between an umbrella and a sewing-machine upon a dissecting-table" – before adding the caveat that what really provides metaphor's creative spark is not so much the conjunction of images as the replacement of one signifier by another in the signifying chain.[6]

The point to emphasize is that the human animal finds in the language it uses to navigate its world both a marvelous adaptive tool and a scourge that rends the very flesh of that world – finds, in other words, the Pharmakon that was both medicine and poison in Plato's myth of the invention of writing, or "the hair of the dog that bit you," in Slavoj Žižek's more playful reference to an alcoholic's go-to hangover remedy:[7] the signifier, by staying the same while referencing something different, opens a hole in the heart of human being, a clearing in the density of saturated existence that both enlightens and conceals, all the while initiating a seismic sliding towards the impression left in its wake. The most profound, the most existential of these initial mortifications are the loss of the mother's body, gender difference, and death – foundational borders of existence and identity that will ramify into a crystalline latticework of distinctions as the living being evolves. For every elucidating rupture, for every internal dissociation that creates an object to reject, know, or love, unconscious traces are deposited in the form of the fantasies that form the landscape of our imaginary – solitary, incommunicable. And yet, living in the social, we are driven to share a reality via the very language that left ours in ruin. And so, language knits back together the tattered tapestry its onset left behind.

The gift of Jodorowsky, in plain sight in his earliest film and writ large in his trajectory as filmmaker, is to explore those tattered remnants of the imaginary in all their traumatic, violent glory, while at the same time gesturing to the larger libidinal drift underlying such fragmentation. Life's journeys, as pathetic and unmotivated as they may seem, suffer from a common structure and often common sets of failures. Art, both its production and its interpretation, can be therapeutic, when it involves a confrontation with the fantasies of coherence that we use to escape a reckoning with the frailty, contingency, and ultimately inexplicability of our existence. The common arc of Jodorowsky's films manages to relate both poles of this experience: the failures that erupt in the imaginary as symptoms and causes of fear, of anxiety, of suffering, or even in the real, as hallucinations, delusions, or world-crushing depressions, inherently hinge on a fundamental fantasy of plenitude and redemption that is constitutively negated by the very nature of human being.

In Jodorowsky's version, Fando and Lis become emblems of gendered humanity. Lis's memories are tinged by horrific scenes of being treated as a doll in a puppet theater as young girl, hounded by various male characters and controlled by an eerie puppet master (played by Jodorowsky, who studied puppeteering and mime in France). As the grown counterpart to Fando, she is confined to a doll-like state, paraplegic and in need of Fando's help to move anywhere. Fando for his part fawns on Lis and tries to prove his relevance to her, pushing her on his cart and repeating the promise that all will be made whole when they finally arrive in Tar. But his attentions also erupt into abuse. He despairs of her immobility and leaves her on the ground, telling her she must crawl. At another time he appears to be trafficking her, inviting a parade of random people (evocative of the theater troupe that molested her in her memories) to admire and paw her naked body like chattel.

Fando's alternating fawning care and abusiveness in turn relates to a series of scenes reflecting his own traumatic fixations around gender identity, separation from his mother, and death. Several scenes explicitly involve graves or imply them. In one, Fando and Lis come upon a hellish mud pit teaming with writhing, naked bodies, their features entirely obscured by the slime they roll about in. Fando urges Lis to submerge herself in it, while Lis resists in repulsion. In another, pivotal scene right before the "third act," Fando recreates the death of his mother, leading a quite obviously living woman from a makeshift hospital bed to a freshly dug grave, embracing her while she thanks him for destroying her, and then placing her in the hole and covering her with dirt as she repeats her grateful words of thanks. Right before he finishes the job, she calls out to him, and her hand rises above the grave to give him something. He takes it from her, and places it on the ground, where a bird quickly takes flight. The card that then appears to mark the end of the second act and beginning of the final act reads: "and when I tried to separate myself from her, I realized that we formed a single body with two heads."

The third act then culminates in Fando's last desperate attempt to climb the mountain and attain the goal of Tar. Unable to do so, he lashes out in fury at Lis, eventually stoning her to death. At which point an enormous crowd appears and carries her to a coffin where they proceed to feast on her. The Christological move then becomes all the sharper as Fando pulls her body from the coffin and bears it like a cross on his shoulders the rest of the way up the mountain. There he places Lis's body in a fresh grave, covered in white stone and lies down next to it, murmuring "Speak to me, Lis, speak to me," over and over. As the ground brush grows over his body, Lis rises naked and fresh from the grave like a newborn Eve. Across from her, another Fando, also naked and clean, stands in a clearing in the woods. Hand and hand they escape together into the forest, as the final card appears, reading: "when their image was erased from the mirror, on the glass appeared the word freedom."

As with the violent rending of bodied relationships, and reality itself, the film's end begs for a Lacanian clarification. For Lacan, the ego – what many other schools of psychotherapy consider it their end and purpose to defend and strengthen – is itself merely the subject's most fundamental defense mechanism against the incoherence and radical contingency that threaten its sense of power and control over the world. Because the shell of the ego bakes into the subject's psychic life the very symptoms that cause the subject (and indeed the social body) to suffer – especially its enslavement to certain norms, such as gender roles and expectations, that perpetuate impossible-because-contradictory models of embodiment and behavior (for woman, purity and desirability; for man, stoic loyalty and unlimited sexual prowess) – the analytic process requires not its strengthening but its (at least temporary) dissolution, a process called subjective destitution. As Žižek puts it, "the psychoanalytic cure is effectively over when the subject loses this fear and freely assumes his own nonexistence."[8] It is only by passing through the fundamental fantasy upholding the ego's coherence and claim to power that something like freedom can be attained. But that freedom comes at a high cost, namely, abandoning the precious image of oneself that has accreted over a lifetime.

In what ways, then, does the filmic trajectory in Jodorowsky resemble or even deploy similar mechanisms to the psychoanalytic cure? It is precisely by staging a subject's fundamental fantasies, whether in the engagement with Surrealist art or psychoanalytic practice, the possibilities of liberation from enchainment to the ego can be realized. And the steps in the one mimic those in other. First, there is transference. In the transference the analysand spells out in a series of stories or vignettes the arc of his or life, the peculiar pitfalls and secrets that may have led to the blockage, the repetition compulsion, now causing the subject to suffer. In this dynamic the role of the analyst is decisive. While he or she in fact knows nothing about the analysand's secrets, the ultimate meaning tying it all together, the transference begins to take shape when the "analyst appears in the guide of the subject supposed to know – to know the truth about the analysand's desire."[9] From the subject's perspective, this is essentially an epistemological problem, one Lacan noted as central to science and philosophy: "Does Descartes, then, remain caught, as everyone up to him did, on the need to guarantee all scientific research on the fact that actual science exists somewhere, in an existing being, called God? – that is to say, on the fact that God is supposed to know?"[10] The truth of my desire is out there; some Other is aware of it, can work it out with enough time, given enough details; and this "subject supposed to know, in analysis, is the analyst."[11] Once the analysand accepts the analyst's power in this dynamic, transference is in full bloom.[12] And here is where the power of the analytic discourse kicks in. Not in the illusion of the transference itself, however; but in the dis-illusion that takes places when the subject comes to the realization that the analyst and the trust he or she has deposited in that role are an empty support, a kind of heuristic replacement. At this point, "this 'epistemological' incapacity shifts into 'ontological' *impossibility*; the analysand has to experience how the big Other does not possess the truth about his desire either, how his desire is without guarantee, groundless, authorized only in itself."[13]

If a sort of subjective destitution is clearly at work in the denouement of *Fando y Lis*, we get a clearer exposition of the role of transference and the subject supposed to know in later installments of Jodorowsky's journey. Indeed, it makes a particularly striking appearance in *The Holy Mountain*. With *The Holy Mountain* Jodorowsky, building on the runaway success of *El Topo*, found the financing to realize his vision with few limitations. With the support of John Lennon and Yoko Ono and produced by Beatles' manager Allen Klein, Jodorowsky created a technicolor phantasmagoria with clear Surrealist influences from Buñuel and Dalí, that has been called the "best surreal film ever" made.[14] The story, to the extent there is one, involves the journey of a Christ-like figure known as The Thief. Beginning with a series of scenes recalling Mexico's violent past and present (including a bloody recreation of the conquest of Mexico with costumed toads and chameleons, as well as scenes reminiscent of the 1968 massacre of protesting students by armed forces in the Tlatelolco Plaza, playing out for the cameras and entertainment of foreign tourists), The Thief allows his body to be used as a model for plaster Jesuses to be sold as souvenirs. He then climbs an enormous tower and enters a tube leading to a giant, rainbow-colored room where he encounters The Alchemist, played by Jodorowsky. In one key scene that follows, The Alchemist asks The Thief if he wants gold. When The Thief replies that he does, The Alchemist has him defecate in a clear bowl, and then initiates an elaborate ritual whereby we see The Thief's excrement transformed into a lump of gold, at which point The Alchemist tells him, "You are excrement. You can change yourself into gold." He then shows The Thief a mirror, and The Thief immediately smashes his image with the lump of gold.

While far from the film's denouement, two central themes enter in this scene. The first is the identification of The Thief's sense of self with both gold and shit. The Thief's journey so far has been motivated in part by material gain. His participation in the circus of toads and chameleons is for paying tourists; his likeness to Jesus is also monetized; indeed, his climbing of the tower is inspired by a desire to find gold there. But more profoundly, perhaps, The Thief engages with The Alchemist in the hopes of finding gold in himself. The precious core of oneself – what Lacan referred to as *agalma* in reference to Alcibiades's term for the fascinating source of Socrates's charisma, "something beyond all good,"[15] that led him and others to be seduced by the philosopher – is instrumental in producing the transference. In this sense it is a precise correlate to the *subject supposed to know*. The Thief, like the analysand, begins by projecting into the person of The Alchemist a kind of wisdom and knowledge about The Thief's self. You are excrement, but you can change yourself into gold, is thus both the promise of the guru/analyst, but also the secret to his method. This love, Lacan says, is "essentially a deception." In locating agalma in him or herself, the analyst triggers the transference and also triggers the emergence of the analysand's fundamental fantasy, "centered on the ideal point . . . placed somewhere in the Other, from which the Other sees me, in the form I like to be seen." The paradox of this central point – that it is something one desires in the other and at the same time a place from which one imagines being seen in an ideal form – engenders a primordial aggression, in which the subject essentially says "I love you, but because I love something in you more than you – the *objet petit a* – I mutilate you." This then is the source of the Surrealists' fragmented bodies, their mortified imaginary landscapes. Descending a level below the slick coherence of social reality, they discover a landscaped shredded by desire, pockmarked by the *objet petit a*, Buñuel's *Obscure Object of Desire* that leads us from one errant and ephemeral satisfaction to the next, in desperate search of something *that is not that*.

Assuming the position of the agalma in the relationship with the analysand is necessary but insufficient in the cure. What comes next is the kicker. For the way to wisdom and self-knowledge to be opened, the analysand must come to the realization that that the analyst is an idiot, and that the longed for agalma is "a gift of shit."[16] Jodorowsky's surrealist expression is a direction recognition of the proximity of violence and enlightenment, and of the role art and therapy have in preventing the "*psychotic passage à l'acte*" precisely by staging the emergence of the fundamental fantasy in art or in the transference and not in the space of social reality. Time and time again violence spasms into reality when the paradoxical and hidden object/cause of desire, whose absence is required for the fabric of reality to cohere, comes too close to the surface, leading to a derealization of reality in which "reality is no longer structured by symbolic fictions; fantasies which regulate the imaginary overgrowth get a direct hold on it."[17] Here we see the perverse "logic" behind Fando's treatment of Lis, alternatively worshipping her and abusing her, promising to serve her and provide for her, and then turning around and trafficking her to pawing, drooling men. The trick to the famous whore/virgin divide is that it isn't a divide at all. Indeed, the misogynist fantasy is structured on the very impossibility of a woman occupying both sides of the coin. The misogynist desires both sides, simultaneously, precisely because they are in contradiction, and then explodes in violence when confronted by the truth of his own fantasy. Herein lies the humor of a scene like that in the 1999 comedy *Analyze This* in which mafia boss Paul Vitti, played by Robert De Niro, seeks help from Billy Crystal's Dr. Ben Sobel:

> —What happened with your wife last night?
> —I wasn't with my wife, I was with my girlfriend.
> —Are you having marriage problems?
> —No.
> —Then why do you have a girlfriend?
> —What, are you gonna start moralizing on me?
> —No, I'm not, I'm just trying to understand, why do you have a girlfriend?
> —I do things with her I can't do with my wife.
> —Why can't you do them with your wife?
> —Hey, that's the mouth she kisses my kids goodnight with! What are you, crazy?[18]

Unfortunately, this comic scene hides a far darker, more frightening truth: that of countless women brutalized and killed each year by so-called jealous partners, whose jealousy is little more than the projection of their own fantasies.

To avoid both eruptions of ego-protecting violence and full psychotic meltdown, Lacan taught that the subject needs to use the transference to come to grips with and expose to the analyst his or her most intimate, awful, mortifying desires; to own them, as it were. In so doing, the subject comes to the realization that "the story I have been telling myself about myself no longer makes sense" and, at least for a brief spell, "I no longer have a self to make sense of."[19]

Jodorowsky illustrates this process as The Alchemist introduces The Thief to a variety of temptations. These come in the form of seven industrialists, each representing a different planet and excessive ego attributes, such as vanity, political power, sexual desire, aggression, control, etc. All, being industrialists, also express acquisitiveness, or greed. The exposition granted to each industrialist gives Jodorowsky carte blanche for his surrealist impulses, which he explores with relish. A female weapons manufacturer sleeps in a sensory deprivation tank with two women lovers and starts each day by awakening her giant sty full of naked male secretaries. An art dealer and his lover fondle painted sculptures made of human parts, which writhe in ecstasy under their caresses, before using a giant shining pole to stimulate an even larger robotic vagina into orgasm. A fascistic police chief initiates a young follower into his militaristic cult with a ritual in which he cuts off his testicles with shears, before adding them in a bottle of liquid to his shrine. His followers then become the army who descends on student protesters, massacring them as their bodies spew multicolored blood and guts.

These industrialists then join The Alchemist and The Thief on their journey, which requires that they first burn all their money, and then burn in effigy wax figures of themselves. Their journey to the top of the Holy Mountain requires them to undergo a series of trials, culminating in what The Alchemist calls the vision of death, ecstatic visions of their worst fears: visions of themselves eating the flesh of living animals; being part of animal copulation; being castrated and hung on a tree filled with chicken carcasses; being covered in tarantulas; sucking milk from the sagging breast of an ancient androgenous person whose breasts then turn into jaguar heads. At the end of their journey, the industrialists gather around a table with The Alchemist, who reveals to them that he is the film director Alejandro Jodorowsky. "We came in search of the secret of immortality," he tells them, "to be like gods. And here we are, more human than ever." Then he continues, "If we have not attained immortality, at least we have attained reality. We began in a fairy tale, and we came to life. But is this life reality? No, it is a film. Zoom back camera." As the camera recedes to reveal a film set, Jodorowsky stands up and bids his fellow actors to accompany him, "We shall not stay here, prisoners," he insists to them, "we shall break the illusion." And then he intones, "Goodbye to the Holy Mountain. Real life awaits us," as they take their leave of the set, and the film fades to white.

In the therapeutic practice he developed, which mixes from his early fascinations with Tarot, radical theater, Surrealism, and a variety of psychoanalytic and philosophical influences, Jodorowsky recreates similar pathways in order to lead his patients "to make peace with [their] subconscious, not becoming independent of it but making it an ally."[20] The mechanism he uses to help them come to this new relation with their subconscious is remarkably similar to the transference as Lacan described it. In Jodorowsky's telling, "I became a screen on which" his patients could "vent their bottled up hatred."[21] To becomes that screen, the pscyhomagicians present themselves "only as a technical expert, as an instructor," and explain to the patients "the symbolic meaning and purpose of every act."[22] This is in contrast to the patients' expectations of a guru, a popular charlatan who "must present himself as a superior being who knows all mysteries."[23] In this sense, his patients follow the path exposited both by *The Holy Mountain* and by the psychoanalytic transference. We, The Thief, the analysand, turn The Alchemist or the analyst into the subject supposed to know. We deposit there our agalma, that which is in us more than us. Its proximity to our social reality causes that reality to give way; the grotesqueries of our deepest fears and desires come to the surface. And then The Alchemist shows us his cards. He was never in control, never had access to agalma. We must face life on its own terms, freed from our ego's carefully constructed prison, yes, but also exposed to all the uncertainties and banalities that existence holds in store.

NOTES

1. This chapter summarizes many of the arguments made in my forthcoming book *Jodorowsky: Philosopher and Filmmaker* (2023).
2. St. Augustine, *Confessions*, 244.
3. Plato, *Symposium*, 183c–193e.
4. William Egginton, "The Psychosis of Power: A Lacanian reading of Roa Bastos's *I, The Supreme*," *Journal of Foreign Languages and Cultures*, vol. 5, no.2 (2021), 4–11.
5. Jacques Lacan, *Ecrits*, trans. by Bruce Fink (New York: Norton, 2002), 417.
6. Lacan, *Ecrits*, 422.
7. Jacques Derrida, "Plato's Pharmacy" in *Dissemination*, trans. by Barbara Johnson (Chicago, IL: University of Chicago Press, 1981), 63–171; and Slavoj Žižek, "The Hair of a Dog That Bit You" in Mark Bracher, ed., *Lacanian Theory of Discourse* (New York: NYU Press, 1994), 46–73.
8. Slavoj Žižek, *The Metastases of Enjoyment* (London: Verso, 1994), 170.
9. Žižek, "The Hair of a Dog That Bit You," 72.
10. Jacques Lacan, *The Four Fundamental Concepts of Psycho-analysis*, trans. by Alan Sheridan (New York: Norton, 1977), 225.
11. Lacan, *The Four Fundamental Concepts of Psycho-analysis*, 225.
12. Lacan, *The Four Fundamental Concepts of Psycho-analysis*, 232.
13. Žižek, "The Hair of a Dog That Bit You," 72.
14. Will Jones, "Why *The Holy Mountain* is the Best Surreal Film Ever," https://www.tasteofcinema.com/2017/10-reasons-why-the-holy-mountain-is-the-best-surreal-movie-ever/
15. Lacan, *The Four Fundamental Concepts of Psycho-analysis*, 255.
16. Lacan, *The Four Fundamental Concepts of Psycho-analysis*, 268.
17. Žižek, "The Hair of a Dog That Bit You," 76.
18. *Analyze This* (dir. Harold Ramis, 1999).
19. Žižek, "The Hair of a Dog That Bit You," 77.
20. Alejandro Jodorowsky, *The Dance of Reality*, trans. by Ariel Godwin (Toronto: Park Street Press, 2014), 311.
21. Jodorowsky, *The Dance of Reality*, 308.
22. Jodorowsky, *The Dance of Reality*, 316.
23. Jodorowsky, *The Dance of Reality*, 316.

CHAPTER 14

Talmudist and Kabbalist Practices in Alejandro Jodorowsky's *Psychomagic, a Healing Art*

Henri-Simon Blanc-Hoang

In his Chilean duology, Jodorowsky returns explicitly to his Jewish roots by creating a Surrealism-inspired biopic of his parents' failed attempts at assimilation into an anti-Semitic environment. His latest film, *Psychomagic, a Healing Art* (2019) seems to be leaning away from identity politics and shifting the focus towards promoting the Chilean-French director's own version of therapy.[1] As its title indicates, and as Jodorowsky himself reiterates at the beginning of the film: "El psicoanálisis fue creado por Sigmund Freud, un médico neurólogo. Sus raíces son científicas. La psicomagia fue creada por Alejandro Jodorowsky, un cineasta y director de teatro. Sus raíces son artísticas." ["Psychoanalysis was created by Sigmund Freud, a neurologist. Its roots are science-based. Psychomagic was created by Alejandro Jodorowsky, a film and play director. Its roots are art-based."][2] At first glance, Jodorowsky's inspiration appears to come from numerous cultural sources, especially from shamanistic traditions found in Asia and among the First Nations of the Americas. However, we shall see that the content and the form of this director's mind-healing techniques that are revealed throughout the film really originate in both Talmudism and Kabbalism. After briefly explaining the difference between those two Jewish traditions of biblical exegesis, we shall show how the major sequences that constitute the "ego-documentary" that is *Psychomagic, a Healing Art* incorporate regular study habits used by both Kabbalists and Talmudists.

For the first unit of every "Psychomagic" séance that Jodorowsky re-enacts in his last film, scholars who are trained in Jewish studies could recognize exegetical strategies that mimic the ones taught in Talmudic schools. At the same time, the content of these mind-healing sessions can also be identified as allegories which help the director's consultees find their inner selves. In this case, it is as if Jodorowsky were duplicating some Kabbalistic rituals. When one considers how Jewish holy texts are studied as part of a general religious practice, the tendency exists to identify a binary system that would oppose two methods of textual interpretation. On one hand, students of the Talmud are formally trained to answer questions of Jewish Law by making sense of the various levels of interpretation they find in the Written Torah, the Oral Torah (no longer transmitted orally), the Mishnah, and the Gemara. On the other hand, Kabbalists would rather look for a deeper, almost secret, meaning hidden in biblical narratives. In fact, these two schools of exegesis complement each other, and Jodorowsky finds his deeper sources of inspiration in these two spiritual heritages when he elaborates his own "art of healing" that he calls "Psychomagic."

THE DIFFERENCE BETWEEN TALMUDISM AND KABBALISM: THE BOOK OF JONAH AS AN EXAMPLE

Comparing and contrasting how Talmudists and Kabbalists explain the narrative of the Book of Jonah can reveal, in fact, how these two schools of interpretation complement each other. Such endeavor will later help us understand how Jodorowsky relies on these two spiritual traditions to elaborate his new art of healing that he calls "Psychomagic."

Talmudic Interpretation of the Book of Jonah

Beyond the idea that demonstrates God's almightiness and that it is pointless not to follow his orders – especially when one is given a prophetic mission – the Book of Jonah also can be used as a primary text by scholars of the Talmud to answer questions about Jewish Law. One would call this kind of biblical exegesis a rabbinic teaching.[3] In fact, during Yom Kippur (the most important holiday in Judaism), it is not uncommon for some rabbis to write for their congregation "legal briefs" on Jewish Law. Since passages from the Book of Jonah are in fact read during the service at the synagogue during this time of the year, rabbis take the opportunity to quote from the biblical text various interpretations that were passed on in the Mishnah and the Gemara – both of which constitute the Talmud. For instance, according to Israel Drazin,[4] one can find in the Book of Jonah justifications for the progressive role that can be given to women as well as for the origins of different rituals. Consequently, although Jonah is not explicitly a legal text, parts of this narrative have become the sources of Jewish Law. According to rabbi Maya Bernstein, by meditating on this text, Jews can learn about forgiveness, humility, repentance,[5] and even why it is fine to say their first daily prayer in the afternoon on Yom Kippur – even though this religious holiday starts early in the day.[6] All these lessons

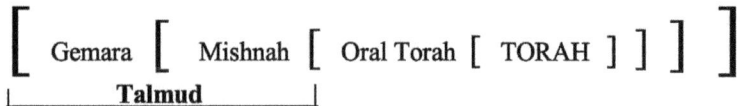

Figure 14.1 The different levels of interpretation of Jewish Law

that rabbis can extract from one biblical narrative are perfect examples of what the Talmud is: a superposition of various levels of textual interpretation (see Figure 14.1). At the first level, is found the Written Torah, then comes its first level of interpretation or what is called the Oral Torah (which exists now in written form), then comes the interpretation of this interpretation (the Mishnah), then the interpretation of the interpretation of the interpretation (the Gemara). In his para-therapeutical practice that he describes in *Psychomagic, a Healing Art*, Jodorowsky relies on a similar structure, but uses his own work as a primary text.

Kabbalistic Interpretation of the Book of Jonah

In his *Zohar, The Book of Splendor: Basic Readings from the Kabbalah* (1949), scholar Gershom Scholem summarizes what the Book of Jonah means for Kabbalists: it is not only an allegory of human life but of the destiny of the Jewish People:

> The story of Jonah may be constructed as an allegory of the course of a man's life in this world. Jonah descends into the ship: this is parallel to man's soul descending to enter into his body in this world. Why is the soul called Jonah? {lit., aggrieved}? For the reason that she becomes subject to all manner of vexation when once she enters partnership with the body. Thus, a man in this world is as in a ship crossing the vast ocean and like to be broken, as it is written, "so that the ship was like to be broken" {Jonah I:4} (76).

As we can see, while Talmudists focus on both orthodoxy and orthopraxy when it comes to Jewish life in our world, Kabbalists are concerned with a more mystical understanding of life not only on Earth but also in the afterlife. This Kabbalistic reading of the Torah is more like an alternate level of interpretation that parallels the work done by Talmudists (see Figure 14.2). To the Theoretical/Speculative/Theosophical Kabbalah ("Kabbalah Iyunit" in Hebrew), one must also add two other famous approaches that are called the Ecstatic Kabbalah and the practical or linguistic Kabbalah ("Kabbalah ma'asit" in Hebrew) which includes specific rituals one must follow to receive help from God – or to protect oneself from a curse.[7]

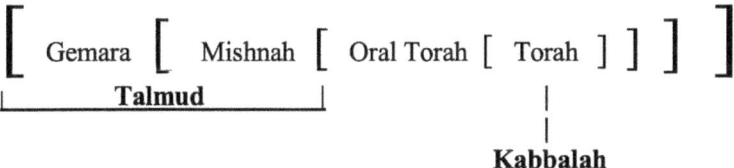

Figure 14.2 How the Talmudic and Kabbalistic readings of the Torah complement each other

In all the instances where Jodorowsky films himself practicing his "art of healing" in his last film, the director relies first on techniques used by students of the Talmud to identify the problems that his consultees must solve. However, the solutions that he prescribes are more in tune with rituals mimicking instructions found in practical Kabbalah. Finally, the final (self?) diagnostics given to (by) his consultees echo more the discovery of a "deeper truth"[8] that is characteristic of lessons that the speculative Kabbalah can teach its devotees.

Psychomagic, a Healing Art could be described as a self-documentary or ego-documentary in which Jodorowsky shows how his mind-healing practice, that he calls "Psychomagic," works. The film includes fourteen episodes or "Psychomagic" sessions/séances, each one consisting of: (1) a short passage from one of Jodorowsky's past works, (2) an interview or (self?) diagnostic of the "consultee," (3) the mind-healing séance itself. Although one could recognize in many of these episodes various elements taken from cultures and religions that still rely on healers, the entire structure of each "Psychomagic" session incorporates in fact techniques inspired by Talmudic and Kabbalistic practices, which gives a unicity to the entire film.

INFLUENCE OF THE TALMUDIST TRADITION IN *PSYCHOMAGIC, A HEALING ART*

What differentiates a film such as *Psychomagic, a Healing Art* (2019) from Jodorowsky's past works (especially his texts) is its director's illusionary self-effacement. In his fictionalized autobiography that was published in 2001, *La danza de la realidad*,[9] the French-Chilean artist includes various examples of successful healing sessions (or "Psychomagic séances") that he conducted.[10] Nevertheless, in his ego-documentary, he lets his consultees speak directly to the camera, as if they were providing a self-diagnostic. With the exception of episode 10, the film does not reveal whether Jodorowsky previously initiated the diagnostic by reading the Tarot or by asking direct questions. However, based on all his previous writings, we could say that such a precondition is very likely. At least, all the witnesses who appear in *Psychomagic, a Healing Art* seem to be convinced of the accurateness of their (self)-identified psychological crisis.

When one considers the entire structure of the Talmud itself, a good description would be to see this study aid as a superposition of commentaries (at least three levels) about a primary text (i.e.: the Torah). When it comes to *Psychomagic, a Healing Art*, each one of the fourteen "Psychomagical" séances that constitutes the film also relies on a primary "text" that functions as a narrative that "illustrates" the emotional and personal problems that the consultee must resolve. Of course, the nature of such a primary "text" is not religious but is a sequence taken from one of the director's past motion pictures – with the exception of episodes 1 and 2, which come from previous documentaries. In addition, these primary "texts" are themselves either film adaptations of someone else's work or of books by Jodorowsky. As a result, this technique used to identify the consultee's personal and emotional struggles models itself according to the process of a Talmudic lesson plan that incorporates commentaries of commentaries of an original source.

The system borrowed from the structure of the Talmud appears immediately in episode 1 ("Two brothers competing for the love of their mother") of *Psychomagic, a Healing Art*. The introduction to this first episode is one of the very few new pieces of footage that Jodorowsky produced especially for this self-documentary – in the remaining episodes the director recycles passages from his other films. In the first scene of episode 1, the film director neither relies on a voiceover nor attempts to give the illusion of speaking spontaneously when he provides us with a definition of his alternate form of therapy. Instead, he is reading from a booklet, but it is impossible to identify the title of the text. This written source could either be the script of the film itself or a manuscript that is completely unrelated. In this first episode, the Talmudic nature/structure of the presentation is perfectly preserved. We first find an "original source" (which might not exist, as it is the case in many of Jodorowsky's works[11]) that the director is quoting and inserting in a new source. At the same time, Jodorowsky also reveals to the viewers the origin of his massage technique that is an essential component of his alternative therapy. However, only his fans can understand that this "autobiographical" element comes from a previous text (*The Spiritual Journey of Alejandro Jodorowsky*, 2005).[12] It is in this book that the director explains in detail where and when he learned that massage therapy can help to heal not only the body but also the mind.

For the first two episodes of *Psychomagic, a Healing Art*, the nature of each unit which composes these two introductory episodes shifts between a documentary and a work of fiction. Nevertheless, the structure stabilizes at the beginning of episode 3 ("A man abused by his father on the verge of suicide"). The two units (the Talmud-inspired presentation and the Kabbalah-based ritual) of episode 1 do not include works of fiction. For episode 2, the Talmudic part comes from an interview that Jodorowsky gave to Spanish TV in 2005. However, its Kabbalistic component is a scene taken from *La danza de la realidad* (2016). Viewers must wait for episode 3 to notice an organizational system that is made up of a sequence from one of Jodorowsky's films (Talmudic structure), followed by a "Psychomagical" session (Kabbalistic model).

As a result, the introduction of episode 2 ("Fear of darkness") is a passage taken from the Spanish TV interview where Jodorowsky explains how he uses his Tarot-reading technique not to foresee the future but to analyze the present (and sometimes the past). In fact, once more, we are witnessing the study of a text within a text. At the beginning of this second episode, Jodorowsky explains how he learned about the tool (a Tarot deck) that he uses to prepare his consultees' diagnostic. In this case again, someone who is watching Jodorowsky for the first time would not understand immediately how the Psycho-mage has adapted the para-science of Tarology for his own therapeutical practice. However, Jodorowsky's fans would notice that his technique of interpretation copies the process of a Talmudic lesson, i.e.: the study of a text within a text within a text (see Figure 14.3).[13] For the rest of the film, the pattern of every episode becomes predictable after episode 3. Every episode first incorporates a theoretical part (that echoes the system of a Tamuldic lesson plan) taken from one of Jodorowsky's previous films. The second unit of each episode thereafter includes a testimony of Jodorowsky's consultee just before the "Psychomagic" session. This séance reproduces the three-step process of a specifically designed ritual which is based on Practical Kabbalah.

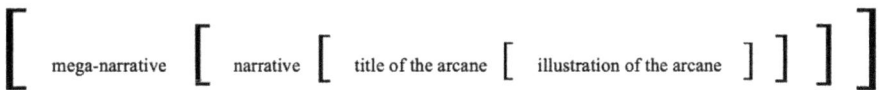

Figure 14.3 The different levels of interpretation of the Tarot, according to Alejandro Jodorowsky

The primary "sources" for episode 3 ("A man abused by his father on the verge of suicide") in *Psychomagic, a Healing Art* are different scenes taken from Jodorowsky's second film, *Fando y Lis* (1968). One would notice that the director reproduces again the multi-level system of textual interpretation that structures a traditional Talmudic lesson plan (see Figure 14.4), since the film itself is an adaptation of Spanish playwright Fernando Arrabal's work[14] of the same title (1962). Moreover, some critics have pointed out that Samuel Beckett's *Waiting for Godot* (1952) could also have been an inspiration for Arrabal.[15] The primary sources of episodes 4-5-6-7-10 are taken from Jodorowsky's next-to-the-last film, *Poesía sin fin* (2016). This work is itself an adaptation of two books by Jodorowsky: the second part of his family saga, *El niño del jueves negro* (1999) and *La danza de la realidad* (2001). Once again, the system of a multi-layered structure is imitated.

Figure 14.4 The multi-level system of textual interpretation for chapter 3 ("A man abused by his father on the verge of suicide") of *Psychomagic, a Healing Art*

Both episodes 8 and 13 use passages taken from *La montaña sagrada* (1973). This fourth film by Jodorowsky is itself an adaptation of an unfinished novel by French writer René Daumal *Le mont analogue* (1944). This film also includes the director's first filmed interpretation of a Tarot reading. In this case too, the existence of a multi-layered structure is unquestionable. Finally, episode 11 recycles as its primary source a sequence taken from Jodorowsky's last Mexican film, *Santa Sangre* (1989) – which some critics consider a color-version remake (with a crimson dominance) of Alfred Hitchcock's *Psycho* (1960),[16] which itself was a film adaptation of Robert Bloch's novel of the same title (1959).

Episode 3 ("A man abused by his father on the verge of suicide") is illustrated by a scene from *Fando y Lis* (1968) in which Fando crazily runs around a crater in circles. A similar scene taken from the same film is used to identify the relationship described in episode 5 ("A couple in crisis"). Episode 4 ("Birth massage") also relies on a scene from *Fando y Lis* (1968) for its introduction – where we are shown a mountain made of horse skulls that is giving birth to Lis. No explanation is necessary, but later the consultee reveals that his emotional suffering originates from a mother who was never affectionate with him. This kind of atmosphere which shows an individual who is trapped in a dead-end space reappears in episode 13 ("Coming out of the closet"). This time, Jodorowsky recycles a scene from *El topo* (1970) in which the main character is trying to escape from an arena. It goes without saying that this carceral environment is supposed to represent the closet where repressed homosexuals are hiding.

The primary source that appears at the beginning of each episode of *Psychomagic, a Healing Art* not only identifies the consultees' mental and emotional state of mind, but also can sometimes prescribe a radical solution to their problem. The title of episode 6 ("An Australian in Paris angry against his family") is associated with a scene taken from *Poesía sin fin* (2016), where a young Jodorowsky cuts the tree that has been growing in his grandmother's garden. This sequence displays perhaps the best example of a multi-layered structure of textual exegesis that is specific to Talmudic studies. To understand this reference in the film, one must read the interpretation (given by Jodorowsky himself) of the title he used for the second book of his family saga, *Donde major canta un pájaro* (1999) [*Where a bird sings best*], which was itself the source of inspiration for *Poesía sin fin* (2016). On the back cover of the novel, the author explains the choice of his book title by quoting a Surrealist verse attributed to Jean Cocteau: "Where a bird sings best is on his family tree" ["Un pájaro canta mejor en su árbol genealógico"] (back cover). Thus, if one wants to be set free from a toxic family, such as in the case of this Australian consultee, the solution is to cut all ties with the specific relatives who caused the problem in the first place.

Overall, the examples taken from *Poesía sin fin* which are also used to introduce several episodes of *Psychomagic, a Healing Art* are quite explicit. Episode 7 ("Menstruation problem") inserts a scene from the director's next to last film in which a poet has sexual intercourse with a female dwarf who is on her period. At the beginning of episode 8 ("A Mexican woman whose fiancé committed suicide on the wake of their wedding") there appears another scene from *Poesía sin fin* in which Jodorowsky as a child initiates a dialogue with his old self (played by the director himself). Literally, two separate entities that represent different stages of an individual's life can talk to teach other. Consequently, the consultee could still indirectly communicate with her dead fiancé. The same idea is proposed in episode 11 ("Arthur Higelin, poet and singer, after the death of his father") where a similar sequence taken from *Poesía sin fin* is inserted at the beginning of the episode. This time, the scene involved is the passage where a young Jodorowsky (played by the director's son) says goodbye to his father (played by Jodorowsky himself) – an event that supposedly never happened, according to the artist.[17] Here, the solution to his consultee's emotional distress lies in the idea that forgiveness really does work sometimes. In the same way that Jodorowsky was able to hug his dead father in the fictional world, Arthur Higelin should reconcile with his dead father who never recognized his talent.

Episode 9 ("A 47-year-old who wants to stop stuttering") presents in its first unit another scene from *Poesía sin fin* (2016) where a young Jodorowsky spontaneously recites some "poesía libre" – a style of free poetry that allows verses to flow out without restriction. Unlike normative speech, free poetry does not depend on a pre-existing set of metric and rhythmic rules or structure to exist. Such practice could therefore become a cure for stuttering. Episode 10 ("A 88-year-old woman deep in depression") relies for its primary text on a scene from *La montaña sagrada* (1973) that describes the work of Sel. This character owns a toy factory that produces play guns for children whose duty is to defend the motherland against an imaginary enemy. In this sequence, Sel makes money by having children conform to the model of a patriotic citizen. Such a situation supposedly reflects the state of mind of Jodorowsky's consultee, who also explains that she has been formatted all her life to fit the model of a devoted wife and mother.

Another scene from *La montaña sagrada* is also used as a primary text for episode 14 ("Walk of the dead in Mexico City"). This time, the recycled sequence represents an attempt to help Mexican people mourn all the deaths that resulted from the War on Drugs. In this case, the scene selected is a passage where live doves (i.e.: symbols of hope and peace) fly away from the dead bodies of political opponents who were murdered by the military of an unidentified Latin American dictatorship. Finally, sometimes a simple analogy with the plot of one of Jodorowsky's films is enough to help his consultee mentally. In episode 12 ("Can cancer be cured?"), the director extracts from *Santa Sangre* (1989) the scene where a character literally struggles against a live python. This physical challenge is supposed to mimic the mental fight that the consultee must initiate to destroy her cancer by the mere force of her will.

In *Psychomagic, a Healing Art*, by associating his consultees' emotional state of mind to a mini-plot taken from one of his previous films (or videotaped conference), the Chilean-French director also gives us an interpretation of his own past works. Consequently, one can notice a double transmission of knowledge. First, Jodorowsky teaches his viewers (especially his fans) a lesson in which he offers a direct interpretation of a sequence found in his previous films. Second, the primary source for every séance of "Psychomagic" is also used to identify the emotional problem that is haunting the consultee who is being filmed – in the same way that a teacher of the Talmud relies on specific passages from the Torah (and its subsequent levels of commentaries) to explain Jewish beliefs and customs.

INFLUENCE OF THE KABBALIST TRADITION IN *PSYCHOMAGIC, A HEALING ART*

It is important to remember that two traditions exist within Kabbalism. First, comes the "Speculative" Kabbalah ("Kabbalah Iyunit" in Hebrew) which is exemplified in the works of Gershom Scholem. This school of interpretation helps its practitioners find an inner truth "encoded" in the Torah that becomes a path to enlightenment. Second, what we call the "Practical" Kabbalah ("Kabbalah ma'asit" in Hebrew) consists of a series of specific pre-established rituals that could be assimilated to some traditional ceremonies one can perform to fight the evil eye. On the one hand, Jodorowsky has inherited from Practical Kabbalah the organizational structure that he applies to his "Psychomagic" sessions. On the other hand, at the end of every episode, the conclusion as well as the state of mind that his consultees describe are more analogous to the kind of "revelation"/"enlightenment" that practitioners of the mystical Kabbalah experience.

As a result, in *Psychomagic, a Healing Art* every testimony incorporates at the end of its corresponding episode a philosophical conclusion provided by Jodorowsky's consultees, where they explain how their healing process opened up for them a new path towards improving their personal life. More-over, the same testimony is preceded by a set of specific instructions. Accord-ing to Faye Levine, "[t]here are a number of recurring ritual procedures which either preface practical Kabbalistic activities or are involved in them directly."[18] These procedures incorporate three steps: (1) the selection of a specific timing – or space because "[d]emons preferred dark, spiritually and literally unclean places" (no page number), (2) a specific invocation, and (3) the use of physical objects and surroundings. In fact, each one of the fourteen episodes that constitutes the mega-narrative that is *Psychomagic, a Healing Art* presents a list of prescriptions that are organized in the same way as the Practical Kabbalistic procedures we have just described.

PSYCHOMAGIC SÉANCE OR PRACTICAL KABBALISTIC ACTIVITY?

Step 1: Spatial and Temporal Selection

The first component of a "Psychomagic" séance that is inspired by the form of a Practical Kabbalistic activity is the choice of a specific time (or place) for the rit-ual to be performed. This spatial and temporal selection must be directly linked to the goal one needs to achieve. The second unit of episode 1 ("Two brothers competing for the love of their mother") actually shows us a direct application of the massage therapy that is mentioned in the introduction, when Jodorowsky reads his definition of "Psychomagic" from his multi-layered source (one oral that is written but not shown, and one written that is shown but unidentified). The second unit displays in its organization the schemata of a ritual inspired by the structure of a séance of Practical Kabbalah. The video itself is of footage taken from an old public conference organized by Jodorowsky, where he appears himself as a "Psychomagic" masseur. Based on the camera angle, we can see that the séance itself takes place in front of an audience. Consequently, the time and space are indirectly revealed. Identifying the specific time of the day in the second unit of episode 2 is self-explanatory since the title of the chapter ("Fear of darkness") explicitly indicates when the ritual must take place (i.e.: at night).

In *Psychomagic, a Healing Art*, the time and place when and where the séances are organized are sometimes associated with the act of (re)creating a (un)happy event that never happened but that must be performed so that the consultees can move on with their lives. This is the case for episodes 8 ("A Mexican woman whose fiancé committed suicide on the wake of their wed-ding") and 11 ("Arthur Higelin, poet and singer, after the death of his father"). For episodes 4 ("Birth massage") and 5 ("A couple in crisis"), the place is a simple bedroom that looks sanitized and brilliantly illuminated like a maternity clinic. Such a setting gives the impression that the sequence is being filmed in a room that was recreated for this purpose. Even Jodorowsky's assistants wear white clothes that are reminiscent of how traditional midwives dress. The moment of the day is important too. The reconstituted birth seems to take place when the sun is at its highest. Jodorowsky's assistants then turn the "newborn" consultee towards the window, facing the natural light. It is worth noting that the English expression "to give birth" is translated in Spanish (Jodorowsky's native tongue) as "dar a luz" (literally, "bring to the light").

In episode 6 ("An Australian in Paris angry at his family"), the spatial and temporal selection (business hours of the post office) that is preferred for the ceremony is in fact purely practical, since Jodorowsky's consultee is later instructed to immediately mail to his family in Australia the objects he used during the ritual. To perform this act, the consultee must also choose a space where people do not hang out (a deserted street in Paris), since one of the objects involves the use of a long hammer. A similar requirement regarding the time of the day is necessary for episodes 2-5-7-8-11-12 and 13, but for the opposite reason. In these chapters, a public must be present, because the "Psychomagic" séances that are inspired by Practical Kabbalistic activities are transformed into public performances/happenings. As a result, the place chosen must be either a busy urban area – especially during a famous event (the Madrid Gay Pride, the Day of the Dead in Mexico City) – or a building specifically reserved to welcome a big audience (a concert hall, an amphitheater).

Step 2: The Use of Objects

The second element taken from the Practical Kabbalistic ceremony that Jodorowsky incorporates as a key component of his séances of "Psychomagic" is the use of physical objects. In this context, the quantity of objects involved varies according to the circumstances and the individual's condition. In episode 1 ("Two brothers competing for the love of their mother"), the items used display similar characteristics to the time and space chosen: they seem to be missing. However, this apparent absence functions to reveal a presence that was not obvious at first because the objects in question are the purple plain clothes that both brothers and Jodorowsky are wearing and need to take off partially. This way, the two siblings can make the massage therapy efficient and reach a moment of reconciliation. Only the woman (Jodorowsky's assistant) who is "acting" as the mother of these two men is wearing different clothes. The fact that these two brothers are wearing the same clothes prepares them to appear as equals in front of their "mother." Once they get rid of the purple objects and are left naked, there is no need for these two siblings to display any kind of artificial equality because their nudity works as a level playing field.

Its second unit probably makes episode 2 one of the most interesting episodes because Jodorowsky applies his own "Psychomagic" technique to himself. The ritual that he creates to cure his "young self" from his fear of darkness in the fictional world is a sequence taken from the film *La danza de la realidad* (2016), his fictionalized autobiography. In this scene, the object that the mother of a young Alejandro incorporates is a can of black shoe polish. Its content is used as paint to cover the entire naked body of her son so that he can blend with the night and be cured of his fear of darkness. In this case we can also notice a typical act of Speculative Kabbalah. If the fear of darkness is a phobia that is real, it is also suggested that this "lack of light" that has young Alejandro live in fear is the anti-Semitic environment in which he grew up. Although the "documentary"–"work of fiction" order is reversed in this second episode, the symbiosis Talmud-Kabbalah is perfectly reproduced. Painting (this time of a golden color) is also used as a physical object in episode 9 ("A 47-year-old who wants to stop stuttering").

Episode 3 ("A man abused by his father on the verge of suicide") includes quite an extensive and significant list of objects: a balloon, a family portrait, some rotten meat, milk, a wooden knife, a transparent salad bowl. For episodes 4 ("Birth massage") and 5 ("A couple in crisis"), the list is rather limited: a pair of scissors, the facsimile of an "umbilical cord" made of fabric, a glass of milk. This is the case too for episode 6 ("An Australian in Paris angry at his family"): a few pumpkins, some family photographs, a hammer. Sometimes, only one object is enough to perform the ritual, such as the cello in episode 7 ("Menstruation problem"), the water bottle in episode 10 ("A 88-year-old woman deep in depression"), or the clothes/costumes in episodes 1 ("Two brothers competing for the love of their mother"), 8 ("A Mexican woman whose fiancé committed suicide on the wake of their wedding"), 9 ("A 47-year-old who wants to stop stuttering"), 11 ("Arthur Higelin, poet and singer, after the death of his father"), and 14 ("Walk of the dead in Mexico City").

Episode 13 ("Coming out of the closet") is quite particular because this séance of "Psychomagic"/Practical Kabbalistic ritual involves the combination of minor objects (scissors, suit, shirt, a tie) and a major one (the wooden closet). In the most extreme case, such as in Episode 12 ("Can cancer be cured?"), it is in fact the elimination of an object that becomes part of the ceremony. When Jodorowsky is about to instruct his consultee and the audience to pronounce the incantation (a simple collective "OM"), he is first provided with a microphone that he immediately refuses. Unconsciously, maybe, negating the very existence of an object can be interpreted as a method to make the cancer disappear.

Step 3: The Incantation

This third component of a Practical Kabbalistic procedure that is the incantation can in fact acquire many forms in a "Psychomagic" séance. In episode 1 ("Two brothers competing for the love of their mother"), the incantation seems not to be explicit until it becomes overpowering. Here, we are dealing neither with written nor spoken words, but with a scream that becomes louder and louder. In fact, such a technique of not using words specifically but of relying on sounds that the human body can produce stands for an alternative to a specific incantation that Jodorowsky utilizes several times in different episodes from *Psychomagic, a Healing Art*. Since the second unit of episode 2 is taken from Jodorowsky's fictionalized autobiography (and not from a documentary), different genres are mixed, such as opera and theater, which explains why the incantation that Alejandrito's mother pronounces is a song. This technique also appears in episode 11 ("Arthur Higelin, poet and singer, after the death of his father").

In episode 3 ("A man abused by his father on the verge of suicide"), Jodorowsky pronounces a voiceless incantation. In this case, the film director blows on the body of his consultee. This act imitates the "Breath of God" from the Book of Genesis that the Creator blows on a lifeless body of clay before it becomes Adam.[19] In this case, the consultee's healing is analogous to a new birth. After this initial psychological shock, the individual finally experiences a revelation of his own and concludes: "Life in Paris is not for me." This three-component ritual that Jodorowsky makes up finds its source in the procedures of Practical Kabbalah. However, this act is only a path towards the individual's enlightenment (i.e.: Speculative Kabbalah) that eventually results in a life-altering decision for the consultee.

The nature of the incantation articulated by Jodorowsky in episode 4 ("Birth massage") is also voiceless. In this sequence, the séance of "Psychomagic" consists in putting an adult woman (who never felt the love of a mother) in the position of a baby who is being born. Once again, the director's assistant mimics the "Breath of God" by blowing on the consultee's naked body which is being placed in a fetal position. An extra sound effect is even added to the soundtrack so that we can hear the air coming out of the assistant's mouth. This type of incantation is also used in episode 5 ("A couple in crisis"), where Jodorowsky makes a man and a woman go through a similar ceremony. Both the woman and the man must relive their birth while the director blows his breath on their naked bodies.[20] Once again, this incantation imitates the act of God that makes life on Earth possible. Thus, the couple is reborn.

If in episode 3 the incantation is voiceless, it is more literal in other parts of the film. Sometimes, it can even become a mantra, such as in episode 9 ("A 47-year-old who wants to stop stuttering"). In fact, this is the case for most of the passages (episodes 4-5-6-8) that constitute *Psychomagic, a Healing Art*. In some examples, the prescribed incantation has a lot to do with the consultee's talent and can become a song, such as in episodes 11 ("Arthur Higelin, poet and singer, after the death of his father") or 14 ("Walk of the dead in Mexico City").

In episode I2 ("Can cancer be cured?"), it is not only Jodorowsky and his con-sultee, but also the entire public who participates in the event and is required to take part in the ritual. Here, the director-healer mixes both the Jewish and Hindu traditions, since the chosen incantation is a simple but collective "OM."

In episode 8 ("A Mexican woman whose fiancé committed suicide on the wake of their wedding"), the incantation is neither pronounced nor sung but becomes a written message. The séance of "Psychomagic" involves cremating a wedding dress, in a real crematorium, set in the Père Lachaise Cemetery in Paris. In this sequence, while the wedding dress is burning, the camera focuses on a quote engraved above the crematorium that is attributed to Socrates and was passed on to us through Plato: "Mais voici l'heure de nous en aller, moi pour mourir, vous pour vivre. Qui de nous a le meilleur partage, nul ne le sait, excepté le dieu." ["The hour of departure has arrived, and we go our ways – I to die, and you to live. Which is better, God only knows."] Curiously, the quote that we found engraved above the crematorium is in fact missing its last part ("God only knows"), probably to make the place non-denominational. However, by cutting the last part of the sentence, the message also changes its meaning, and could be translated as: "The hour of departure has arrived, and we go separate our ways – I to die, and you to live. May the one who gets the best deal share [it]."

In the case of this woman whose fiancé committed suicide on the wake of their wedding, healthy advice for her would be to continue with her life after a mourning period. This is where the written incantation begins to make sense: "May the one who gets the best deal share [it]." After burning the wedding dress that she never used (end of the mourning period), this consultee might be now ready to share her life with someone else . . . A similar system of refer-ring to an unspoken but written incantation appears in episode I3 ("Coming out of the closet"). During the Madrid Gay Pride, a political message, printed on the T-shirt of one of the participants ("Legalize Gay") becomes the focus of the camera while Jodorowsky and his assistants are getting ready to set fire to a wooden closet – from which a gay couple (i.e.: the consultees) is literally supposed to have come out.

Eventually, the people who ask Jodorowsky for help do not always need to be instructed at all times with a specific incantation that they have to pro-nounce during the séance of "Psychomagic." In episode IO ("A 88-year-old woman deep in depression"), the consultee loudly vocalizes her admiration for the old tree which she was given the responsibility to care for (and visit) frequently in the Jardin des Plantes in Paris. By expressively, and spontane-ously, saying to the old tree "I see that you are beautiful," this woman becomes suddenly aware that a new cycle is beginning for her, and that she did not waste her life – despite her advanced age and the unsatisfying relationship she had with her absent husband.

CONCLUSION

By analyzing the structure of every single episode that constitutes *Psychom-agic, a Healing Art*, we can see that Jodorowsky imitates the Talmudists' study habits when he identifies both an origin and a solution for his consultees' emo-tional distress. Moreover, the director relies on his past works as the primary texts to illustrate a psychological condition in the same way that Talmudists refer to the Torah when they explain Jewish Law. Jodorowsky can even propose a "healing" for his consultees by directly quoting passages from his own cine-matographic works. However, when we watch the healing process that follows, Jodorowsky's influence does not come from Talmudism but from Kabbalism – especially if we refer to the Kabbalah ma'asit (i.e.: Practical Kabbalah). In this case, the healing ritual that Jodorowsky elaborates finds its inspiration in the three components that make up a séance of Practical Kabbalah.

Contrarily to his two previous films *La danza de la realidad* (2013) and *Poesía sin fin* (2016), *Psychomagic, a Healing Art* does not make explicit references to Jodorowsky's Jewish heritage. At first glance, viewers who are not familiar with his work might be tempted to conclude that this ego-documentary borrows from spiritual traditions that originated in Asia (Buddhism, Hinduism) or the Americas (shamanism). In addition, because *Psychomagic, a Healing Art* does not depend on a fictional plot per se, but looks more like a documentary, one could almost consider this film as apocryphal – especially since the 88-year-old director appears only in two scenes and accepts a kind of self-erasure for the rest of the film. Nevertheless, throughout his life Jodorowsky gave many con-ferences that were filmed, and this is not the first time that he performed his "Psychomagic" acts in front of a camera. If we consider Jodorowsky's autobio-graphical novels about his family (*Donde major canta un pájaro*, *La danza de la realidad*), *Psychomagic, a Healing Art* fits perfectly with the director's previous two films and even ends the circle.

Because of its eclectic presentation, *Psychomagic, a Healing Art* seems to have been put together quickly, especially since this work includes passages from other of Jodorowsky's past films as well as extracts from some of his conferences and documentaries. However, nothing could be further from the truth. At first glance, viewers who are familiar with the director's past works might be tempted to conclude that this ego-documentary does not seem to fit very well with the Jodorowskyan canonical filmography. However, if one remembers the director's generational novels about his family history (*Donde mejor canta un pájaro* [1992] and *El niño del jueves negro* [1999]), his autobiography (*La danza de la realidad* [2001]), as well as the subsequent film adaptations of all these texts, *Psychomagic, a Healing Art* is in perfect harmony with the rest of Jodorowsky's work. In fact, by studying his fictionalized autobiography, we can see clearly that the director was already announcing a mixture of different genres (plot-based film and doc-umentary-like film), which is why this last film "ends" the circle of his oeuvres.

NOTES

1. Although *Psychomagic, a Healing Art* was released in 2019, Jodorowsky first mentioned the project of directing a motion picture about his own version of therapy in 2006. During an interview with Ben Cobb, he explained that he would begin filming what would become *Psychomagic, a Healing Art* if he did not get enough money to make the movie *King Shot*: "I am still searching for the money. I need $5 million and I have one. But I have one! That's something . . . one million dollars! I am happy because if I don't do *King Shot* then I will do a documentary on psychomagic. I will do something, no? It is good. I. know I can do something." Ben Cobb, *Anarchy and Alchemy: The Films of Alejandro Jodorowsky* (London: Creation Books, 2007), 264.

2. According to Brian Lancaster, an alternative to Freud's psychoanalysis that was more based on Jewish spirituality had already been proposed in the past, such as Roberto Assagioli's "psychosynthesis": "Assagioli seems to have drawn on the kabbalistic understanding of the division of the soul. He posited three realms of the unconscious: a lower unconscious, identified with bodily functions; a middle unconscious, dealing with present experiences and their relations to 'I'; and a higher unconscious concerned with intuitive and spiritual functions. Psychosynthesis is directed to the integration of these levels, and especially to forging a synthesis between the personal self and the transpersonal self. The emphasis on synthesis, and on the psychological means of promoting it, leads to some stimulating parallels between Assagioli's school of therapy and Kabbalah. More than this, Freud's psychoanalytic theory – very much the trigger for all subsequent schools of therapy – displays a number of significant resonances with key themes in rabbinic Judaism and Kabbalah. There is a profound psychological edge to Kabbalah, which gives it a special value in the quest for self-betterment" (41). *The Essence of Kabbalah*, 2006.

3. Israel Drazin, "Unusual Explanation in Midrashim of Jonah," https://booksnthoughts. com/unusual-explanations-in-midrashim-on-jonah/ (October 18, 2021).

4. Israel Drazin summarizes a commentary from the Babylonian Talmud which quotes the Book of Jonah to argue in favor of non-traditional roles for women: "Erubin 96a discusses whether women are obligated to observe biblical positive commands that are not limited to a particular time. It mentions that King Saul's daughter wore tephilin (traditionally worn only by men) and the sages did not prevent her, and the wife of Jonah attended the festival pilgrimage and the sages did not prevent her." Drazin also quotes the Mishnah to explain the symbolism of some specific rituals: "Mishnah Taanit 2:1 discusses the order of the worship service for fast days. Among much else, it states that the people placed wood ashes on their heads just as the people of Nineveh did, and God saw the Ninevites' sackcloth and their fasting and that they turned from their evil ways and did not destroy Nineveh." https://booksnthoughts.com/unusual-explanations-in-midrashim-on-jonah/ (October 18, 2021).

5. "The book [of Jonah] reminds us of God's infinite mercy [according to the Mishnah:] 'Israel said to God, "Master of the Universe, if we repent, will you accept it?" God responded, "Would I accept the repentance of the people of Ninveh, and not yours?"' We read Jonah to be reminded that if God could forgive Ninveh, of course God can forgive us." Maya Bernstein, "Jonah and Yom Kippur," https://www.myjewishlearning.com/ article/jonah-yom-kippur/ (October 18, 2021).

6. "One should always take special care about the afternoon prayer. For even Elijah was favorably heard only while offering his afternoon prayer. As we read of Jonah being answered from the belly of the fish, we are reminded that we too can be saved, even as the day begins to wane." Maya Bernstein, "Jonah and Yom Kippur," https://www. myjewishlearning.com/article/jonah-yom-kippur/ (October 18, 2021).

7. Faye Levine, "Practical Kabbalah: Things They Did Not Teach You in Hebrew School," http://kabbalah.fayelevine.com/practice/pk015.php (October 18, 2021).

8. Hoping that every individual can find his inner/deeper truth or "enlightenment" is also a constant in Jodorowsky's works. "Y es que, sin duda, y como no para de repetir nuestro hombre, iluminarse es importante: 'El Dios interior, nuestro ser esencial, nos lanza un anzuelo, a nosotros. Nos dice: ¡aquí estoy, dentro de ti, reconóceme, ven a buscarme, yo soy tú y tú eres yo, realiza la unidad con tu parte divina!'" ["And, without any doubt, and as our man keeps repeating, reaching enlightenment is important: 'The interior god, our essential being, is sending us a hook. He is telling us: Here I am, inside of you, recognize me, come and get me, I am you and you are me, re-unify yourself with your divine part!'"]. Hazael González, *Danzando con la realidad, las creaciones artísticas de Alejandro Jodorowsky* (Palma de Mallorca: Dolmen Editorial, 2011), 72.

9. Not to be confused with the film of the same title, especially since the movie is a partial adaptation of the book.

10. See the table of contents in *La danza de la realidad* (2004), especially "Actos psicomágicos transcritos por Marianne Costa" (396–403).

11. Robert Neustadt, "Alejandro Jodorowsky: Reiterating Chaos, Rattling the Cage of Representation," *Chasqui*, vol. 26, no. 1 (May 1997), 56–74.

12. See the chapter entitled "From Skin to Soul" in Alejandro Jodorowsky, *The Spiritual Journey of Alejandro Jodorowsky* (Rochester, VT: Park Street Press, 2005), 99–124.

13. One must understand that a Tarot card includes at least three narratives. First comes the image itself that usually illustrates a specific scene (level 1) that the Tarologist must interpret. Then, comes the name/title of the card (level 2) that the Tarologist must also explain. In fact, the title of the arcane is by itself already an interpretation of level 1 (the illustration). Eventually, comes a specific exegesis (level 3) that reveals how these two levels are connected to the consultee's situation. Last but not least, a Tarot reading also includes a mega-narrative (level 4) that connects together all the cards/situations that were selected randomly. Thus, this type of Tarot reading performed by Jodorowsky reproduces the techniques used to study the Talmud and its different levels of interpretation (the Written Torah, the Oral Torah, the Mishnah, and the Gemara). It is worth observing that in *Poesía sin fin*, Jodorowsky spells Torah "Torat." If one relies on the French rule of pronunciation, final consonants are silent. By spelling the word Torah with a final "t," it can be read right to left (as in Hebrew) and will be pronounced "Tarot." Jodorowsky is famous for playing with the rules of phonetics in his works and conferences: "Camen-vert," "OM"/"FAM," etc . . . . Finally, when it comes to the twenty-two arcanes of the Tarot, various authors, such as Samaël Aun Weor, have also written about this divinatory art's connection with Kabbalah: "Tous les kabbalistes se basent sur le Tarot, il est nécessaire de le connaître et de l'étudier à fond. L'univers fut conçu à travers la Loi du nombre, de la mesure et du poids; les mathématiques forment l'univers, et les nombres sont par conséquent des entités vivantes." ["All Kabbalists find their inspiration in the Tarot, it is necessary to know it and to deeply study it. The universe was conceived through the Law of numbers, of weights and measures; mathematics shape the universe, and numbers are consequently living entities."] Samaël Aun Weor, *Tarot & Kabbale* (Québec: Editions Thoth, 1988), 2.

14. Although Arrabal did enjoy Jodorowsky's adaptation of his play, he admits that he does not understand it, and that the day he will understand it he will cease to enjoy it. Louis Mouchet, *La Constellation Jodorowsky* (Wide Management, 1993), 1 hr., 30 mins.

15. Puma Torres, Paúl Fernando, and Carla Gabriela Campaña Yépez, *Análisis comparativo entre dos obras del Teatro del Absurdo: "Esperando a Godot" de Samuel Beckett y "Fando y Lis de Fernando Arrabal*, Universidad Central del Ecuador, 2018: "al haberse catalogado a esta última obra como un plagio de la primera" ["this last work has been

16. catalogued as a plagiarism of the first one"] (Abstract), http://www.dspace.uce.edu.ec/handle/25000/17320 (October 10, 2021).

16. "Santa Sangre is in many ways a novel retelling of Hitchcock's Psycho (1960), with that film's psychosexual subtext here put on full display with overt symbolism." David Church, "Jodorowsky, Alejandro," *Senses of Cinema* (February 2007), https://www.sensesofcinema.com/2007/great-directors/jodorowsky/ (October 10, 2021).

17. In *La danza de la realidad* (2004), Jodorowsky describes his abrupt departure for Europe this way: "Me estaba yendo también, de cuajo, de mi familia: nunca más los volví a ver" ["I was also tearing myself apart from my family: I never saw them again"] (182).

18. Levine, "Practical Kabbalah: Things They Did Not Teach You in Hebrew School."

19. The idea of pronouncing an incantation to bring life to an inanimate object originates in the Jewish legend of the golem: "The first friend circled the Golem seven times while reciting certain holy letter combinations. The Golem began to glow. The second friend did the same thing, and the glow was replaced by a watery vapor. Then the Maharal also circled the Golem seven times and the three of them cried out, 'And God blew the breath of life into his nostrils.' The Golem's eyes then opened." Allen H. Lipis, "The Golem of Prague," *Atlanta Jewish Times*, December 22, 2020.

20. According to Rabbi Gershon Winkler (who also considers himself a Jewish shaman) it is sometimes necessary to "redirect the God Breath": "Jewish shamanic healing is therefore a science of helping someone to shift a misbalanced soul-aspect manifestation. Of someone who is emotionally ill it might be said that their soul-aspect *ruach* – the force which stirs the God Breath through one's being – is out of synch or in an uncontrollable, chaotic spin. In such a case, the shaman might choose to redirect God Breath or energy flow so that it manifests more in the intellect or the body, depending on the personality involved." Gershon Winkler, *Magic of the Ordinary, Recovering the Shamanic in Judaism* (Berkley, CA: North Atlantic Books, 2003), 132.

Index